LOBBYING IN AMERICA

Selected Titles in ABC-CLIO's
CONTEMPORARY
WORLD ISSUES
Series

For a complete list of titles in this series, please visit **www.abc-clio.com**.

Books in the Contemporary World Issues series address vital issues in today's society, such as genetic engineering, pollution, and biodiversity. Written by professional writers, scholars, and nonacademic experts, these books are authoritative, clearly written, up-to-date, and objective. They provide a good starting point for research by high school and college students, scholars, and general readers as well as by legislators, businesspeople, activists, and others.

Each book, carefully organized and easy to use, contains an overview of the subject, a detailed chronology, biographical sketches, facts and data and/or documents and other primary-source material, a directory of organizations and agencies, annotated lists of print and nonprint resources, and an index.

Readers of books in the Contemporary World Issues series will find the information they need to have a better understanding of the social, political, environmental, and economic issues facing the world today.

LOBBYING IN AMERICA

A Reference Handbook

Ronald J. Hrebenar and
Bryson B. Morgan

**CONTEMPORARY
WORLD ISSUES**

A B C CLIO

Santa Barbara, California
Denver, Colorado
Oxford, England

Copyright 2009 by ABC-CLIO, Inc.

Library of Congress Cataloging-in-Publication Data
Hrebenar, Ronald J., 1945–
  Lobbying in America : a reference handbook / Ronald J. Hrebenar and Bryson B. Morgan.
      p. cm. — (Contemporary world issues series)
  Includes bibliographical references and index.
      ISBN 978-1-59884-112-1 (hardcopy : alk. paper) — ISBN 978-1-59884-113-8 (e-book)   1. Pressure groups—United States.   2. Lobbying—United States.   I. Morgan, Bryson B.   II. Title.

  JK1118.H849 2009
  328.73'078—dc22

                          2008048563

13   12   11   10   09   1   2   3   4   5

ABC-CLIO, Inc.
130 Cremona Drive, P.O. Box 1911
Santa Barbara, California 93116-1911

This book is also available on the World Wide Web as an eBook.
Visit www.abc-clio.com for details.

This book is printed on acid-free paper ∞
Manufactured in the United States of America

Contents

List of Tables

Preface

As Alexis de Tocqueville, the French political scientist, wrote in 1834, "In no country in the world has the principle of association been more successfully used . . . as in America" (Heffner 1956, 95). Another political scientist, Arthur Bentley, wrote more than a century ago, "When groups are adequately stated, everything is stated" (Bentley 1949, 208). Many believe this statement is even truer in contemporary American politics. The United States in the 21st century appears to be awash in interest group politics. Every major and minor policy initiative debate is organized and dominated by interest groups supporting or opposing it. Our current political leaders frequently discuss the prospects and problems of our present political environment in terms of "special interests" and "lobbyists."

Interest group politics is even more on our minds because of its newly expanded role as the "deep pockets" and general supporter of our political party campaigns. As parties continued their decline from their once preeminent role in our national campaigns, interest groups moved in to fill the void. Now, various interest groups and movements attach themselves to many of our campaigns years before election day and promote their causes in a relentless manner in the national media, by lobbying in Washington, D.C., and the various state capitals, and by organizing and implementing candidate campaigns across the United States.

Lobbying and interest groups in the United States have also been in our consciousness in recent years because of the frequent cases of corruption at the highest and lowest levels of U.S. politics. The Jack Abramoff, Randy "Duke" Cunningham, and Bob Nye scandals in 2006–2007 brought the words *bribery, lobbyist, member of Congress,* and *prison* to the front pages of newspapers over and over again. The rewards associated with successful lobbying campaigns have become astronomical. Abramoff, for example, had billed his Native American tribe clients $85 million over a few years. In 2006, Abramoff pled guilty to three felony counts and agreed to make restitution of at least $25 million that he had defrauded from his clients—mostly Native Americans. Rep. Randy Cunningham (R-CA) received millions of dollars in bribes from the defense industry lobbyists seeking his favors.

American interest group politics and lobbying have had a long and complex history. The interest group system continues to be the world's most fully developed and serves as a model for measuring the development of interest group systems and democracies around the world. This book provides the reader with a comprehensive examination of the world of lobbying in the United States and around the globe. A wealth of information and data about lobbying is contained in the following eight chapters and glossary. We have not ignored the more controversial aspects of the attempts made to influence public policy, but we have tried to present the various sides of these debates and let the readers decide how they feel about them.

Chapter 1 provides a broad framework for understanding the nature of interest groups and lobbying in the United States. Once the reader has a firm grasp of the fundamentals of this world, he or she can proceed to Chapter 2, "Problems, Controversies, and Solutions," which presents important debates about the impact of lobbying on modern election campaigns, public policy development in Washington, D.C., and the problems of controlling the possible excesses of interest groups. Even if we can all agree that serious problems exist in the interest group and political system, can we ever agree on which of the possible remedies could be adopted? Chapter 3 expands the focus to compare the American interest group and lobbying patterns to those of other nations, especially the developed democracies of Europe and Asia. Chapter 4, "Chronology," is a selected set of political and economic events in American history that help the reader understand how interest group politics and lobbying have developed over the decades. It illuminates the great diversification of interests in our increasingly complex society and the growing role of government in providing services and regulation of the economy and lobbying.

Chapters 5 through 8 provide the reader with an extremely useful collection of information about lobbying. It is the most up-to-date and comprehensive collection available of accessible and practical information for the general reader or serious researcher on this topic. Chapter 5 presents biographical notes on 44 individuals who have played significant roles in our interest group system. Chapter 6, "Data and Documents," presents a treasure trove of information on lobbying. It also contains seven documents that present key scholars' interpretations as well as some classic pieces from Tocqueville and James Madison. Chapter 7, a directory of organizations and other entities, offers a road map for readers who may wish to contact organizations that interest them. With tens of thousands of political organizations operating in the United States, we obviously cannot feature all of them, but we have tried to focus on the most important and influential groups representing key interests and sectors. With the ubiquitous availability of the Internet, readers can learn much about the most powerful groups and lobbyists in the United States with the mere click of a computer mouse. Chapter 8, "Selected Print and Nonprint Resources," offers a list of books, videos, and Web sites for readers to continue to explore the world of lobbying and interest group politics. Fifteen films are listed, and these all can be used in classrooms at the junior high school, high school, and college/university levels to help students understand the sometimes complex and confusing realm of group politics. Finally, we have provided a glossary of terms and concepts.

We wish to express our sincere appreciation for the support and understanding extended to us by the editors of ABC-CLIO, including special thanks to Mildred Vasan, who encouraged us to undertake this project, and Kim Kennedy White, who gave us invaluable advice on how to improve our manuscript. We also wish to thank the students of the University of Utah who have taken Interest Groups and Lobbying and Political Management courses in the Department of Political Science and have served internships on the state, national, and international levels through the Hinckley Institute of Politics. Without the feedback from these students, this book would never have been possible.

References

Bentley, Arthur. 1949. *The Process of Government*. Bloomington, IN: Principia Press.

Heffner, Richard, ed. 1956. *Alexis de Tocqueville: Democracy in America*. New York: Mentor.

1

Background and History

All political societies, ancient or modern, have had or currently
have interest group politics and lobbying. Imagine being
transported back to the earliest human societies that began to
develop into specialized economic and political roles. Hunter-
gatherers came to compete with warriors, agricultural workers,
priests, governmental leaders, and bureaucrats for the scarce resources of the community. To paraphrase the definition of one famous political scientist, Thomas R. Dye, politics is the allocation of
governmental resources; it is who gets what, when, where, why,
and how (Dye 1995). Ancient Rome was famous for the various
conflicts among the Roman Legions, aristocrats, and economic
elites. Throughout history, even the powerless—the serfs and
peasants—could participate in interest group politics by rioting,
demonstrating, and even revolting. (They were not always successful in these tactics. Sometimes they paid with their lives for
their decisions.) Politics in those times often was truly a "winner-
take-all" game.

Beginning with England, a more modern style of group politics began with the Magna Carta (1200s) and the expansion of
participants to include more than the royal family; friends; and
supporting economic, political, and military groups. As societies
became more complex and economies more diverse, the interests
that demanded a place at the decision-making tables greatly increased. With the enhanced role of Parliament in England, there
was an arena for lobbying by the various interests.

The most English of the British Empire's colonies were those
in North America, and they inherited both the range of interests
and the legislative arenas for the development of interest group

1

politics. The 13 British colonies in what became the United States developed a lively style of politics by the mid-1700s, and various economic interests such as planters, importers, exporters, shipowners, small businessmen, farmers, and religious groups made demands on the colonial assemblies and British governors. The 13 colonies were even developing a significant manufacturing base.

James Madison and the "Dangers of Factions"

Following the American War of Independence (1776–1783), the new American nation operated under a pre-Constitution document called the Articles of Confederation. Interest group politics among the 13 newly independent former colonies (now states) was mostly conducted on the state level because the structure of the national government prevented significant decision making. The Articles provided for an extremely weak national government with a largely symbolic president and a Congress that had no real taxing power and a need to have all decisions made by unanimous vote. By the mid-1780s, it had become clear to some national leaders such as James Madison that the key issues that faced the new national government could not be successfully addressed under the Articles. Among the challenges the new nation faced were economic, security, and political issues.

The economic position of the new states was precarious. The Continental Congress issued government bonds to cover the costs of the War of Independence against the British. The outstanding amount of these bonds was about $75 million, a very substantial amount of money—about one-seventh of the total property value of all 13 colonies. The revenue streams of the national government consisted of customs taxes and revenue from postal stamps. Any additional funds had to be requested from the states, which were understandably resistant to the idea of such financial transfers. Many of the bonds had been bought by "speculators," who went from house to house offering small amounts for bonds that many people had concluded were not worth much. These speculators represented an interest that demanded that the national government be reformed so it could raise tax money that could pay off, among other expenses, these war bonds. Several states, such as Rhode Island, were on the edge of fiscal bankruptcy. Their state-issued currencies were not accepted by citizens of other states. Some states had raised barriers around their borders, which prevented the development of national markets. Clearly, for these economic reasons, various business and financial interests supported a substantial revision of the national governing document.

The security realm also experienced serious problems. The Peace Treaty of Paris that ended the War of Independence had given the new American nation the Northwest Territory—the region that is today's midwestern states of Ohio, Michigan, Indiana, and Illinois. However, the region continued to be occupied by British troops in forts, and the American military had been disbanded. Besides issues of national honor, why was this occupation important? American investors and settlers were pushing west over the Appalachian Mountains, and profitable migration into the Ohio River Valley could not be accomplished as long as the region was occupied by the British. Additionally, and far more important, the world was aflame with war among the major superpowers of the 18th century: Great Britain, France, and Spain. One very important reason why the British gave up on their American colonies in 1783 was that much more serious threats to British interests were posed by France (led by Napoleon), and other sites were compromised, such as those affected by the ongoing battle to control India and Asia. The 13 American colonies on the Atlantic coast of North America were a relatively minor irritant and distraction compared with the dangers in Europe.

For these and other reasons, James Madison led a movement to call a convention in Philadelphia in the summer of 1787 to revise the Articles of Confederation. This action was highly irregular and not part of the written procedure for revising the Articles. In fact, the goal of revising the fundamental document for the American national government was quickly dropped at what is now called the Constitutional Convention. The Articles were too weak to use as a foundation for an effective national government. James Madison had spent the previous year researching various governments and constitutions and was prepared to help write a strong new constitution with sufficient limitations to protect liberty.

Madison's subsequent propaganda campaign in support of the proposed constitution marks the beginning of the discussion of interest group politics in the United States. Madison is considered the "father of the American Constitution" and, in reality, the father of interest group studies. The pro-Constitution propaganda campaign took many forms, but the most important was a series of 85 essays written by James Madison, Alexander Hamilton, and John Jay. (Madison later went on to become the nation's fourth president; Hamilton, the first secretary of the treasury; and John Jay, the first chief justice of the Supreme Court.)

The essays have come to be known as the Federalist Papers and collectively are now considered to be the finest piece of political writing in American political history (Wills 1982). They tried to defend the crucial elements of the proposed constitution. Of the 85 essays, the most famous is Madison's Federalist No. 10; it warns the nation of the dangers of "factions." Madison addressed No. 10 to the people of New York, one of the states that appeared to be most hostile to the proposed constitution. The opening sentence clearly describes the central point of his argument: "Among the numerous advantages promised by a well constructed Union, none deserves to be more accurately developed than its tendency to break and control the violence of faction" (Ketcham 2006, 84).

Madison's description of *faction* is basically what we will come to call "interests," or "interest group politics": "By a faction I understand a number of citizens, whether amounting to a majority or minority of the whole, who are united and actuated by some common impulse of passion, or of interest, adverse to the rights of other citizens, or to the permanent and aggregate interests of the community" (Ketcham 2006, 84).

Madison's significant contribution in No. 10 is his argument concerning the problems of trying to eliminate the negative outcomes of interest group politics. "There are two methods of curing the mischiefs of faction: the one, by removing its causes; the other, by controlling its effects" (Ketcham 2006, 85).

Again, two methods of removing the causes of faction exist: "the one by destroying the liberty which is essential to its existence; the other, by giving to every citizen the same opinions, the same passions, and the same interests. It could never be more truly said, than of the first remedy, that it is worse than the disease. Liberty is to faction what air is to fire, an aliment with which it instantly expires. But it could not be a less folly to abolish liberty, which is essential to political life, because it nourishes faction, than it would be to wish the annihilation of air, which is essential to animal life, because it imparts to fire its destructive agency" (Ketcham 2006, 85).

In other words, the problems of factions (interests) can be avoided, but the method of avoidance would kill liberty and thus is completely unacceptable to the liberty-loving American citizenry. However, the second method he analyzes to control the "mischiefs" of factions is not acceptable either. "The second expedient is as impracticable, as the first would be unwise. As long as the reason of man continues to be fallible, and he is at liberty to exercise it, different opinions will be formed" (Ketcham 2006, 85).

Madison identifies the causes behind the formation of different opinions. It is property that ensures a division of the society into different issues and parties. So the causes of faction are based "in the nature of man" and the "most common and durable source of factions has been the various and unequal distribution of property" (Ketcham 2006, 85). Since property in a free society and economy will always be distributed in unequal amounts and types, factions will always be present.

Since, as Madison argued, no cure exists for the causes of faction, one must focus on methods for reducing the negative impacts of factions (or interests) on the political system. This philosophy is another of Madison's great contributions to the establishment of the American political system: the complex or large republic. "A Republic . . . promises the cure for which we are seeking." Madison designed a republic, not a democracy. Madison's Republic is a representative government, not a government of direct citizen decision making. The representatives would use their wisdom to discover the true interest of their country. Madison suggested his design was the best compromise: a large republic where the various interests could be countered in the national government and a series of state legislatures (small republics) where local and specific interests would be important (Ketcham 2006, 87–88).

So Madison argued that the advantage his republic had over a democracy was in controlling the effects of factions. He gives an example of a religious sect becoming a political faction in a given part of the republic, noting further that "a variety of sects dispersed over the entire face of it, must secure the national Councils against any danger from that source" (Wills 1982, 48).

James Madison's Constitution of 1787 set the stage for what would become interest group politics in the new American government. We are not saying such interest groups and their politics did not exist before 1787, but after 1787, the structure and rules of the new Constitution guided the development of American

politics and government into a particular pattern much like a valley guides water into a riverbed. Before we move on to others
who have commented upon the historical development of American interest group politics, we would be remiss if we did not include the adding of the Bill of Rights and especially the First
Amendment to the Constitution in 1791.

Madison, Hamilton, and Jay promoted the adoption of the
proposed constitution in the Federalist Papers. Opponents to the
adoption came to be called the Anti-Federalists, and their collected propaganda efforts demanded that several fundamental
problems existed in the Madisonian design. The Anti-Federalists
were especially concerned that the new national government had
too much power or the potential to acquire too much power at
the expense of the liberties of the American people. Why did the
constitution writers fail to include a "bill of rights" protecting the
American people from abuses by the new national government?
After all, they correctly noted that most of the 13 states had such
protections. The Anti-Federalists had other concerns as well,
such as a president with the potential to have too much power, a
judiciary appointed for life, and a federal government with areas
of responsibility that were too vague. Actually, the two groups
supporting and opposing the Constitution represented two col-
lections of very different interests. The Federalists were mostly
property owners, creditors, and merchants, while the Anti-Federalists were mostly small farmers, debtors, and small shopkeep-
ers (Ginsberg 2007, 53).

One of the arguments Madison and some of the Federalists
(not including Hamilton, who, in Federalist No. 84, argued that a
bill of rights was not needed) made to obtain final ratification for
the Constitution was to address the need for a federal bill of
rights to protect against federal government abuses.

Madison led the fight for the Bill of Rights that was passed
by Congress and adopted by the states by 1791. For the purposes
of this analysis of the development of lobbying and interest
group politics in the United States, we will examine only the First
Amendment, which reads as follows:

Amendment I
    (Freedom of Religion, of Speech and of the Press)
    Congress shall make no law respecting an establish-
ment of religion, or prohibiting the free exercise thereof;
or abridging the freedom of speech, or of the press; or of

the right of the people to peaceably assemble, and to petition the government for redress of grievances.

All of the First Amendment applies to our subject in various
ways. By the 1790s, the diversity of religions in the 13 states was
such that few people considered replicating the normal relationship between government and religion—the establishment of one
religion as the official "state religion" of the nation. The United
States had sizable Protestant communities representing mainstream Protestant organizations as well as many of the smaller
dissident groups such as Quakers and Puritans. If you add the
growing Catholic population centered in Maryland, Jews, and
other groups, the establishment of a national religion was a political impossibility in 1790. The "free exercise" clause tried to prevent any one religion from imposing its beliefs upon others. Some
of the battles regarding the relationship between government and
religions and the issues of free exercise of religion continue to be
very significant political issues into the 21st century.

The next four clauses of the First Amendment all directly re-
late to how government came to view interest groups and lobbying. The "freedom of speech" clause has been interpreted by the
U.S. Supreme Court to cover political speech (such as lobbying)
and recently to protect the spending of money in attempts to influence political campaigns as well as lobbying. "Freedom of the
press" also guarantees that interests (including the media as an
interest itself) can make their political demands and communications without governmental obstruction. But it is the final two
clauses, which protect the right of the people to assemble and petition government, that have enshrined the lobbying game as a
fundamental part of American politics. The assembly clause has
been read to mean Americans have a right to join organizations
that have political agendas, and the petition clause has been read
as a prevention of almost all attempts to rein in the various strategies and tactics found in modern lobbying. We will discuss these
aspects of the First Amendment in Chapter 2, where we consider
the important issues regarding interest groups and lobbying in
contemporary American politics and government.

Evidence of the development of interest group politics in the
new United States can be found in the writing of the French aristocrat Alexis de Tocqueville, who toured the young nation in
1831–1832 and later wrote the first great book about the nature of
political life in the United States. His book *Democracy in America*,

detailing his observations, was first published in 1835 and re-published in 1840 and many times since then (Heffner 1956). Central to Tocqueville's concerns regarding the new nation were the American combination of the concepts of democracy and equality and, more specifically, the American thinking that equality means freedom and democracy means liberty. Additionally, Tocqueville viewed with some fear the dangers of the "tyranny of the majority." Had the United States so structured its politics and society to favor the masses to the detriment of important, but narrower, interests?

Tocqueville noted that the Americans used associations more than other major nations at that time. "Wherever, at the head of some new undertaking, you see the government in France, or a man of rank in England, in the United States you will be sure to find an association" (Heffner 1956, 198). In Tocqueville's section on political associations in the United States, he wrote one of his most famous and oft-quoted comments:

> In no country in the world has the principle of association been more successfully used, or applied to a greater multitude of objects, than in America. Besides the permanent associations, which are established by law, under the names of townships, cities and counties, a vast number of other are formed and maintained by the agency of private individuals . . . . If some public pleasure is concerned, an association is formed to give more splendor and regularity to the entertainment. Societies are formed to resist evils, which are exclusively of a moral nature, as to diminish the vice of intemperance. In the United States, associations are established to promote the public safety, commerce, industry, morality, and religion. There is no end which the human will despairs of attaining through the combined power of individuals united into a society (Heffner 1956, 95).

What Are Interests, Interest Groups, Lobbies, and Lobbyists?

People participate in politics either as individuals or as formal or informal members of organizations. Individuals can have an impact on political decisions by the act of voting or can affect public opinion through such means as writing letters to the editors of newspapers or magazines. But the most effective way people can have a voice in politics is by joining a group of like-minded individuals and using the power of their group to magnify their political voices. Such organizations that have engaged in political activities to affect public policy decision making have been identified by many different names during the more than 200 years of U.S. history. Some of these names carry negative connotations because of their linkage to various lobbying scandals, including the terms *trust, vested interest, special interest,* and *pressure group.* Each of these terms comes with a public perception of unsavory tactics or a lack of concern for a broader public interest. Even the word *lobby* carries a bad image in many people's minds. In this book, we use the most neutral term, *interest group,* which David Truman defines in his classic study *The Governmental Process* as "any group that is based on one or more shared attitudes and makes certain claims upon other groups or organizations in the society" (Truman 1971, 13). We derive two key ideas from this definition. First, the organization is composed of individuals (or other organizations) who share some common characteristic or interest. For example, the American Federation of Labor and Congress of Industrial Organizations (AFL-CIO), a giant labor union confederation, shares the interests of its members on a wide range of economic, social, and political objectives that affect working people in the United States. Second, only those associations that engage the political system and seek to affect public policy are considered interest groups under this definition.

We must also differentiate among interest groups and lobbying and social and political movements (Meyer 2007). Movements or social movements are *emergent groups* that propose change and need to become political groups to effect change. Social movements have spontaneity and some structure. Sociologists tend to study social movement, and political scientists tend to study interest groups. Eventually, some social movements evolve into political interest groups with a well-defined membership, regular funding, a permanent staff, and knowledge on how to operate within the political system. Jo Freeman suggests that such types of social action can be seen as points along a continuum (Freeman 1983). At one end are those relatively unstructured social actions such as a riot; at the other end are the established, structured interest groups; and in the middle are the social movements having spontaneity and some structure, but not a well-defined formal organization. A social movement may have one or several core organizations within the larger movement. People who consider themselves part of a social movement often share identity as part of a group focusing on a particular concern. Social movement politics is often outside the mainstream of politics, and thus political movements are forced to rely on disruptive tactics to publicize their demands. If you cannot win in the legislatures or courts, you have to try to rally public opinion to your side by disruptive strategies and tactics.

In the 1960s and 1970s, most of the major political movements were found on the liberal or left end of the political spectrum and associated with such causes as women's rights, sexual rights, civil rights for minorities, environmental rights, the antiwar movement, and animal rights. All of these movements are still in existence in the 21st century, but the most significant change has been the rise of a number of major conservative, or right-wing, movements since the 1970s. The new conservative movements have focused on anti-abortion law, antipornography, anti-gay marriage, and anti-immigrant (especially anti-illegal immigrant) stances.

If a movement is successful in achieving its basic political goals, it will frequently evolve into one or more influential interest groups that have significant power to affect policy making in various governmental sites. On the other hand, unsuccessful movements tend to disappear as a result of cooptation, lack of interest, or even repression. We discuss movements in this book, but our primary focus is on the interest groups embedded within the broader movements. Some recent research has noted the difficulty in clearly separating interest groups from social movements. Costain and McFarland (1998) have argued that the two are really quite similar in many aspects and that they should be called "interest organizations." But they do argue that a very fundamental difference exists between interest organizations and political parties.

Interest groups are not usually political parties, and political parties are not usually interest groups. On rare occasions, interest groups and political parties do reflect the same organization. In the United States, several interest groups have become political parties in order to use the political campaign opportunities in elections to further their goals. Among the examples of these merged organizations are the Socialist and Communist parties as well as the Libertarian and La Raza parties. These are really interest groups of an ideological bent presenting themselves as political parties to gain attention for their ideas.

Interest groups and political parties both serve as communications links between citizens and their government, but they are very different. Political parties have as their major reason for existence the objective of capturing control of the institutions of government. Parties want to occupy government physically, whereas interest groups want to influence some of the decisions made by government. In addition, parties focus their attention on elections and the selection of candidates to fill public offices. They are highly regulated by state laws and, in terms of membership, are usually broad-based coalitions of individuals who frequently share only one common objective, the capturing of government. Interest groups, in contrast, are almost totally free from legal restrictions on their activities and focus mainly on the public lawmaking phase of the governmental process.

We mention from time to time some nonpolitical interest groups because they serve important roles in the social system of the United States. Many of the thousands of social, youth, and sport groups found in the United States, such as Elk, Moose, Masons, and Boy Scouts and Girl Scouts, play important social roles but very seldom get involved in politics. However, in general we will not spend much time with those groups that do not participate frequently or effectively in the political process. In addition, thousands of groups exist that may on a very rare occasion come into contact with the political system on a very unusual issue, but for our purposes, we will not focus on these groups.

American society seems to be well represented by the tens of thousands of groups that operate in the nation. But some interests that are very difficult or seemingly impossible to organize into effective organizations participate in the political process. We call those interests that have not effectively organized *potential groups.* These are a segment of people who share a common interest but who are not yet organized and usually are not a regular part of the political process. Although it is difficult to discover major interests that have no formal organizational representation, certainly some sectors are underrepresented, such as children. Children's interests have been largely represented by their parents, as in the case of various conservative Christian groups forming to represent parents in their concerns over the nature of their children's education in the public schools. Other interests that have not organized well to represent their political interests include single (never married and divorced) people. As a group, single people have almost no voice in Washington despite being 40 percent of the U.S. population.

In recent decades, organizations have been formed to represent many previously unrepresented interests of society. Senior citizens have America's largest and, maybe most powerful, lobby in the AARP (American Association of Retired Persons). The AARP grew from 1 million members in 1967 to more than 36 million members in 2007. A very large group of fundamentalist, evangelical, "born again" Christians has been organized into several organizations beyond their usual church memberships. The late Rev. Jerry Falwell founded the Moral Majority to act as the political agent for this previously unorganized interest and claimed 400,000 members and a multimillion-dollar budget in 1980. Although the Moral Majority died as an organization in the late 1980s, it was successfully replaced by the Christian Coalition, which became a powerful force in conservative politics in the early 1990s. The Christian Coalition claimed more than 2 million members in 2005. Other groups have also recently formed to try to organize additional members of evangelical Christians. Dr. James Dobson, a Christian activist, organized the most political evangelical group of the 1990s, Focus on the Family. Various estimates have placed the potential number of born-again Christians at between 30 million and 65 million Americans—potentially one of the largest interest sectors in the United States. Such Christians have been increasingly organized by interest groups in recent decades.

Other ethnic and religious interests have also become organized in recent years. Asian Americans have been difficult to organize except for the Japanese, who organized under the Japanese American Citizens League. However, recent new Asian organizations, such as the Asian American Association and the Organization of Chinese Americans, have moved to represent the interest. After 9/11, various groups of Islamic Americans felt the need to organize and protect their interests. Among these new American Muslim groups was the Free Muslim Coalition Against Terrorism.

Political interest groups are the groups we will be looking at in great detail. These are the groups that frequently participate in lobbying the government. This category can be conveniently divided into two subcategories: *self-oriented* and *public interest* groups. Self-oriented groups seek to achieve some policy goal that will directly benefit their own membership. Usually these groups attempt to portray their political objectives as being in the interest of the general public and not just helpful to the group. Public interest groups (PIGs) seek benefits that will not advance their membership directly but will be enjoyed by the general public. The abolitionists of the 1850s sought an objective that would not directly benefit their membership, for none of them were slaves. Environmentalist groups seek clean air and water for all, not just their members. Many American groups claim to be PIGs because of the more favorable public image of such groups.

Thousands of American Interest Groups

No one really knows how many active interest groups are currently operating in the United States. However, of the three levels of American politics—national, state, and local—the best estimates regarding numbers of groups have been made on the national level. The *Encyclopedia of Associations* has enumerated more than 26,000 national nonprofit organizations (Hunt 2004). The largest category of groups is that of trade, business, and commercial, with 3,757 groups representing 17 percent of the total in 2005.

This summary of national groups includes many organizations that never become actively involved in mainstream patterns of politics. How many of the 26,000 national-level groups are frequently active is unknown at this time. On the other hand, we do know that more than 30,000 clients or interests have registered with the U.S. Congress under the provisions of the lobby registration requirements.

More and more groups are moving their headquarters to Washington, D.C. Of the groups that have been founded since 1945, most had headquarters in Washington at some point in time. In 1960, Washington was home to 67 percent of America's voluntary associations; by 1980, the total had increased to more than 88 percent. A study by the Greater Washington Board of Trade noted that the number of trade and professional associations located in the Washington area had increased from 1,700 organizations employing 42,600 people in 1977 to 2,000 organizations employing at least 50,000 people in 1980. It noted that one or two new associations arrived every week (*New York Times* 1980). According to the more recent count of the National Trade and Professional Associations of the United States, 7,400 national associations were headquartered in Washington, D.C. A walk around the northwest quadrant of that city reveals building after building with offices containing from one to dozens of groups or associations. The U.S. capital sometimes seems filled with lobbyists and lawyers—and these are not necessarily different professions. One street in the northwest quadrant of Washington, D.C., has come to symbolize the concentration of interest groups and lobbyists there—K Street. In fact, K Street was the focus of an HBO miniseries entitled *K Street: Politics from the Inside Out.*

On the state level, a clearer picture is emerging of the number of groups that are the result of lobby registration laws that have been enacted in various states. One interesting finding is the numerical domination of business, banks, and economic groups among the state-level registrants. The number of local-level groups is impossible to determine because of the ephemeral nature of many local groups. Many deal with specific local problems and may be founded and dissolved within the same calendar year. Additionally, almost no reporting requirements are in place for local-level groups in the United States. Despite these issues, estimates indicate that more than 200,000 different organizations exist at the state and local levels of American politics.

Patterns of Interest Group Proliferation

The interest group universe in the United States seems to expand in surges several decades apart. U.S. history has seen several periods of high group formation separated by longer periods of relatively small increases in the number of groups. Political scientist David Truman noted, "the formation of associations tends to occur in waves" (Truman 1971, 59). James Q. Wilson subsequently noted that three great waves of association formation occurred between 1800 and 1940 (Wilson 1995, 198). The first wave occurred between 1830 and 1860 and saw the establishment of the first national organizations in American history. The Young Men's Christian Association, the Grange, the Elks, and many abolitionist groups were formed during the three decades before the Civil War. Later, during the 1880s, a second wave was a result of the industrialization of the United States. Also at this time, economic associations were formed to represent the interests of both labor and business (AFL, Knights of Labor, and many manufacturing associations), and some of the most familiar present-day associations, such as the American Red Cross, were created in this era. The years between 1900 and 1920 can be seen as the period during which the greatest number of organizations was formed, including the U.S. Chamber of Commerce, National Association of Manufacturers, American Medical Association, National Association for the Advancement of Colored People, Urban League, American Farm Bureau Federation, Farm Union, American Cancer Society, and American Jewish Committee. Whereas Truman and Wilson saw three major waves of group formation in American history, the current authors saw that a similar increase in the number of groups occurred in the 1960s and 1970s. This expansion was largely based on an increase in cause-oriented and economic organizations reflecting the social activism and increased governmental activity of the past 30 years.

What explains the increase in the number of political interest groups during the first several decades of the 20th century? A number of societal changes seem to have facilitated the association explosion (Wilson 1995). Nationwide organizations could be established because communications of nearly every sort became easier as radio, telephones, railroads, and national newspapers and magazines allowed people to participate in the new national organizations. As government escalated its regulation of the business world, the business world organized to deal with the governmental demands. Economic specialization resulted in the creation of many new economic associations. Additionally, new immigration contributed to the increased heterogeneity of the American population. "Organizations become more numerous when ideas become more important . . . widespread organizing seems always to be accompanied by numerous social movements" (Wilson 1995, 201). Each of these great organizing periods was simultaneously a period of great social unrest and social movement.

Lobbying Power Is Built upon Interest Group Characteristics

A lobbying campaign's success or failure will be based upon the foundation of its interest group's organizational characteristics. What, then, is the basis of that foundation? Membership characteristics, the structure of the organization, and the quality of the leadership and staff are fundamental to a group's power.

The first place we should look for power potential is in the nature of its membership. Every group is advantaged and disadvantaged by its membership. A huge, powerful group such as the AARP has tremendous financial resources and the potential to convert its millions of members into a potent lobbying force; on the other hand, because it is so huge, it will have a difficult time developing a membership consensus to support a particular lobbying objective. Even a much smaller group, such as the American Civil Liberties Union (ACLU), with a membership that is highly educated and generally left of center, sometimes has to avoid certain issues because the membership is so divided on them.

Organizations with largely middle and upper social-economic class memberships seem to have additional resources associated with that income and social status that can be converted into lobbying resources. Common Cause, the largely middle-class political reform organization based in Washington, D.C., with state-level units in many states, has members who are willing and able to be activated into the political process. These characteristics tend to produce high degrees of personal efficacy and ego strength. The higher a person's education level and income, the more free time he or she has, and thus the greater his or her sense of obligation (or guilt) to participate. Often this equation can translate into more interest in politics and even past experience in politics. All of these factors tend to produce "the upper class bias of interest group participation" (Schattschneider 1960, 31–32).

The resources of interest groups are many and varied. No one group has all of them, and some groups have only one or two, but all groups have some resources available to support them. As noted, the most fundamental resource for any interest group is its membership. Rich or poor, active or passive, many or few, happy or unhappy, political or nonpolitical, interested or disinterested—all of these characteristics will either enhance or reduce the potential for converting the membership into a lobbying resource. Consider the following membership characteristics that may be enormously useful in lobbying. First, special knowledge or education may directly apply to a particular issue. For example, the American Medical Association, arguably the most important national organization of medical doctors, has dominated the political debates on health care in the United States for at least the past 50 years and, in reality, much earlier.

Another example is the small group of atomic scientists, producers of the *Bulletin of the Atomic Scientists* who have had a very powerful presence in the debates on nuclear weapons and the dangers of nuclear war.

Second, celebrities who join a group can greatly increase the potential of the group's ability to achieve its political goals. Robert Redford, the famous Hollywood actor and director, has brought enormous publicity and media attention to various issues related to the environmental movement. More recently, Angelina Jolie, the actress, has turned her attention to the plight of people in the underdeveloped world and has spent a great deal of time in Cambodia, Africa, and India. Everywhere she goes, Jolie garners media attention for her and her issues.

Third, the passion of members for the cause can be an enormously important resource. Even a small group with very few members can have a significant impact on an issue, especially if the members are willing to take extraordinary efforts to promote their cause. One recent example of this characteristic was personified by the members of various radical animal and environmentalist groups who were willing to take violent actions to promote their cause, including burning new luxury homes in areas that the members believed should be protected from development. In 1998, the Earth Liberation Front was associated with the arson of expensive houses in Vail, Colorado. In some respects, an organization with a few completely dedicated members may be able to have more impact than a much larger organization with a largely apathetic membership.

Fourth, the geographical distribution of an organization's membership is important. For example, organized labor's membership is unevenly distributed across the United States. While strong in the Northeast, it is weak in the South and Southwest. In states such as Michigan, Pennsylvania, New York, and Nevada, organized labor is a major political force, whereas in the Deep South and most of the Mountain West it exerts very little political influence. Another interest group whose influence is not consistent across the country is the ACLU; it is almost nonexistent in conservative states such as Utah. Some interests, such as those of schoolteachers, real estate brokers, bankers, small businesspeople, and mass media, are found in every congressional district and legislative district in the United States. But sometimes, a concentration of members in a few places can be very useful. Muslim Americans have found that their relatively small numbers are more politically useful because of their concentration in a few places such as Michigan and California. Jews have long magnified their political power in American politics because of their heavy concentration in New York City, Los Angeles, and Miami. The expansion of the auto industry out of Michigan to many sites in the South and West has increased its political power in recent years.

What other resources are potentially important to interest groups seeking to play the lobbying game? Money, of course, comes to mind immediately. "Money is the mother's milk of politics" (Hoover Institution 2008). This comment, by Jesse Unruh, the former speaker of the California State Assembly, indicates the relationship between government and the lobbying world and the connection between the two: money. Of course, the bigger the group, the more likely it is to have money, such as the AARP, whose annual income from all of its activities is in the hundreds of millions of dollars. The AFL-CIO labor confederation is also in that financial category. Major business groups such as the Business Roundtable, the National Association of Manufacturers, and the Chamber of Commerce have large organization revenues for possible lobbying campaigns. Major trade associations that represent large business sectors such as oil, autos, computers, and airlines can tax its members for lobbying. The beneficial attribute of money is that it can be converted into almost every other resource useful for lobbying. With money, an organization can buy skilled leadership and professional staff, public opinion polling, scientific research, public relations campaigns, "volunteers," and media access. Clearly, money is the universal resource of interest group politics and campaigns. We are not saying that having large financial resources guarantees lobbying success; on occasion, a large bankroll does not result in a successful outcome. The failure of the very rich oil companies to open up the northern Alaska coast to oil exploration is one example of a situation in which money has not yet produced political victory. But money wins much more often than it loses, and therefore, it is always advantageous to have money to launch a lobbying campaign.

The large size of an organization does not automatically convert into lobbying power. The two largest interest groups in the United States, the AARP and the AFL-CIO, have had unexpectedly poor lobbying records in recent years. The lobbying problems of the AFL-CIO are obvious. The organization is firmly attached to the Democratic Party, which was in political exile in

Washington, D.C., from 1995 to 2007 in Congress and from 2001 to the present (perhaps to 2009) in the White House. Organized labor has also suffered a 50-year decline in its membership, from its peak of representing 33 percent of the nonfarm labor force in 1955 to less than 13 percent in 2007. Only 8 percent of the non-governmental sector workforce is unionized, and labor unions enroll only a small percentage of youthful workers. The Republicans who controlled the federal government considered themselves at war with organized labor, and thus the past decade or so had seen labor not on the offensive, trying to get new benefits, but desperately on the defensive, trying to keep its enemies from passing more laws that will injure organized labor.

The AARP does not engage in partisan political battles in Washington, D.C., very often because, at 36 million members (both Republicans and Democrats, liberals and conservatives), getting the membership to support a controversial lobbying position is very difficult. It did throw its lobbying power behind the extension of Medicare to include prescription drugs in 2004, giving the George W. Bush administration an important victory that helped it keep control of Congress in that year's elections. Later, as the various problems with that new law became apparent, the AARP may have had doubts about that lobbying campaign.

What Kinds of Groups Do Americans Join?

Americans are joiners. Most belong to a church, temple, or mosque. Millions belong to labor unions. Additional millions belong to thousands of trade and business associations related to their place of employment. A political science professor at a major university may carry up to 10 memberships related to his or her teaching or research specializations. But the single most frequently joined organization is a church. Churches usually do not participate directly in the lobbying process, but when they do decide to lobby, usually on so-called moral issues, they encourage their membership to establish new political action groups that frequently enjoy church support. Churches have been involved in the American political process throughout the nation's history, participating in such religious lobbying efforts as abolition, women's voting rights, Prohibition, gambling, civil rights, as well as anti–Vietnam War, busing, gay rights, pornography, and abortion campaigns. Clearly, since the 1960s, churches have become more active in the lobbying process and consequently more significant as a type of political organization.

Concerned about perceived threats in issue areas related to education, the role of religion, sexuality in media, wars, homosexual rights, and others, the New Christian Right emerged as a formidable political movement by 1980. New Christian Rights groups that have been particularly active during the George W. Bush administration have included Focus on the Family, the Traditional Values Coalition, and the American Family Association.

Millions of Americans belong to sports associations and school service groups, and although the sports associations do not normally participate in lobbying, school groups have been increasingly active as the education process has become a central part of the so-called culture wars between liberals and conservatives. Most of the remaining association categories, such as hobby, literary, fraternal, youth, and service groups, participate very infrequently in politics. That leaves the heavyweights of the lobbying game: business, labor unions and professional, veterans, political, farm, and ethnic groups. These are the 800-pound gorillas of the lobbying game.

One membership characteristic that may be either positive or negative to building a lobbying campaign is *overlapping memberships.* Americans have multiple identities and multiple interest group memberships that may come into conflict with one another and result in *cross-pressuring* of an individual.

Take the hypothetical case of a university professor—a political scientist. A contentious congressional election is being held in the professor's home district between a Democratic candidate who supports womens' rights, especially abortion rights, and a Republican candidate who argues that abortions are wrong. Since the majority of political scientists tend to vote for Democratic candidates, one would expect the academic to support the Democrat, but multiple identities have brought cross-pressures into the decision. Our academic is also a practicing Catholic and comes from a labor union family. The professor's church is urging a vote for the pro-life Republican candidate; the professor's father and mother are urging support for the union-endorsed Democrat. What to do? Our academic can select among several choices. If the identity or associational pressures are relatively equal and cannot be resolved in terms of one coming to be the dominant pressure, our cross-pressured academic may just decide not to vote in that particular contest. Or the professor may decide to emphasize one of the memberships over the other and reduce commitment to the less significant membership.

If the stress levels rise to crucial levels on additional issues, our academic may have to make a decision about the multiple identities and membership because they are in conflict.

Cross-pressuring is thus another characteristic of interest groups that may be a problem or an advantage for an organization. Its effect depends on the number of individuals exposed to cross-pressuring in an organization, their commitment to the organization, and how leadership deals with the problem. Internal group cohesion is very important to a group's survival (Truman 1971). Sometimes, a group must accept a split on an important issue that is central to the group's mission. In the 1970s, the ACLU lost thousands of members when it decided to defend a Nazi group that wanted to parade in a largely Jewish suburb of Chicago. Yet, on other less central issues, such a cross-pressured organization may decide to drop the issue or perhaps redefine it in such a way that it reduces the cross-pressures. Often, multiple memberships have a reinforcing impact on the political commitment of individuals or organizations. A person with multiple memberships will usually belong to various organizations that hold the same policy positions. In such situations, the individual willingness to participate in political activities is enhanced.

Lobbyists, Lobbying, and Political Campaigns of All Types

Interest groups have, generally speaking, two broad strategies at their disposal when attempting to influence the formation of public policy: direct and indirect lobbying. Direct lobbying is the strategy preferred by the vast majority of interest groups because it is simpler, less dangerous, and less subject to misinterpretation than indirect lobbying. By *lobbying,* we mean the communication of data or opinion by someone other than a citizen acting on his or her own behalf to a governmental decision maker in an effort to influence a specific decision. Direct lobbying usually uses the organization's designated agent in the lobbying process, a lobbyist who may be a staff member, an elected leader, a member, or a hired professional.

Direct Lobbying
Categories of Lobbyists
There is no "typical lobbyist." Lobbyists come from a wide variety of backgrounds and professions. Some people think former politicians make the best lobbyists; others believe lawyers or former bureaucrats make better lobbyists; some argue that a good lobbyist comes from within the interest group. In terms of conventional wisdom, general agreement has been reached on what skills the ideal lobbyist should have. The "ideal lobbyist" should have knowledge of four subjects: the legislative and political process, the law and legal process, the subject matter of concern to the lobbying organization, and public relations techniques (Milbrath 1963, 61). Most organizations seeking a lobbyist tend to look at persons who are or were in government, at lawyers, or at lobbyists in other organizations.

The following are some, but certainly not all, of the major categories of lobbyists: former politicians and bureaucrats, lawyers, public relations persons, accountants, and association personnel.

One of the most visible categories of lobbyist both in Washington and the various state capitals are former elected politicians. After retirement or electoral defeat, they decide to stay in Washington or their state capitals and work the political process from the lobbying position, which is considered the more lucrative end of the process. The numbers are significant—several hundred former congresspersons and senators serve as lobbyists in Washington—but tend to appear rather small compared with the city's total of more than 30,000 lobbyists. What these former official-lobbyists lack in numbers they make up for in clout, or influence. Major lobbying firms and political law firms in Washington will pay top dollar for the services of those recently holding significant positions of political power. Salaries for those in this category have been running in the "mid-six figures" to highs of several million dollars a year. These former politician-lobbyists are expected to deliver inside knowledge, exceptional access, and subject matter expertise in such a quality to make these salaries a good investment for the groups or associations.

The recent big turnover years in the U.S. Congress (1994 and 2006) saw a significant increase in the number of former members of Congress and senators seeking and gaining employment on K Street. If the former official also happens to be a lawyer, he or she is even more highly coveted because he or she adds a marketable skill to the other aspects brought to the position. Foreign economic and security interests seem to automatically assume that former elected officials retain their clout and can get things done for their country. After all, that is the way it is done back home in their own countries. U.S. senators seem to do quite well in this category because of their very high name visibility.

Within this category of elected officials working as lobbyists, an often overlooked collection of lobbyists are those we call "inside lobbyists." An *inside lobbyist* is a supporter of an interest who also happens to hold a congressional seat. Some legislators naturally represent with great vigor the dominant interests of their states or districts. One might expect the senators from Michigan, for example, to be on the side of the automobile manufacturers, just as one might expect the senators from Utah to represent the interests of the Mormon Church. Incidentally, this natural representation phenomenon was the reason Congress had difficulty passing the Farm Bill in 2007. Every state and every rural district had its special piece of the pie to protect from possible changes and reforms. Other interests seek representation by inside lobbyists because of the personal characteristics of the members themselves. Israel's interests have long been watched over carefully by Connecticut's Democratic, now Independent, Sen. Joseph Lieberman. Certain occupations and their interests are also represented by members in the legislature who come from those occupations. Military veterans were once well represented in Congress in the 50 years following World War II, but lately their inside numbers have been significantly reduced, and some say that veterans affairs and concerns have suffered as a result of the reduction of the size of the veterans' inside lobby. It is difficult to determine whether such a large inside lobby makes a great deal of difference on veterans bills, however, for such bills normally receive near-unanimous congressional approval, especially in time of war.

In recent decades, inside lobbyists are also frequently found in the White House and executive branch's various departments. The Reagan, Clinton, and George W. Bush administrations were filled with activists from a wide range of special interests. Several hundred members of the George W. Bush administration in the White House and in departmental appointments actually served as lobbyists for the interests that now petition the offices they administered. This situation is called by many in the reform community "putting the fox in charge of the chickens."

But in terms of actual numbers, many of the lobbyists in Washington and state capitals such as Sacramento, California, and Austin, Texas, are increasingly the former bureaucrats who work for the legislatures and executive branches. As far back as the late 1950s, former executive branch officials represented about 40 percent of lobbyists in Washington (Milbrath 1963). These former bureaucrats and politicians frequently were lobbyists themselves before they entered government. Additionally, they retain their contacts and knowledge of the governmental decision-making process. Thousands of lobbyists fit this pattern of working some years in government and then moving to the lobbying world. Some move back and forth several times, and this "revolving door" tends to produce huge salary jumps every time they return to the world of lobbying. The bigger the reputation or name of the appointed government official, the more money he or she can claim as a lobbyist. Perhaps the king of the lucrative revolving door was former secretary of state Henry Kissinger, who advised former president Richard Nixon on the opening of China in 1973 and then moved on to become one of the most successful advocates for the Chinese government at the time.

Since lawmaking in Congress is so complicated and largely mysterious to many outsiders, former legislative staff members are highly prized as lobbyists by many interest groups. They bring legislative and political skills, contacts, and subject matter expertise. A glance at the lobbying pages of the *National Journal* or *Congressional Quarterly Weekly Report,* two of the U.S. capital's weekly magazines of record, would give one a sense of the number of former legislative and executive branch staff members who have decided to become lobbyists.

The White House has a huge lobbying corps but is carefully shrouded under the label Office of Congressional Liaison. White House lobbyists are relatively new, a phenomenon of the last quarter century, but a great proliferation in "liaison lobbyists" has pushed federal government lobbying into a $15-million-a-year business. In addition to the president's direct lobbying team, all of the departments and agencies of government have their own lobbying teams. The Pentagon has 50 persons on its liaison staff on Capitol Hill; the State Department, 25; the Central Intelligence Agency, 6; and the Department of Health, Education and Welfare, 20. Many of these high-profile government lobbyists then move on to become richer private lobbyists. In some administrations, a trend appears to be emerging that the eagerly sought-after lobbying jobs inside the White House and the various departments require about two years of credential building before the "big move" to a more lucrative private lobbying position. Turnover is quite high in these jobs, but even for those who stay to the end of a presidential term or even two, the outside jobs as lobbyists are still available for most.

Private-Sector Lobbyists

Let us now turn to the more private-sector supply of lobbyists, the major law firms and public relations firms that fill the city of Washington, D.C. The "top dogs" of Washington lobbyists are a very special band of lawyer-lobbyists who function as the "lobbyist's lobbyists." A roll call of these super-lobbyists in the past two decades includes such power luminaries as Clark Clifford, Paul Warnke, Joseph Califano, Thomas Corcoran, and Thomas Austern. Affiliated with the most prestigious Washington law firms, these men seldom participate in the direct contacts other lobbyists perform daily. Historically, they have been unwilling to even register as "mere" lobbyists.

> Under law, anyone who seeks to influence the passage or defeat of any Federal legislation must register with the Clerk of the House of Representatives and the Secretary of the Senate. He must file quarterly reports detailing the interest represented and the amount of money spent. Clifford and other lawyers avoid registration in a perfectly legal manner: they sit in their offices two miles from Congress and tell the client what sort of legislation is needed, and exactly how he should go about obtaining it. Then they shake his hand at the door and send him a bill. Clifford was careful never to approach a Congressman face-to-face on behalf of a specific client (Goulden 1972, 259).

The number of lawyers admitted to practice before the federal courts of the District of Columbia increased from just under 1,000 in 1950 to 61,000 in 1990. Many think more than 100,000 lawyers work in the U.S. capital, and many of these are lawyer-lobbyists. Often successful lawyer-lobbyists deny that they ever practice their lobbyist skills. Robert Strauss, former chairman of the Democratic National Committee and former trade representative and ambassador to Russia, argues that he is not a lobbyist, although many would have labeled him one of the best lobbyists in the history of the city.

Many of these super-lawyer lobbyists have served as cabinet-level officials in a variety of administrations and offer their clients a wealth of political wisdom. Some earn unbelievably high hourly rates for their lobbying advice, while others charge flat fees. Lobbyists in Washington often earn annual salaries of $1 million or higher. Some can command huge yearly retainers from foreign and domestic interests that run into the hundreds of thousands of dollars.

Charles D. Ablard, a Washington lawyer-lobbyist, argues that a lawyer-lobbyist is far more useful than a nonlawyer lobbyist. They are trained to provide legal analysis and to gather and interpret facts. They can draft bills, be convincing witnesses at hearings, and even help write a bill's report at the end (Ablard 1970, 641–651). The increased role of Washington's lawyer-lobbyists can also be seen by the large number of non-Washington law firms that have opened up branch offices in the city in recent years.

Specialists in image building have also entered the world of lobbying in the United States. These *public relations (PR) lobbyists* usually work out of the largest public relations or advertising agencies on Madison Avenue in New York City and are frequently in the employ of foreign governments. But many of America's top corporations and interest groups will add a PR team to their lobbying operations if necessary. These PR firms offer a set of lobbying skills that most traditional lobbying shops cannot begin to envision. Public relations lobbying is heavily focused on mass media. The PR lobbyists often come out of newspaper and TV advertising backgrounds rather than the traditional Washington, D.C., backgrounds. The PR targets are either governmental decision makers or general public opinion. The elite opinion leaders are targeted by using media found in only a handful of cities or even just in the area around Washington, D.C. The public may be targeted using nationally available newspapers such as the *New York Times* and *USA Today* or increasingly specific cable TV networks such as MSNBC or FOX News.

One of the most important PR firms is Burson-Marsteller, a large New York PR firm that performed PR and lobbying tasks for the Argentine government. Many of the PR-challenged regimes in Africa, Asia, and South and Central America have spent million of dollars hiring Burson-Marsteller or another of the famous PR lobbying firms. The award-winning political comic strip *Doonesbury* featured one of its most interesting recurring characters, Duke, in an August 2007 series titled "Duke, the Washington Super Lobbyist." His specialty? Representing the world's tyrants; as Duke put it, "Who knew I'd be so good at reframing evil?" (Trudeau 2007).

One of the great Washington, D.C., PR stories involves a major PR triumph during the Gulf War in 1990–1991. After the Iraqi invasion of Kuwait in 1990, the Kuwaiti government-in-exile contracted with Hill and Knowlton to develop a PR campaign to increase support in the United States for the liberation of Kuwait. A front group was formed, Citizens for a Free Kuwait, financed almost entirely by the Kuwaiti government. Hill and Knowlton was paid $11.5 million for its PR lobbying. On October 10, 1990, a 15-year-old Kuwaiti girl testified to Congress that she witnessed Iraqi soldiers removing Kuwaiti babies from incubators and leaving them to die on a hospital floor. The story became a major part in the rising American support for the liberation of Kuwait. The girl turned out to be the daughter of the Kuwaiti ambassador to the United States, and no direct evidence was found to support the charges (Center for Media and Democracy 2007).

These elite PR firms tend to get hired by the traditional lobbying shops that need expertise beyond their abilities. However, a growing number of full service lobbying firms have within their own ranks a wide range of lobbying skills and resources. A good example of a complete-service lobbying firm is Black, Manafort, Stone and Kelly. This nonpartisan firm is made up of four conservative Republicans and a former Democratic Party finance chairman. Among their clients are Trans World Airlines, the Tobacco Institute, Salomon Brothers security firm, and an Angolan guerilla movement. Black, Manafort, Stone and Kelly provides a wide range of services, including campaign management, lobbying, polling, marketing, fund-raising, advertising, and public relations.

Many of Washington's most successful lobbyists belong to small firms offering one or two lobbyists. Since more than 90 percent of Washington lobbyists work for law firms, trade associations, or corporations, the "boutique lobbying firms" often specialize in a particular issue or in a particular industry. They spend a large part of their time monitoring the actions of Congress or the departments that could affect their clients. Others write speeches or editorial page articles for their clients. The boutique firms' clients have much closer working relations with the small firms than with the full-service firms. Since these smaller boutique firms have one or only several clients, they can work full time on a client's issue if necessary.

In-House Lobbyists

The majority of association lobbyists who work in Washington and the state capitals across the country are *in-house lobbyists.* Larger and richer organizations have lobbying departments or legislature liaison staffs that work full or part time as lobbyists for their organizations. Smaller organizations usually have association managers or executive directors who can take the job of lobbyist when needed. These in-house lobbyists bring their knowledge of the interest area of the organization. Some groups, usually the more political and ad hoc ones, use volunteer lobbyists, drawn from their active memberships. Many groups dealing with moral, religious, women's, and environmental issues have used amateur lobbyists either by choice or because they lack finances to pay for professional, full-time lobbyists.

Sometimes *amateur lobbyists* can be effective if they possess special talents or resources. The top 180 American corporate executives who are members of the Business Roundtable can access the Washington, D.C., power elite because of the prestige of their positions. When these chief executive officers call on politicians, the latter group listens.

This summary of lobbyist categories is not exhaustive. Lobbyists are working in Washington who come from almost every possible background and have a variety of college degrees, ranging from English literature and microbiology to political science and law.

New Trends in Lobbyist Training and Makeup

A significant professionalization of the lobbying business has taken place in recent decades. Master's degree programs in lobbying have been established in a number of universities in the eastern part of the United States, including one in Washington, D.C., at George Washington University's Graduate Program in Political Management. Many of the students who enroll in these programs are already working in the policy-making process in one capacity or another but seek the professional credentials to move up to higher-level positions and responsibilities.

In addition, the American League of Lobbyists (ALL) has been created, which is dedicated to improving the image of lobbying as a profession. Hrebenar and Thomas have found that lobbying on the state level has become more professional in recent years as better-trained, better-educated, and higher-paid lobbyists have become more common in many states, and the contract professional, multiclient lobbyist has emerged in almost all the larger states and in many of the smaller states as well (Hrebenar and Thomas 2004). Although lobbying has long been dominated by males, a significant increase has been seen in the number of female lobbyists in Washington and in the state capitals. This increase is partly related to the increased status of lobbyists, the decline in unsavory lobbying techniques, and the increased expectations regarding special skills to be an effective lobbyist. The growing corps of female lobbyists has generally excellent political and educational backgrounds.

The Lobbyist's Role

What do lobbyists do? In fact, lobbyists may assume only a few major roles. Some are *contact persons,* who offer access to significant government decision makers. The quality of the person-to-person relationship is the important aspect here. A much smaller number of lobbyists serve as *strategists,* who plan lobbying campaigns. Far more common are the *liaison* lobbyists. In their *watchdog* subrole, the liaison lobbyists listen and collect information about what is occurring in their assigned territory—be it Congress, the regulatory agencies, or the White House. Their job is to alert their clients to potential dangers or opportunities. The other major subrole of the liaison is that of *advocate.* Advocates perform as the popular stereotype pictures them: visiting politicians and bureaucrats, presenting data, and testifying at committee hearings.

The primary job for most lobbyists is to persuade policy makers to support their organization's policy objectives. So getting access to these decision makers is one of the keys to successful lobbying. Whether it is true or not, most legislators and bureaucrats think of themselves as extremely busy people, and with tens of thousands of lobbyists prowling the corridors of Washington, getting access can be very difficult.

Historically, bribes and parties were common ways to gain access not only in Washington but in many of the state capitals as well. Although these practices have not completely disappeared, they have certainly become much less common and important than in the past. The new lobbying laws and occasional increased media focus on lobbying have made direct bribery rare (but recent congressional scandals indicate that it still exists) and placed all sorts of restrictions on entertainment as a lobbying technique. Reflecting on what lobbying was like in the late 1800s, George Thayer described the half century following the 1876 election as America's Golden Age of Boodle. "Never has the American political process been so corrupt. No office was too high to purchase, no man too pure to bribe, no principle too sacred to destroy, no law too fundamental to break" (Thayer 1973, 37). But lobbying style in Washington has changed over the past 100 years. Milbrath concluded that by the 1960s, "bribes, broads, and booze" are near zero in influence effectiveness (Milbrath 1963, 274–276).

Certainly, money has not disappeared as an access-creating tool. A much more subtle and legal form of "indirect bribery" has evolved, and it is almost as effective as the older, coarser forms of blatant direct cash bribes it has replaced. Indirect bribery is most often found in the campaign contribution. Both sides of the exchange claim no direct relationship exists between the money the official receives and the decisions he or she makes as an official. As Hillary Rodham Clinton (D-NY) said during one of the Democratic Party presidential debates in 2007, she can take the money from the special interests such as insurance companies and it does not affect her votes in the Senate. Various political science studies have found some relationship, a mixed pattern, and even no relationship between campaign contributions and official votes (Maisel and Brewer 2008, 181). In reality, it is almost impossible to prove a quid pro quo exchange unless the lobbyist or official is incredibly careless or stupid, but almost everyone believes the money buys extraordinary access for the interest to the official and perhaps some special attention to the requests for assistance. If you listen to the politicians and the lobbyists, they almost always talk about the money creating access and not buying votes.

The Abramoff lobbying scandals of 2005–2006 involved free golfing trips to Scotland for high-level congressional leaders and selected lobbyists as well as free air travel on corporate jets in addition to tens of millions of dollars paid to several lobbyists in exchange for getting special policy favors from government officials. The reforms that were enacted in 2006–2007 have, at least for the moment, ended those types of trips and severely cut back on golf trips as an access-creating tactic.

The newer forms of access creation now center around low-cost social events and information-providing seminars. More and more, the lobbyists seek to provide help to legislators such as useful information and data on key issues and even help to write legislation for the legislators to introduce. Information and research have increased in value as money (outside of campaign contributions) has decreased in value. Information and person-to-person persuasion are at the core of direct lobbying.

Indirect Lobbying

The core element of indirect lobbying involves stimulating the grassroots or third parties into the lobbying game. It is used by lobbies to supplement their direct lobbying. Indirect lobbying takes many forms. Here we mention such tactics as using coalitions, initiatives and referendums, boycotts, demonstrations, and media lobbying because they are important parts of contemporary lobbying.

Media lobbying campaigns come in a variety of specialized forms. They try to generate positive feelings toward the group or conduct defensive or offensive campaigns to support a given policy objective. These campaigns can be seen on broadcast television and cable television, in newspapers and magazines, on the Internet, and even in handouts or fliers placed on the windshield of your car. The electronic and print versions of these communications can be very expensive and thus are largely the tactics of the larger, richer associations. Small or poorer associations try to seek free media on newscasts, public television and radio, and other such media. Free media can be sought by many groups that are small, politically impotent, or on the fringe of the mainstream political process where the use of normal paid media are out of the question. How does a group get free media attention? Demonstrations, protests, boycotts, and even forms of "cause terrorism" can and often do get the free media's attention. The big drawback is that the group cannot control the message found in such free media coverage. Violence and forms of cause terrorism are usually the last gasp of interest groups committed to a cause but unable to make acceptable levels of progress. Recent examples of this tactic have been the anti-abortion movement, the animal rights movement, and the radical environmental movement. In general, during the history of the United States, interest groups that are the victims of violence tend to fare better in the long-term achievement of their policy goals than those groups that commit the violence.

Interest groups will often band together in coalitions to multiply their lobbying resources to achieve a policy goal. Many of these coalitions will have dozens of informal members, and several are ad hoc, lasting only for the duration of the campaign and sometimes ending in failure. Coalitions offer an interest group several clear advantages. One is an efficient division of lobbying resources. Some organizations have special ties with one political party or congressional caucus and can use these resources to influence their special target. Labor unions can always have special access to the Democratic Party caucuses, while the business and fundamentalist religious groups have excellent access to the Republican Party caucuses. Groups with mass memberships can conduct more effective grassroots lobbying; groups with substantial research departments can collect data and publish information necessary to support a campaign. Coalitions can spread the risks and costs among the members. By sharing costs, a given group can participate in more campaigns or participate more powerfully in fewer efforts.

Most interest groups have to decide whether joining or even creating a coalition is worth the effort. A group may be able to achieve its goals by participating in a coalition of like-minded organizations or those that have similar goals. For some groups, joining a coalition may reveal to other groups some of a group's secrets and lobbying strategies and tactics. This approach also makes a group vulnerable to being identified with other groups that may have less than sterling reputations or leadership. Guilt by association is a danger in some coalitions. Finally, coalitions often cannot effectively control all of their members and the tactics they choose to use to further their objectives.

Coalitions are often brokered by a lobbyist who may specialize in putting together those kind of legislative coalitions. Often front groups are used to hide the real membership of a coalition. Groups that may have PR problems (such as the tobacco industry) try to create coalition names that have a good or nice feel to them, such as the Calorie Control Council, a coalition in which the soft drink industry participates.

Boycotts are very popular tactics for interest groups in conflict with other powerful organizations in American society. Most boycotts fail to achieve their political objectives. One of the biggest boycotts in American history was the Equal Rights Amendment supporters' boycott in the 1970s of the states that did not support the amendment. The boycott failed to win approval of the amendment but helped create an environment in which many of the new laws passed by states following the boycott helped to move society closer to the political goals of the movement.

More demonstrations and protests are held in Washington, D.C., than in any other American city, and perhaps any other city in the world. Every day, an average of three demonstrations take place outside of the White House and at other sites in the city. Some of them (especially the civil rights marches of the 1960s and 1970s) have involved more than a million people.

Lobbying in the United States has become a huge business involving battles over governmental public policies, and trillions of dollars in appropriations, contracts, and profits are up for grabs. Between 1998 and 2006, the American Medical Association spent more than $1.5 million on lobbying the federal government, and that total placed it second on the biggest-spender list to the $3.17 million spent by the U.S. Chamber of Commerce. Overall, lobbying expenditures of groups lobbying the federal government totaled $2.55 billion in 2006—up from $1.45 billion in 1998. Several billions of additional dollars were also spent on the state level in lobbying (Center for Responsive Politics 2007). These lobbying expenditure totals represent the huge role played by lobbyists and lobbies in the United States, and they indicate the challenges and dangers such expenditures create for American democratic politics and responsible, honest government. We address these issues in the next chapter.

References

Ablard, Charles D. 1970. "The Washington Lawyer-Lobbyist." *George Washington Law Review* 38 (2): 641–651.

Bentley, Arthur F. 1949. *The Process of Government*. Bloomington, IN: Principia Press.

Center for Media and Democracy. 2007. "How PR Sold the War in the Persian Gulf." [Online article; retrieved 8/16/07.] http://www.prwatch.org/books/tsigfy10.html.

Center for Responsive Politics. 2007. "Lobbying Database." [Online information; retrieved 8/16/07.] http://opensecrets.org/lobbyists/index.asp.

Costain, Anne E., and Andrew S. McFarland. 1998. *Social Movements and American Political Institutions.* Lanham, MD: Rowman & Littlefield.

Dye, Thomas. 1995. *Politics in America.* Englewood Cliffs, NJ: Prentice Hall.

Freeman, Jo. 1983. *Social Movements in the Sixties and Seventies.* New York: Longman.

Garson, G. David. 1978. *Group Theories of Politics.* Beverly Hills, CA: Sage.

Ginsberg, Benjamin. 2007. *We the People.* New York: W. W. Norton.

Goulden, Joseph C. 1972. *The Super Lawyers.* New York: Dell.

Heffner, Richard D. 1956. *Alexis de Tocqueville: Democracy in America.* New York: Mentor.

Hoover Institution. 2008. "Jesse Unruh, Coming to Terms: A Money in Politics Glossary." [Online article; retrieved 8/16/07.] http://www.campaignfinancesite.org/structure/terms/m.html.

Hrebenar, Ronald J., and Clive S. Thomas. 2004. "Interest Groups in the States." In *Politics in the American States,* edited by Virginia Gray and Russell L. Hanson, 100–128. Washington, DC: CQ Press.

Hunt, Kimberly N. 2004. *Encyclopedia of Associations.* Farmington Hills, MI: Gale-Thomson.

Ketcham, Ralph. 2006. *Selected Writings of James Madison.* Indianapolis, IN: Hackett.

Maisel, Sandy, and Mark D. Brewer. 2008. *Parties and Elections in America.* Boulder, CO: Rowman & Littlefield.

Meyer, David S. 2007. *The Politics of Protest: Social Movements in America.* New York: Oxford University Press.

Milbrath, Lester. 1963. *The Washington Lobbyists.* Chicago: Rand McNally.

New York Times. 1980. August 18.

Schattschneider, E. E. 1960. *The Semi-Sovereign People: A Realist's View of Democracy in America.* New York: Holt, Rinehart and Winston.

Thayer, George. 1973. *Who Shakes the Money Tree?* New York: Simon & Schuster.

Thomas, Clive S. 2004. *Research Guide to U.S. and International Interest Groups.* Westport, CT: Praeger.

Trudeau, Gary. 2007. *Doonesbury,* August 6. [Online cartoon; retrieved 8/16/07.] http://www.doonesbury.com/strip/dailydose/index.html?uc.fulldate=20070806/.

Truman, David. 1971. *The Governmental Process.* New York: Alfred A. Knopf.

Wills, Garry. 1982. *The Federalist Papers by Alexander Hamilton, James Madison and John Jay.* New York: Bantam.

Wilson, James Q. 1995. *Political Organizations.* Princeton, NJ: Princeton University Press.

2

Problems, Controversies, and Solutions

A re interest groups and lobbyists important in your life? We provide some perspective to show how interest groups and lobbyists affect the everyday lives of Americans. In February 2008, a man shot 16 people, killing 5, at Northern Illinois University in De Kalb. This tragedy followed the shooting and killing of 32 people at Virginia Polytechnic Institute and State University in Blacksburg in 2007. While a Fulbright professor at the University of Vienna in the fall of 2007, one of this book's authors, during every speech or lecture, fielded a question from a student or a member of the audience concerning how such mass killings could happen over and over again in the United States without the government taking steps to prevent them.

In fact, the answer is quite simple. In the United States, millions of people value their ownership and possession of guns as so important that they oppose effective gun control laws. Many of these progun people have joined together in interest groups that lobby state and federal governments against any gun control laws. These organizations are among the most powerful found in the United States, and they are extremely active in election campaigns at both the state and national level. In general, but not completely by any means, the Democratic Party tends to favor gun control laws and the Republican Party tends to oppose them. During the administration of President George W. Bush and the Republican control of Congress, previously passed laws banning the private ownership of automatic weapons were allowed to

lapse. Many thought the Democrats would move to pass more effective gun control laws when they regained control of the U.S.
Congress in the November 2006 elections, but the Democrats
dropped gun laws from their list of priorities for the 2007–2008
session. Why? The Democratic margin of control in both chambers was razor thin: one seat in the Senate and a bit more than a
dozen in the House. Many of the new Democratic seats won in
2006 came from states with a progun electorate, and the Democrats, fearful of losing seats in the 2008 elections, decided not to
address the issue of gun control. One of the most powerful progun organizations is the National Rifle Association (NRA), with
more than 3 million members. It has long raised millions of dollars for progun candidates (almost all Republicans) and actively
opposed the candidacies of antigun candidates. In 2000, the NRA
proudly proclaimed it was a decisive actor in Al Gore's defeat in
the presidential election. It spent considerable resources mobilizing hunters and other progun voters in a number of key states,
including Gore's home state of Tennessee and West Virginia—
two states in which Gore should have done well given past voting patterns. He lost them both, and with them the presidency.

The NRA claimed victory and enhanced its reputation as an
interest that can stop antigun legislation and defeat antigun candidates in elections. Whether this reputation is warranted is not
the point, as many people, including many politicians, believe it
is true. The perception of interest group power is the important
point to remember. Despite the fact that public opinion polls indicate that a strong majority of Americans favor stronger gun
control laws, the intense minority has been able to win on this
issue year after year because of its strong interest organizations,
strategies and tactics, and lobbyists.

Another story from 2008 can also help to illustrate how interest groups and lobbyists can affect everyday life. In February,
a California meat company issued a recall of 143 million pounds
of beef. Much of the meat had been used in school lunch programs and had already, according to reports, been consumed. It
brought back to Americans' attention the ongoing issue of the
safety of the U.S. food supply, especially the meat supply. In the
United States, 23 recalls of beef were announced in 2007 related
to the potentially deadly strain of *Escherichia coli*; 8 were announced in 2006, and 5 were issued in 2005. Prior to 2007, Japan
banned the importation of American beef products because it
was convinced of a significant danger of U.S. beef imports caus-

ing bovine spongiform encephalopathy, or "mad cow disease." Japan demanded that every cow be inspected for the disease, but the U.S. meatpacking industry protested that such inspections would be too expensive and insisted the meat supply was safe. The U.S. Department of Agriculture, the supervisory body for the American food supply, supported the meat industry, and when one meatpacker said it planned to inspect every cow in the process, the government forced it to stop. The meatpacking industry has had many friends in the federal government and has successfully resisted effective inspection. In fact, during the administration of George W. Bush, the inspections have become less stringent than in previous years (Schlosser 2002).

On the other hand, hundreds of interest groups are actively representing many millions of people seeking a wide range of policy outcomes such as protecting the environment, human rights, job protections, better transportation systems, and many other causes beneficial to society. The essence of all modern politics is based on individuals banding together to pursue some political, economic, or social objective in the political arena to determine who gets what, when, where, and why. Individuals simply do not have sufficient power to accomplish these goals by themselves, and thus groups are formed to allow them to succeed. But the act of forming groups changes the dynamics of the political process because groups can possess incredible political power and can be used to advance or inhibit the public good. Interest group politics can be a blessing and a curse. The issue of the potential dangers and advantages associated with interest group politics and lobbying continues to be an ongoing unresolved part of the U.S. political dialogue.

To Control the Mischiefs of Factions?

We turn to James Madison in his role as the author of the Federalist Papers No. 10 to begin our discussion of the problems associated with American interest groups and lobbyists. Madison's No. 10 is perhaps the most famous political writing in the United States' more than 230 years of history as a nation. (The complete Federalist No. 10 is reprinted in Chapter 6, along with selections of other important documents related to interest groups and lobbying.) First, it warns of the dangers of interest group politics; then it discusses how such dangers can be contained (Ketcham

2006). Before anyone had invented the phrase *interest group politics* or the word *lobbyist*, Madison understood the process of interest aggregation and articulation and the threat it posed for democratic government in the new nation.

What is the problem, according to Madison? The problem is selfish interests, to put it in simplest terms. Today, we would contrast the so-called special interest groups with the public interest groups. The first category of groups tries to get something for themselves by working against the second, which are trying to get something for the nation. Of course, the issue is more complex, as we will discuss later in this chapter. Sometimes, the selfish groups are doing very positive things for the larger society even while pursuing their own interests, and, unfortunately, some (and perhaps many) of the public interest groups are pursuing hidden agendas disguised as being in the interest of broader society.

Madison, knowing his history of the brutal wars of Europe, understood that factions in a society were caused by all sorts of passions based on religion or political identities. But he chose to focus on factions (we call them interest groups today) that are based on economic interests, and he argued that the source of factional politics was property (or wealth or economic interests). In other words, Madison saw the source of interest group politics in the world of business and economics. America in the late 1780s was overwhelmingly agricultural (perhaps by a 99 to 1 ratio), and the needs of the large landowners, plantation owners, and farmers, and the businesses that supported them (including shipping companies and banks as well as local stores), were Madison's target when he talked about the property sources of factions.

That factions were a great danger to the new American democracy Madison had little doubt. He argued that his constitution, with its well-constructed republican form of government, could "break and control the violence of faction." Already, he knew factions played a damaging role in the colonial legislatures, as he noted that a "factious spirit has tainted our public administrations."

As noted in Chapter 1, Madison argued that the causes of factions cannot be removed because they are rooted in the nature of human beings. Liberty to hold different amounts of property or different opinions must be preserved, so the only remedy is to try to control the damaging effects of factional politics. We can say that Madison is the founder of the Big Institution, a conservative school of thought on how to control the "mischiefs of factions." He argues, in effect, not for special laws to limit what factions can and cannot do in the political arena but for the general structure of U.S. government based on the Constitution to provide a set of checks and balances and separation of powers coupled with American federalism to control factional problems. More than 220 years later, conservatives in the United States are essentially making the same arguments on the need to preserve liberty and the continued reliance on the broad-based controls provided by the constitutional system established in 1787.

Madison did understand what the liberals in the 21st century would be calling severe problems of the excessive political power and influence of interest groups and their money. He pointed out, for example, that the property owners (landed, manufacturing, mercantile, and moneyed interests) naturally came to government with their requests for legislation. He also anticipated the current debate between Democrats and Republicans regarding the growing inequality of income and wealth in American society and the role that tax policy and interest groups play in it. "The apportionment of taxes on the various descriptions of property . . . there is no legislative act in which greater opportunity and temptation are given to . . . trample on the rules of justice. Every shilling with which they over-burden the inferior number, is a shilling saved to their own pockets" (Ketcham 2006, 86).

Madison dismisses the idea that the elected representatives of the new American republic might always function to "discern the true interest of their country, and whose patriotism and love of justice, will be least likely to sacrifice it to temporary or partial considerations" (Ketcham 2006). In theory, that is possible, but he notes, on the other hand, "men of factious tempers, of local prejudices, or of sinister designs, may by intrigue, by corruption . . . then betray the interest of the people" (Ketcham 2006). For Madison, the solution was the "big republic" with all the institutional safeguards he and the founding fathers wrote into the Constitution. Yet, during the next two centuries of American political history a big republic by itself has not been able to contain the dangers of factions.

As James Madison struggled with this question in 1788, we do the same today. These are the questions we discuss in the rest of this chapter: Do interest groups have too much power? If so, does this power significantly undermine democratic procedures? If so, what can be done to cure "the mischiefs of factions"?

Interest Groups, Money, and the Question of Excessive Influence in the Policy-Making Process

The nature of American politics has fundamentally changed in recent decades. Now, political campaigns are omnipresent features of our politics and not just restricted to a couple of weeks in November every other year. More important, the political parties' campaigns and the interest groups' campaigns have now merged to the point that we have trouble separating one from the other (Burbank, Hrebenar, and Benedict 2008; Rozell, Wilcox, and Madland 2006; Herrnson, Shaiko, and Wilcox 2005).

The American political system has always had trouble figuring out the proper role of money in our elections and lobbying processes. As a generalization, the United States has taken a hands-off approach and assumed that the "marketplace" of politics would self-regulate the process and any excesses would eventually be reduced by the public reacting to them and forcing a different behavior. However, as politics and political campaigns became more expensive, politicians were forced to seek reliable sources of money, and the richer interest groups were more than happy to loan and give them money to run their campaigns (Nelson 2005).

Political campaigns were quite inexpensive until the late 1800s. Presidents from George Washington through Abraham Lincoln and into the early post–Civil War administrations ran very cheap campaigns, with most of the expenses coming at the two parties' national nominating conventions. But that all changed in 1896, when Republican William McKinley was elected after what has been called the first modern presidential campaign. McKinley had the first modern campaign manager, Mark Hanna, and Hanna ran the first really effective "shakedown" of American business to run a national election campaign. Hanna decided that McKinley needed a national campaign with a national organization and as much media exposure as he could afford. The problem was how to pay for such an effort. Hanna knew the answer. Who had money and the need to have access to the federal government policy-making process? Big business. The decade of the 1890s was also a period of great industrialization in the United States and saw the growth of huge corporations and larger conglomerates called "trusts." Standard Oil, railroads, steel companies, and powerful banks were building a new America, and they were ready to invest in a political party that pledged to help them build this new economic model. The choice of party was simple in 1896. The Democrats had never really recovered from being on the wrong side of the Civil War, and after 1876, they had settled into being the party of the South and rural interests. In 1896, the Democrats nominated William Jennings Bryan, an evangelical Christian, who ran a campaign that reflected a near total lack of support for the industrialization that was sweeping the nation. Hanna went to the various leaders of industry and made his case. In essence, Hanna said, fund us and we will protect you from the likes of Bryan and others who may threaten the processes that will make the United States a great power. Hanna came up with an imaginative funding formula based on the wealth of a given company, and he asked companies to contribute a set percentage of that wealth to the McKinley campaign. He accumulated more than $3.5 million for the 1896 campaign, an unheard of amount for that time (about $82 million in 2006 inflation-adjusted dollars). With that money, Hanna hired 1,200 staff members for the campaign and outspent the Democrat Bryan's campaign by a 12 to 1 ratio. The modern national political campaign was born, and the essential linkage to interest groups and their contributions was firmly established (Hamilton 2006).

The next century saw presidential and congressional campaigns get more expensive, but the next great change occurred in the 1950s with the introduction of television to the list of communications tools used by campaign managers in statewide, congressional, or presidential elections. Although print media of all sorts could be somewhat costly and radio a bit more, television advertising required much more in production and broadcasting costs. Beginning with the 1952 Dwight Eisenhower–Adlai Stevenson presidential race, television grew to become the primary communications conduit between serious candidates and the electorate. By the 2000 George W. Bush–Al Gore and 2004 Bush–John Kerry campaigns, the two candidates were spending hundreds of millions of dollars to win their party's nominations and then hundreds of millions of dollars more to contest the general election. By late 2007, the various Republican and Democratic candidates for the presidential nominations of 2008 had spent more than $80 million in Iowa and New Hampshire, at a rate of $400,000 a day in media ads per candidate in those two states. In the 2006 congressional elections, a typical U.S. Senate campaign cost more than $7 million, and a typical House of Representatives election cost well over $1 million. Of course, contested races in the big population states such as California and New York could cost well over $20 to $30 million. Some of these campaigns could be paid for by rich candidates out of their own pockets. Republican Mitt Romney funded his own campaign in the 2008 presidential nomination process. However, almost all campaigns are financed by candidates asking interest groups and their members to make campaign contributions. By 2008, to finance a typical campaign for a U.S. Senate race, a candidate had to raise $20,000 a week every week for his or her six-year term in the Senate.

A modern American campaign is financed by a mixture of interest group political action committee (PAC) money; contributions from members and families of members of supporting interest groups; some individuals from the home state or home district; and, if absolutely necessary, the candidate's own money. In 2006, candidates for the Senate and House spent very little of their own money on their campaigns. House Democrats contributed only 0.3 percent of their total funds, House Republicans only 1.7 percent. Even in the Senate races—the Senate having been long perceived as a home of many millionaires—Senate Republicans gave from their own money only 0.7 percent of their funds and Senate Democrats, 3.2 percent. Clearly, the vast majority of congressional campaign money must be coming from sources other than the candidates' bank accounts.

Thus, the first question we examine in this chapter is the magnitude of the financing role played by interest groups and lobbying in modern political campaigns. Then we examine the controversy over whether this role of financing political campaigns has allowed powerful, wealthy interest groups to buy their policy preference outcomes in the halls of governmental policy makers of all types. A discussion of the various attempts to control interest group influence in the policy-making process is presented next. Then we address a series of questions about what these issues mean for democracy in the United States.

One could begin a discussion of money and politics with the classic quote by the former speaker of the California State Assembly, Jesse Unruh, that "money is the mother's milk of politics" (Unruh 2008). With money one can buy almost every item useful in politics or political campaigns. It can buy organization, skilled consultants, pollsters, media consultants, direct mail specialists, volunteer coordinators, get-out-the-vote workers, media production and exposure, and the private jets that allow the candidates to travel around a state much faster than their opponents. Money can be used to change a candidate's image. Candidates running for the 2008 presidential nominations spent tens of millions of dollars running carefully crafted television ads that sought to make them look tougher, smarter, more knowledgeable, and more sympathetic than their rivals.

However, just spending huge amounts of money does not guarantee an election victory. The history of modern American political campaigns is littered with campaigns that outspent their opponents and lost. Two factors help to control the pure power of money in politics. One is that the money has to be well spent. Millions of dollars can be wasted easily in a campaign, and, especially with media taking more than half of total campaign expenditures, the wrong message on the media will do a campaign no good. Second, as many Madison Avenue advertising executives have discovered, the expenditure of huge amounts of money on advertising a fatally flawed product usually will not produce successful outcomes.

Corporate America, or big business, is a major source of political funding for presidential and, in fact, almost all campaigns in the United States. The 2008 presidential campaign is expected to be a $1 billion campaign. In fact, by February 2008—10 months before election day—the cost of the 2008 presidential election had already exceeded the total costs of every other presidential election in history except the 2004 election. The presidential candidates in 2004 spent a total of $718 million. The top interests giving money to the 2008 candidates were lawyers and law firms, followed by retired persons, securities and investment companies, real estate, the health care industry, energy, and entertainment. The single biggest corporate contributor in 2007 was Wall Street's Goldman Sachs, with a total of nearly $1.5 million—71 percent of which was contributed to Democrats. As one commentator noted, "No matter who becomes our next president, Wall Street will have an indebted friend in the White House" (OpenSecrets.org 2007c). When Wall Street collapsed in 2008, the federal government was quick to intervene and to provide up to $700 billion in funds to try to save the financial industry.

Looking at the 2006 congressional elections, powerful and wealthy interests were major money sources for both political parties' candidates. The top 10 were realtors, Wall Street, beer wholesalers, homebuilders, labor unions, auto dealers, bankers, communications companies, teachers, and health companies. Some of the statistics on campaign funding and interest groups are somewhat misleading. If one merely looks at PAC contributions as interest group money and then compares them to the funding amounts from individuals and parties, the impact of interest groups is underestimated. The fund-raising technique of bundling helps mask interest group contributions. *Bundling* is where a group or an individual solicits "friends and family" to make individual contributions through the bundler. Often these friends and family come from the interest or industry but are usually reported as individual contributors. For example, brokers for a Wall Street firm will collect money from their spouses (and even children), coworkers, and friends "on the Street"; bundle it together; and contribute the total to the candidate with the identity of the interest or corporation clearly identified in the process.

The financial numbers recorded in recent American elections leave no doubt that interest groups and lobbyists have become very significant campaign finance contributors. But is it a serious problem? Most liberals would say "yes," and most conservatives would say "no."

Controversy: Are Interest Groups a Threat to American Democracy?

Interest groups become controversial when people assert they are dangerous to American society or democracy. The lawyer, judge, and author Catherine Crier is one who strongly makes the case against interest groups and lobbyists (Crier 2002). Crier writes that our elected politicians pretend to pay attention to average citizens, "yet all the while, they madly cater to the powerful interests in Washington." She notes that several avenues of corruption give interest groups great power in the policy-making process. First, corporations are legally treated as individuals, and they can contribute thousands of dollars though corporate PACs. The idea that corporations should participate in American elections as political contributors is controversial, as is the interesting interpretation that a corporation should be treated as an individual in American law in all aspects, rather than just those necessary to operate as corporations. The question then arises, should corporations be allowed to make contributions to political candidates and thus use their great financial muscle to influence public policy far more than the constituent citizens of the democracy?

Second, the revolving door of lobbyists and public officials allows interest groups to place their representatives into policy-making positions when their party wins elections. Every president has about 4,000 appointments to fill positions within his or her administration. Interestingly, the United States is the only advanced democracy to allow such political appointments for bureaucratic policy-making and leadership positions as well as ambassadorships and judgeships. Many of the persons seeking these jobs are already living in Washington, D.C., and working as lobbyists or think tank policy researchers—waiting for the right administration to come to power and for their appointment to the White House, department, or advisory committee slot. The George W. Bush administration filled hundreds of key positions in the White House and federal bureaucracy with interest group representatives. In many cases, "the foxes were put in charge of the chickens." That is, the interest that is supposed to be regulated by government now runs the governmental office that is supposed to regulate it. From the group's perspective, this is just about a perfect outcome. One of the best (or worst, depending on your perspective) examples of such political appointments was Ron Brown early in the Bill Clinton administration. Brown managed to span nearly every power position in the lobbying game in Washington, D.C. He held the chairmanship of the Democratic National Committee and was a lobbyist and an adviser to the Clinton presidential campaign all at the same time in 1992. He was then appointed by President Clinton as the secretary of commerce, where he could make many decisions affecting his previous clients.

Although one can find similar patterns to that of Brown's course through government in all presidential administrations, the extent of the pattern in the George W. Bush administration was extraordinary. Haley Barbour, for example, took over the chairmanship of the Republican Party in 1992; then established a power-lobbying firm in Washington, D.C., Haley Barbour and Associates; was a confidant of President George W. Bush; and finally ran for and was elected governor of the state of Mississippi. Following the Hurricane Katrina disaster in 2005 on the Gulf Coast, Governor Barbour's lobbying firm still had his name on the door, and he was able to secure what some people noted was a disproportionate share of the disaster aid for his state, while Democratic New Orleans still lies in ruins three years later. Clearly, lobbying and powerful lobbyists did make a difference in the lives of the millions of people who lived in that area.

It is interesting to contrast the appointments of the Clinton and George W. Bush administrations in terms of their interest group relationships. Clinton's pattern was one of appointing people to key positions with policy agendas in support of the agencies and seeking to enhance the agencies' power to deal with the agendas of their interests. For example, he appointed the head of the League of Conservation Voters (a proenvironmentalist group) to be secretary of the Interior; the head of the Wilderness Society was appointed to be the chair of the White House Environmental Council. Democratic presidents tend to think government should help their causes in an activist manner, while Republican presidents appoint people who generally try to reduce the role of government in implementing the programs of their agencies. For instance, Bush appointed Gail Norton as secretary of the interior after a long career as a lobbyist working for various businesses seeking to reduce or eliminate regulation of their industries. Most of her top appointments to policy-making and -implementing positions in her department came from the energy industries, and many were top lobbyists for the coal, mining, and oil industries. The former lobbyists then were able to make the regulations they had previously tried to influence as lobbyists. In the Environmental Protection Agency, following the appointment of former New Jersey governor Christine Todd Whitman, most of the top appointments went to lobbyists for the chemical industry, the timber industry, or the oil industry. According to Crier, a fundamental difference exists between a Democratic and Republican presidential administration (Crier 2002).

But that is not to say that these corporatist interests cannot work well with both political parties in power. The truth is, they usually prefer to work with Republican administrations, but they can almost always find a way to work with the Democrats when they take power in the U.S. Capitol. For example, in 2006, the media discovered that some of the New York City hedge fund brokers were making yearly incomes in the *billions* of dollars but were paying federal income taxes at a 15 percent rate. How could these billionaires be paying a lower tax rate than the average American wage earner? Somehow, Congress allowed financial experts to consider this huge income as dividends rather than salary, and dividends are taxed at 15 percent, not 35 percent as with wage income. The Democrats, the party not in power before the 2006 congressional elections, used this policy as an example of how the Republicans favor the extremely rich and business interests and how the Democrats, as the party of the working men and women, would change it if they won the 2006 elections. After the Democratic Party became the majority in Congress as a result of those elections, some people expected its members in Congress to raise the tax levels on these types of income, and several Democratic leaders in the House actually did try to do so. However, some of the senior Democratic leadership in the Senate, including Sen. Charles Schumer (D-NY), chair of the Democratic Senate Campaign Committee, the big fund-raising committee that helped win six new Senate seats for the party in the 2006 elections, and Sen. John Kerry (D-MA), the 2004 Democratic presidential nominee, apparently were open to different points of view from the financial interests headquartered in New York City and Boston. The financial interests, which gave huge amounts of money to the Republicans when they ran Congress in the 1990s, shifted millions of dollars to the Democrats when they seemed on the verge of regaining power in Congress in 2006. Furthermore, they continued to give significant funding to the major Democratic presidential candidates in 2007 as it became more and more clear that the Democrats might win the White House in 2008. In 2007, securities and investment firms contributed $28.6 million to candidates for federal offices, and 56 percent of that total went to Democratic candidates. Back in the 2000 election cycle, the securities/investment sector contributed almost $96 million, and 54 percent went to Republican candidates (Open Secrets 2007c). To put the story in focus, senators Schumer and Kerry began to express some doubts about dealing with this problem without more research and some careful thought. Remember, "money is the mother's milk of politics," and those with huge amounts of money will always have a strong and influential voice in American governmental policy making. A handful of people making millions of dollars in political contributions can trump the votes of millions of citizens.

The case of interest groups being a danger to democracy is echoed by Charles Lewis (1996) of the Center for Public Integrity in his book, *The Buying of the President*. Lewis argues that the presidential candidates for both parties' nominations have to raise so many millions of dollars to compete against each other that they have to sell their political souls to the special interests willing to support them with all types of resources, especially money. The 2008 presidential nomination races are excellent cases in support of this argument. All through 2007, the candidates were judged by only a handful of criteria, but one of the most important was how many millions of dollars they raised in a given three-month period. Those who raised the most money were considered to be serious candidates, and those who could not raise large amounts were largely ignored by the media. Before the 1996 presidential election, Lewis asked in his book, "Have they—the big contributors, the mega-lobbyists, K-Street, Wall Street, the white envelope crowd—bought the next president yet? The hopeful answer is no, not yet, although they're certainly trying. But the cynic would say yes, realistically, because that's the way Washington and the two-party system have come to work" (Lewis 1996, 1). By 2008, the cost of the complete set of presidential nomination and general election campaigns had risen to $1 billion. Reformers in 1974 thought they had dealt with this problem with public funding for the general elections and matching public funding for the nomination contest. But the big money interests and the political parties and most of the major candidates discovered they could be more effective asking interest groups and their members for political contributions and not be limited by the rules of the public funding law. By 2008, the law was effectively dead, with none of the major candidates using the public money option in the nomination stage of the process.

The big money interest groups had won, but there is even more to the story than just the nomination and general election presidential campaigns—there are the two party presidential nominating conventions. One of the 1974 reforms was an attempt to take away financing of the two party conventions from the interest groups and let the public tax funding pay for most of the conventions' costs. The idea behind the reform was that the two parties received so much money from interest groups to run their conventions that, after normal politics resumed in the halls of Congress and the executive branch, the elected party officials could not say "no" to the major contributing interests. In the 2004 election year, each party received almost $15 million for their conventions, and according to the intent of the law, this was to be the total funding for each convention. However, a Federal Election Commission (FEC) (run by the two parties with an equal number of Democrats and Republicans appointed to the agency) ruling created a huge loophole by allowing so-called soft money (campaign money unregulated by federal laws) to be spent by corporations, unions, and wealthy individuals in support of activities and events at the conventions. The Republicans spent more than $101 million at their 2004 convention, and the Democrats spent $72 million. The great portion of those amounts came from special interests seeking to create access or gain even more access with federal government officials in the coming years after the election. Some interests were happy to spend millions of dollars to support both the Democratic and Republican conventions. That way, they could not lose, regardless of which party won the election. Telecommunications companies such as AT&T, which had important legislation and regulatory issues coming up on the federal level, spent millions to support both parties over the years. Rest assured that the telecommunications interests were not the only ones spending their money at the conventions. In addition, lavish parties and receptions were thrown where the wealthy and powerful interests could wine and dine the politicians and cement personal relationships on which later lobbying campaigns could be based.

Another part of that 1971 effort to reduce the role of interest group money and influence in the presidential general election campaigns was a check-off taxpayer-supported (referring to the check box on federal income tax returns asking taxpayers if they would like to donate $2 to the funding of presidential campaigns) fund of public money that was to pay for the two general elections campaigns for the Democratic and Republican nominees and make the candidates dependent on the public money, not the special interest money. In 2004, the two party candidates, George W. Bush and John Kerry, were eligible for almost $75 million each to fund their general election campaigns for president. Both accepted the government funding, but each was allowed by the law to raise funds until the day they formally accepted their party's nominations (Nelson 2005). The final combined totals for both campaigns was approximately $700 million. Additional tens of millions of dollars were spent by the so-called 527 organizations (interest groups and advocacy groups unregulated by campaign finance laws), such as Swift Boat Veterans for Truth and Moveon.org, supporting the Republican and Democratic sides, respectively. Without doubt, the reforms have completely failed and the interest groups have won the question on how American elections would be financed. No other advanced democracy on the planet allows such interests to buy influence with their political leaders.

The defenders of the American style of interest-financed political campaigns begin with the decision of the U.S. Supreme Court in 1976 (*Buckley v. Valeo*). This decision on the constitutionality of the 1971 campaign finance law had many parts, but it reaffirmed the central idea that government should not place significant restrictions on any form of political speech, and spending money in support of one's preferred candidates or parties is a form of political speech (Cato Institute 2001; Claremont Institute 2002). Based on this decision and reinforced by later decisions on the John McCain–Russ Feingold Bipartisan Campaign Reform Act of 2002 (BCRA) (*McConnell v. Federal Election Commission*), a candidate could spend as much of his or her own money to win elected office as possible (as did Mitt Romney in the 2008 Republican presidential primary process, who spent from $35 million to perhaps $100 million of his own wealth in his failed campaign), and interest groups and wealthy individuals can spend their wealth in independent efforts to influence election outcomes. The government can limit direct contributions to candidates but not independent forms of political communications during campaigns.

The Buckley decision also allowed interest groups to air so-called issue ads, as opposed to campaign ads. The key difference was that the interest groups could present information on a candidate for federal elected office and policy issues as long as they did not expressly advocate voting or not voting for the politician. Footnote 52 of the decision listed the magic words that constituted "express words of advocacy": "vote for," "elect," "support," "cast your vote for," "vote against," "defeat," and "reject." Such issue ads can be and are largely paid for out of union and corporate funds. The McCain-Feingold BCRA tried to put an end to the use of these types of interest group political communications in the final days before an election. More than 80 organizations opposed the BCRA in court, including the NRA, which ultimately was settled by the Supreme Court. The case, *McConnell v. FEC*, resulted in the Court's supporting most of the key elements of the act, including the ban on soft money to political party organizations, and affirmed the regulation on issue ads in the periods immediately before an election. However, a later Supreme Court 5–4 decision in 2007, *Wisconsin Right to Life v. FEC*, exempted issue ads from the BCRA ban. Interest groups were back in business producing and broadcasting political ads in federal election campaigns as long as the "magic words" were not included in the ad.

As long as the Supreme Court continues to regard political money as political speech and thus allow it to receive the highest level of protection, significant efforts to limit the impact of interest group money will be unsuccessful. However, it should be noted that conservatives and most Republicans in general oppose almost all restrictions on political communications, while liberals and Democrats tend to support efforts to restrict the role of interests and group money in political campaigns. The presence of interest groups and their money in the political process is one of the most controversial issues relating to interest groups in American politics.

To Regulate or Not to Regulate

For the players in the game of interest rules and regulations (the interests, the lobbyists, and the political decision makers), almost no significant incentive exists for establishing any meaningful set of restrictions on lobbying. Almost all the powerful interests want to be able to flex their economic muscles to get more favors from government; almost all the lobbyists want to use those resources and techniques to gain access to the politicians and bureaucrats; and the politicians and bureaucrats either greatly enjoy the benefits they get from the lobbying game or even see themselves as future lobbyists, and thus they do not want to limit themselves in their future occupations. Lobby lawmaking is like the campaign finance laws, redistricting laws, and campaign activity lawmaking processes. Their rules and restrictions give or take away political advantages in elections and political campaigns and thus can make or break those campaigns and affect who controls the government and the decisions it makes. The battles between lawmakers and lobbying interests are often the most bitter and fundamental of American politics.

Periodic scandals will force the players to pretend they want to reform the lobbying process. In 2006, for example, a huge lobbying scandal swept across Washington, D.C., pounding the George W. Bush White House and even threatening the decade-long Republican majorities in Congress. For a while, it appeared to be a "perfect storm" of congruent forces that would inevitably produce a set of effective lobbying laws. However optimistic the reformers were in early 2006, by late summer (just before the 2006 congressional midterm elections) the Republican leadership in both the Senate and House had concluded that reforms were not a very high priority for even an institution termed to be a "do-nothing Congress." Another window of reform opportunity had closed without success. If the excesses of the Abramoff scandals could not produce reform, one wonders what could. Later, in 2007, the Democratic congressional leadership addressed the issue of lobby regulations, and later in this chapter we see how effective they were in enacting real reforms.

In almost every Congress since 1911, lobby laws have been on the congressional agenda. However, only one comprehensive (albeit flawed) lobby regulation law had been enacted by Congress before the 1950s. Beginning in the 1970s, a protracted battle was waged in Congress over the enactment of a more stringent and effective law to expose or control certain lobbying activities. Finally, in late 1995, a part of that battle was won when some revisions to the 1946 lobbying registration law were enacted.

Meaningful lobbying reforms are very difficult to enact. First, as we noted, almost all the powerful actors in the lawmaking process are really opposed to effective lobbying laws. Second, the proponents have great difficulty proving a cause-and-effect relationship between lobbying and corruption because the proof of such corruption, while clear to many, is especially difficult to obtain unless the actors are caught in the act of exchanging money to directly purchase a governmental decision, law, or preferment. Almost all involved are too smart to be caught by that requirement. In political science terms, the researchers and proponents of lobbying reform can sometimes prove a correlation, but almost never a causal relationship. In other words, the acts of lobbying and financial contributions seem to be associated with various decisions made by government, but one cannot prove beyond a shadow of a doubt that the lobbying and money results directly in the decisions.

Sen. Edward Kennedy (D-MA) has argued that the pattern of lobbying in Washington, D.C., appears to be corrupt, and thus just the appearance of corruption should be sufficient to justify the regulation of lobbying.

> Fortunes are won and lost on the basis of a single arcane
> sentence in a lengthy complex bill or a Treasury regula-

tion. Page after page of the Internal Revenue Code is dotted with the fingerprints of lobbyists—special tax provisions written into the law for the benefit of a single company or individual. It is difficult enough under the present lobbying law to identify the beneficiaries of such favored tax treatment. It is virtually impossible to trace the way by which they suddenly surface in a committee bill or conference report (Kennedy and Stafford 1976).

The First Amendment to the Constitution is actually the major obstacle to effective lobbying regulation. The words *lobbyist* and *lobbying* (as well as *political party*) do not appear anywhere in the U.S. Constitution. But the meaning of the First Amendment regarding speech and petition has been expanded to cover almost all types of contemporary lobbying. The First Amendment guarantees the people the right to freedom of speech and the right "to petition the Government for redress of grievance." Many people, both liberals and conservatives, worry about the constitutionality of lobby legislation that would restrict the right to petition (or lobby) a citizen's elected representatives. Even liberal organizations such as the American Civil Liberties Union have expressed serious doubts about the necessity for new lobbying regulations. They argue that reporting (not even regulating) all aspects of the lobbying effort could place such a burden on lobbying organizations as to hinder their First Amendment right to petition government.

Because of these concerns, most lobbying laws have focused on disclosure of lobbying activities, rather than trying to limit or restrict them. The reformers would like an effective registration law that would force all lobbyists seeking to affect decisions made by governments to register, to list the issues they are working on, and to disclose the financial resources they expend in these lobbying efforts. Additionally, proponents favor a requirement that all contacts between lobbyists and governmental decision makers be logged and reported on a regular basis.

The response of Congress to the issue of registration of lobbyists and the reporting of their activities can be divided into two major eras. The first era encompasses the first 146 years of the federal government's history, during which *no legislation at all* was enacted to regulate lobbies. Beginning in 1935, the second period has produced several new laws, each of which suffers from serious inherent defects.

No national-level law attempting to regulate lobbying and lobbyists has ever been very effective. Despite the frequent calls for such reforms, all the laws that have been enacted have all included loopholes that make them ineffective. Many campaign legal experts think the lawmakers and lawyers create new lobbying laws that are designed to fail. To understand this opinion, consider the attempts to "control the dangers of factions" right up to the current day and see why they have been failures. Perhaps Madison was correct in both his concern about the dangers of lobbying and the great difficulty in trying to control those dangers.

From the 1790s to the early 1900s, almost no demand or support existed for anything like lobbying control laws. It was not until the 1930s that Congress enacted the first piece of legislation in this area (Hrebenar 1997). The new lobbying regulations were fragmented and inadequate. The initial two pieces were enacted in the mid-1930s in reaction to scandals and excesses in lobbying efforts by public utility holding companies and the maritime industry. Some members of Congress referred to the electric power industry in the United States as the most diabolical lobby, the most powerful—and the greatest—political machine ever created under the American flag. The Public Utilities Holding Company Act of 1935 included a requirement for reports by industry lobbyists to the Securities and Exchange Commission (SEC) before attempting to influence Congress, the SEC, or the Federal Power Commission. This was the first piece of legislation ever enacted by Congress that was directly applicable to lobbying activities in government.

A year later, a scandal in the shipping industry occurred around the granting of maritime mail hauling contracts and the lobbying that took place to influence a maritime subsidy bill. Congress added a lobby registration provision in the Merchant Marine Act of 1936, which required lobbyists of shipping corporations and shipyards receiving governmental subsidies to report their income, expenses, and interests on a monthly basis.

The great weakness of these two early efforts to regulate lobbying was their limited coverage to just two industries among thousands and the almost complete lack of any enforcement provisions if any wrongdoing occurred. The stated goal was to shine public and media attention on these lobbying practices, but not only did the reports produce no media attention but the public was actually barred from viewing them. Government officials ruled that the reports were "internal memoranda containing confidential business information" and therefore not open to the public (Hrebenar 1997, 272). Thirty years later, the passage of the Public Information Act of 1966 opened such reports to the public.

Even worse was to be discovered, however. The Maritime Administration had decided that several of the leading shipping lobbies did not have to file any reports. In these aspects, these two groundbreaking lobbying control laws became the model for those that were to follow. The pattern is clear. A scandal happens, reforms are demanded, a law is passed, no real regulation occurs, and lobbying continues without any real restrictions.

World War II was about to erupt in Europe and had already been raging in Asia for several years. In 1938, Congress tried to control the propaganda activities in the United States of agents of various European governments, particularly those of Germany and Italy. The Foreign Agents Registration Act of 1938, or the McCormack Act, was an attempt to force the registration of any-one representing a foreign government or organization. The objective of the periodic reports was that "the spotlight of pitiless publicity will serve as a deterrent to the spread of pernicious propaganda." Enforcement was first given to the State Department and in 1942 (after the United States entered the war), enforcement was shifted to the Justice Department and has remained there to the present day.

Many amendments have been passed to the McCormack Act since the 1940s, but most have reduced its scope or effectiveness. For a long time during the Cold War, the government seemed only interested in tracking agents representing Communist nations. Substantial amendments were made in 1966 that sharply reduced the scope of the act, and not surprisingly, agent registration fell off sharply from that year forward. One of the most important changes was to redefine *agent* to include clear political activity. Lawyers were exempted if they engaged in routine legal activities for their foreign clients. This exemption alone allowed thousands of lawyers in Washington, D.C., who regularly represented foreign interests to deal with the U.S. government.

Lobbying by foreign governments and the hiring of lobbyists by foreign interests have a long and important history in the United States. Most of the cases never rise to the media's or public's attention. One early case was the Imperial Russian government's hiring of a former U.S. senator for $30,000 to lobby for the American purchase of Alaska in the mid-19th century. Like spies, most agents of foreign governments who lobby in the United

States have no interest in being identified as such and try to resist laws that would identify them as agents of foreign governments or interests. Internationally famous people such as former secretary of state Henry Kissinger have been called by some as the People's Republic of China's most effective lobbyist; his response is that he is just a consultant, and he does not release the client list of his very successful consulting business, Kissinger Associates. The McCormack Act was a symbolic demonstration of America's attempt to remain neutral in the emerging war in Europe and an official warning to other nations to stay out of U.S. politics. No evidence indicates that many of the tens of thousands of agents of foreign interests ever registered under the McCormack Act. The Washington, D.C., law firms represent thousands of foreign interests ranging from nations around the world such as China and obscure islands off Central America to multinational corporations in Japan and Africa. Many of these lobbyists do not register because they claim the exemptions written into the legislation in 1966 allow them to act for their clients without filing. Enforcement by the Justice Department is nearly nonexistent and thus encourages noncompliance.

Very seldom do the McCormack Act and the question of lobbyists representing foreign interest come to the public attention. Libya hired Billy Carter, the brother of President Jimmy Carter, as a lobbyist. When this was discovered, Billy was forced to register belatedly as an agent of Libya, as were some other lobbyists for foreign interests who had neglected to register. It was an embarrassment to the president and his family but resulted in no major changes in the lobbying laws.

Sometimes changes in the Internal Revenue Code will affect lobbies and what they can do. Sections of the Revenue Acts of 1938 and 1939 denied tax exemptions to corporations that devoted a "substantial part" of their activities to propaganda and lobbying and denied income tax deductions to taxpayers for contributions to charitable organizations devoting "substantial" parts of their activities to lobbying. These Internal Revenue Service (IRS) provisions, 501(c)3 and 501(c)4, essentially created two types of interest groups: the 27 types of nonprofit groups, largely religious, scientific, or educational (501(c)3) whose lobbying is largely educational, and the people and organizations who give money to them, can deduct those contributions from their taxes, and those groups that can lobby extensively (501(c)4). But the people and organizations who gave them money cannot deduct those contributions from their taxable income. Examples of the latter more restricted types of groups would include the AARP, National Rifle Association, Moveon.org, and the Christian Coalition. Status as a 501(c)3 organization is important to many interest groups who want to receive funding from individuals and foundations.

Until 1946, the lobbying regulation laws were responses to specific scandals or narrow problems, and little demand was seen for any type of comprehensive lobbying control law. However, after World War II, a major reorganization of the federal government took place, and a lobbying law was part of the effort. In the 1946 Federal Regulation of Lobbying Act, Congress attempted to formulate a comprehensive piece of legislation to cover lobbying of Congress. The four-page law was quickly drafted and added to the Legislative Reorganization Act of 1946. In fact, very little attention was paid to this part of the larger piece of legislation. In the final committee report, only 3 pages of 40 were directed at the lobbying issue. The 1946 lobby law was the first attempt at broad-based lobbyist registration, and it provided for the registration of any person hired by someone else for the principal purpose of lobbying Congress and that quarterly financial reports of lobbying expenditures be submitted as well. The central idea related to efforts to secure the passage or defeat of any legislation by Congress.

The Federal Regulation of Lobbying Act was quickly challenged in the federal court case *United States v. Harriss,* which involved an indictment of a New York cotton broker for hiring others to lobby Congress and failing to register or submit financial reports. In a lower court ruling, the act was declared unconstitutional because it was too vague to meet the requirements of due process and because the reporting and registration requirements violated First Amendment rights. In 1954, the U.S. Supreme Court reversed the lower court's decision and ruled the law to be constitutional but proceeded to attempt to redefine some of its vague terms in a highly restricted manner. In this judicial attempt to redraft Congress's errors, the Supreme Court ruled, first, that the act is applicable only to persons or organizations whose *principal purpose* is to influence legislation. Second, it interpreted the act to cover only a person who "solicits, collects, or receives" money or anything of value for lobbying; finally, it ruled that the lobbying activities covered by the act included only *direct communications with members of Congress* on pending or proposed legislation.

The following, then, is a summary of the major loopholes of the 1946 Lobbying Act:

1. Many lobbyists refused to register, because they claimed lobbying was not their "principal purpose."
2. Other lobbyists did not register because they used their own financial resources to lobby and therefore did not "solicit, collect, or receive" money for lobbying.
3. No grassroots or indirect lobbying was covered by the act. This was an especially serious weakness in this lobby law because large organizations spend millions of dollars to initiate grassroots lobbying campaigns, and these efforts were never reported under this law.
4. The Supreme Court's decision that only direct contacts with Congress must be reported excluded such activities as testifying before congressional committees.
5. By restricting the law's focus to direct contacts with members of Congress, the act excluded lobbying of the congressional staff of the individual representative or the professional staffs of committees.
6. The law covered only congressional lobbying, and thus lobbying of the White House, the various executive departments, regulatory agencies, the courts, or any other governmental organization was exempt. However, these arenas are where most of the crucial decisions are made in Washington, D.C.
7. The decision on what to report under the financial reporting provision was basically left up to the lobbyist to determine. Some lobby organizations reported all of their lobby-related expenditures to Congress, while others reported only a small portion.
8. Investigation and enforcement of the provisions of the act were almost nonexistent. Reports received were merely filed away.

The Lobbying Act, then, was essentially a law that registered a small percentage of the lobbyists working in Washington, D.C., and accounted for only a very small percentage of the total lobbying expenditures.

The next major attempt to regulate lobbying did not occur for nearly 50 years. During that period, major reform groups such as Common Cause and Congress Watch were formed and had lobbying reform as one of their top priorities. Not even among the reformers, however, did a consensus regarding the exact nature of a lobbying reform law emerge. Vague general agreement existed that any new law must not inhibit the constitutionally guaranteed right of citizens to petition their government. Beyond this broad point, little agreement has been achieved on how a new law should be designed. Some advocated including grassroots lobbying; others demanded a more comprehensive registration requirement; most wanted to include the executive branch; and a few (but very few in Congress) wanted the establishment of a regulatory body, such as the Federal Election Commission, to investigate violations and initiate complaints. Also, ideas were floated about logging lobbyist and governmental officials' contacts and tracking down the real sponsors of "front groups" that had names unrelated to the real interests.

Over the years, strong reform bills were defeated one after another, and gradually, more moderate (and much less effective) reforms bills were introduced into Congress but were defeated by conservative filibusters. The fact that about 80 percent of the Washington, D.C., lobbyists were not registered by the early 1990s increased the pressures for some type of reform.

The 1995 Reforms

The Republicans took control of Congress in 1995, and, as part of their campaign promises, two major reforms were passed. Congress finally passed rules that restrict gifts from lobbyists. Both chambers agreed to end the fruit baskets and other small gifts left in the Congress members' offices, lavish dinners, and free recreational ski trips for the members of Congress and their staffs with lobbyists. The new rules barred House and Senate members from accepting all gifts, meals, and trips except those from family members and friends. The Senate allows gifts of value of less than $50, with $100 total limits from a single source in a year. The House allows no gifts of any value from a lobbyist. Exceptions are found in the rules, such as allowing trips and attendance at events connected to the lawmakers' official duties, such as throwing out the first pitch at a baseball game. The exception for trips is a big loophole in that it allows all-expense-paid trips that are for fact-finding purposes or associated with official duties such as to speak about Congress before a convention. Trips such as these that take place overseas are limited to seven days, and domestic trips are limited to four days, excluding travel time. These changes were important steps toward reducing (not eliminating) the role of money in creating access.

In 1995, the 1946 Federal Regulation of Lobbying Act was repealed and replaced by the new Lobby Restrictions Act. Many, but not all, of the 1946 loopholes were closed. Most significant of the remaining loopholes was the exclusion of grassroots lobbying and lobbying by religious groups from the provisions of the new law. The following are the major provisions of the 1995 lobbying restriction law:

- It covered all lobbyists who seek to influence Congress, congressional staff, and policy-making officials of the executive branch including the president, top White House officials, Cabinet secretaries and their deputies, and independent agency administrators and their assistants.
- Lobbyists must register with the clerk of the House and the secretary of the Senate within 45 days of being hired or within 45 days of making their first lobbying contact to a covered official.
- Semiannual reports must be filed, including a list of the issues lobbied on, a list of the chambers of Congress and agencies contacted, the lobbyists involved, and any involvement of a foreign entity. Representatives of U.S. subsidies of a foreign-owned company and lawyer-lobbyists for foreign entities are required to register.

The loopholes left are still significant. All grassroots lobbying is exempt from reporting requirements. Because many lobbying campaigns are heavily dependent on grassroots lobbying, this exception is a fundamental and deliberate loophole. Another major weakness is the exemption of religious groups from the reporting requirements. By 1995, religious groups, liberal and conservative, had become some of the most powerful lobbying organizations in American politics, and to exempt them is to acknowledge the lack of commitment in Congress to make an effective lobbying law. The opposition to closing these huge loopholes was so strong that if they were included in the bill, it would never have passed. Finally, an effective monitoring and enforcement agency was not included. Participants got the message that the 1995 law was merely a stopgap measure and real lobbying reforms would have to wait for some serious lobbying scandal to provide the political support for a new law.

The 2007 Reforms

The series of lobbying scandals in 2005–2006 forced the closing of some of the loopholes left in the 1995 lobbying reforms. The excesses surrounding lobbyist Jack Abramoff included stories of luxurious golf trips for congressional leaders to Scotland paid for on the lobbyist's credit card and the overcharging of his Native American tribe clients. These revelations also occurred at the same time the media focused on the earmarking of a major federal budget bill that contained thousands of pieces of "pork" secretly inserted into the bill. *Pork* refers to money added to an appropriations bill for some special project in a congressional member's home district that may or may not be needed but will probably help get the member of Congress reelected. Added to these incidents was the scandal involving Rep. Randy "Duke" Cunningham (R-CA) in late 2005 in which this ranking member of Congress traded defense contracts for at least $2.4 million in bribes from lobbyists. Cunningham, a former U.S. Navy fighter pilot, resigned his seat in Congress and was sentenced to jail. About the same time, Rep. William Jefferson (D-LA), a graduate of Harvard Law School and Louisiana's first black member of Congress since Reconstruction, was targeted by federal investigators for taking money in exchange for using his congressional clout to arrange business deals in the United States for various African businessmen. Jefferson denied that he had done anything improper, but Federal Bureau of Investigation agents searched his home and found $90,000 in cash in his freezer. More evidence continued to be unearthed by the media. Two hundred organizations paid more than $20 million for congressional trips in the five-and-a-half-year period after January 2000, but none of the groups bothered to register as a lobby. For example, one Chinese business group paid more than $1.6 million for free trips for members of Congress. All of these various events created the strong perception that corruption and lobbying in Washington, D.C., had become too prevalent to ignore any longer and something had to be done to erase that image.

As in the previous lobbying reform debates, many ideas were suggested, including a ban on free travel by governmental officials on corporate jets, a ban on free vacations for government officials to foreign and domestic resorts paid for by lobbyists, the establishment of a strong watchdog agency to monitor and enforce lobby laws, the prohibition of all gifts from lobbyists to government officials, and the extension of the length of time a member of Congress or government official has to wait to begin lobbying after he or she leaves governmental service from one year to two years. The majority Republican leadership in both the House and Senate hoped to wait out the media's coverage of the scandals or, if absolutely necessary, make as few changes as politically possible. The House eventually passed its lobbying reform bill, but it did not include a ban on gifts, did not extend the waiting period to two years, did not eliminate the earmarks so beloved by lobbyists and members of Congress, did not extend existing reporting requirements to grassroots lobbying campaigns, and did not provide for any enforcement agency. It did require members of Congress and their aides to attend ethics training classes. It also attempted to regulate the 527 nonprofit groups (named after the provision in the IRS code). The 527s are a favorite target of conservative Republicans, because they perceive the 527s as being more advantageous for the Democrats than the Republicans.

The Democrats won majorities in both chambers in the 2006 congressional elections, and one of their very top campaign priorities was the passage of a new lobbying and ethics bill. They were able to claim a victory when Congress passed a variety of lobby reform laws and rules in the summer of 2007, and President George W. Bush, while complaining of some of the details on the earmarking question, signed the bill into law in September 2007. The new law is called the Honest Leadership and Open Government Act of 2007. It included several parts, which are summarized below:

- *Slowing the revolving door* of government officials to the lobbying world, but not restricting lobbyists from coming into government. The "cooling-off period" for senators becoming lobbyists is now two years before they can directly lobby Congress. Senior executive branch members are prohibited from lobbying their department or agency for two years. House and Senate members who become lobbyists are prohibited from lobbying the

Senate (for ex-senators) or their old committees (for ex-House members).

- *Ending the K Street Project.* The K Street (the street in Washington, D.C., on which many lobbying firms and associations have their headquarters) Project was an attempt by Republican members of Congress to control the hiring of new lobbyists on K Street by threatening to exclude any firm from their decision-making process that does not hire Republican lobbyists. Now those members or staff members of Congress who try to control lobbying firms in such a way can be fined and imprisoned for up to 15 years.
- *Prohibiting gifts by lobbyists.* Gifts and travel paid for by lobbyists are not allowed.
- *Full disclosure of lobbying activity.* Regular lobbying expense reports by lobbyists must be submitted.
- *Greater transparency for bundling lobbyist campaign donations.* Lobbyists now have to disclose contributions to such recipients as presidential libraries and inaugural committees.
- *Denial of congressional pensions to members convicted of bribery.*
- *Payment of fair market price for trips on noncommercial aircraft required.*

In addition to these provisions in the law, the House amended its ethics rules as follows:

- Sets rules for House members to negotiate for future employment while a member of the House
- Sets new rules prohibiting lobbying contacts with spouses of members who are lobbyists
- Prohibits House members from attending parties at the national party conventions that are held in honor of the member

The following are changes in the Senate's ethics rules passed in 2007:

- Prohibits "dead of the night" additions to conference reports unless 60 members of the Senate approve them.

- Eliminates floor, parking, and gym privileges for former senators who become lobbyists.
- Prohibits lobbyists from planning and sponsoring senatorial travel (Campaign Legal Center 2007).

Many changes have been initiated, and several of them will be very good for opening up the lobbyist-legislator information and contact process. But one very glaring omission remains: no enforcement provision has been established in the new law or the rules changes. In essence, the lawmakers will police their own behavior. Many reformers demanded an independent investigation and enforcement body, but the congressional leadership was not interested in going that far in the reforms. In a very short time, the Washington, D.C., media were speculating on whether the lawmakers and the lobbyists would slip back into old habits with no repercussions. But "something was done" and "heat was off" until the next big scandal.

Other Attempts to Regulate Lobbying

A number of additional laws on the federal level also affect lobbying activities. Political campaigns, as noted earlier in this chapter, provide wonderful access, creating opportunities. So much suspicious money flowed into the 1972 Richard Nixon presidential reelection campaign that the Federal Campaign Act of 1971 (amended in 1974 and 1976) provided for public matching funding of small contributions as well as public funding for the two parties' national nominating conventions. The process worked fairly well until the late 1990s, when George W. Bush decided to avoid the public funding of his nomination campaigns and public resistance grew to "checking off" a couple of dollars to fund the program, which made public funding ineffective in recent campaigns. Another way interest groups transferred money to their favorite politicians was to give them thousands of dollars for giving speeches to their groups. But since 1989, earnings from such honoraria, usually obtained by speaking before interest groups, have been banned by House and Senate rules.

Lobbyists are also affected by the 1978 Ethics in Government Act, under which most federal officials who leave office are somewhat restricted in their lobbying. Various time limits ban executive branch employees from lobbying on issues they worked on while in office, but the most visible time limit is the one-year ban on senior governmental officials lobbying their former departments or agencies after they leave office. Usually, this restriction is not very effective, because no ban exists on such a person consulting or advising a client on strategies and tactics as long as he or she does not directly lobby his or her old office during the cooling-off period.

Lobby Laws on the State Level

Although most of the stories we read about lobbying are focused on the federal level, much lobbying in the United States occurs at the state and local levels of politics and government. The states are far ahead of the federal government in registering lobbyists and reporting their activities. All of the 50 states require the registration of lobbyists—admittedly with varying degrees of effectiveness. Much variation exists among the states as to who must register as a lobbyist. Almost all the states require some form of reporting of lobbying expenditures.

California has been one of the most effective states controlling the excesses of lobbying. Proposition 9 was passed in the June 1971 election to provide for detailed regulation of lobbying, campaign spending, and the standards of conduct of public officials. Detailed accounts of lobbying expenditures to influence California state government are required, and gifts larger than $10 to any public official in any month are prohibited. Various lobby laws have been tried out at the state level over the past several decades. The Center for Public Integrity has monitored lobby laws on the state level since 2003 and concluded that the states have far outpaced the federal levels in lobby laws (Center for Public Integrity 2004).

Controversy: Has the Interest Group and Lobbying System Fundamentally Changed?

American interest group politics and lobbying changed in the 1960s. That decade marked the boundary of different political eras in many respects. The 1960s saw the end of the Democratic Party's domination of national-level politics that had existed since 1932. At the same time, it represented the end of the once solid Democratic South and began the emergence of the Republican Party Southern strategy and its eventual alliance with Southern evangelicals from the Ronald Reagan presidency in the 1980s and the solid Republican Party South by the 2000 elections. In terms of pure interest group politics, the 1960s began an era that was characterized by an enormous explosion in the number of interests formally represented in the political arena by political organizations. Before the 1960s, a relatively small number of political organizations, big labor unions, and business organizations dominated the political system. Emerging from the political chaos of the 1960s, many new organizations were formed and prospered as people struggled to deal with a wide range of social and political problems. New groups formed in response to the decaying state of American politics in the 1960s. The country was seen as collapsing under the assault of the extremely unpopular Vietnam War and movements that represented women, blacks, Hispanics, environmentalists, and many other interests demanding significant change. Many of these new groups represented other interests that had not previously organized, such as senior citizens, the poor, animal rights proponents, farmworkers, and children. Supporting this phenomenon were many new governmental programs that emerged from the various movements of the 1960s. Politics became more open as political parties reformed and the legislatures, both federal and subnational, became more open and accessible to their citizens. Thousands of PACs formed by corporations, unions, and single interests became the financial muscle of special interests in election campaigns.

The changing American interest group system has resulted in a number of different repercussions. One positive impact is the greater democratization of American politics. One can now seriously make the statement that almost everyone and every interest are now represented in the American interest group and lobbying system. This mobilization of previously unmobilized interests means the promise of democratic representation is closer to being fulfilled than ever before in U.S. history.

Interest groups now use the most modern technology to facilitate communications from their members to their government and from government to the interest's membership (Loomis and Cigler 2007). The Internet and e-mail have and will continue to change the nature of politics in ways we have not experienced since the rise of television a half century ago. Interest groups can now communicate with up to tens of millions of their members (the AARP, for example) in the span of a single second. These communications changes have increased flexibility of interest groups in choosing among a number of strategies and tactics available to influence public policy. Even changes such as the spread of cable television to most households in the United States has increased interest group power, as groups can more easily microtarget a narrow sector of the society with their political message. Democracy has also improved from the perspective of government officials in that their constituents (often organized and led by interest groups) can now much more easily communicate their policy desires to their elected representatives.

On the other hand, many argue that the changes that have occurred since the 1960s have negatively affected the democratic system. Critics accuse the so-called single interest groups with fragmenting the democratic consensus and establishing a pattern of deadlock in the legislative process. Regarding this criticism, it is difficult to determine whether the current pattern of hyper-partisan politics found in Congress and Washington, D.C., in general, is the result of the actions of the interest groups or the political parties or even other forces such as the mass media. The cause and effect are difficult to prove, like many other aspects of interest group politics, such as the real impact of interest group financial contributions to governmental officeholders. What we cannot ignore is the fact that we have entered a significantly more contentious era of politics in which it is much more difficult to enact significant policy changes through the representative political process.

It is also clear that it is easier to stop something from happening than to make it happen. Bill and Hillary Clinton's attempts to change America's health care insurance system in 1993–1994 met with failure largely because of how easy it is to block significant new ideas. When the Democrats took majority control of Congress in 2007, most of their new initiatives were easily blocked by the Senate Republicans using the filibuster threat coupled with President George W. Bush's vetoes. The Democrats' reign began with high public support, but by early 2008, the public's rating of the job performance of Congress was actually below that of President Bush.

The media tend to portray the interest group universe as divided into public interest groups and single interest groups. Essentially, the former are labeled as good and the latter as bad.

Good and bad is not a fair description of the system, however. Many of the so-called public interest groups that purport to represent the broader interests of society are in reality single or special interest groups disguised as one of the good guys. But in all fairness, even the single interest groups seeking a very narrow public policy preference may at the same time represent millions of people, and the policy positions they support may also be in the public's interest.

The public interest is very difficult to define. What one person argues is in the public's interest, another will strongly argue against. Many would argue that more cooperation in the public arena, more willingness to put aside one's "selfish" agenda, and more willingness to work for a broader agenda should take place even if one's group does not get the exact policy preference it may desire (Yarrow, 2008).

Concerns over the dangers of selfish interest groups have produced a major new political movement called the "communitarians." Dr. Amitai Etzioni, a political scientist, is the leader of the communitarian movement, and he has written extensively on organizations and interest groups (Etzioni 1982). Etzioni sought to raise the concept of community and individuals' responsibility to the larger community above their own selfish interests. He argues that "me-ism" has been elevated to the group level, and the balance between special interest groups and the community has been lost. To restore the balance, Etzioni advocated increasing the power of political parties (a community type of organization). During the bitter interest group and political party battles of the 1990s, other authors agreed with that conclusion. Francis Fukuyama (1995), in his book *Trust*, argued for a stronger civil society based on intermediate institutions. Robert J. Samuelson (1995) concluded that when citizens join interest groups, a style of politics is created where lobbyists come to dominate the policy-making process. And Jonathan Rauch (1994), in his book *Demosclerosis*, saw stalemates in politics caused by interest groups and argued that the United States should place the needs of society above the demands of interest groups.

Deadlock, stalemate, and immobility—as the United States decided on the new president in 2008, some political analysts (including this author) warned that regardless of who gets elected, the political parties and powerful interest groups have sufficient power to stop all significant reforms in terms of new public policies such as universal health care insurance for all Americans.

The interest group/political party deadlocks produce a political environment where the United States as a whole finds itself unable to deal with, much less solve, chronic public problems such as slow economic growth, a rotting national infrastructure, growing economic inequality, environmental concerns, and fundamental social issues. Many individuals see this power of special interest groups to block legislation as unacceptable to their own interests and a very real danger to the United States. So many well-organized groups now exist and political leadership is so weakened that it has become virtually impossible to formulate meaningful legislation and to guide it safely through the legislative maze. When one dispassionately evaluates the two recent presidential administrations of Bill Clinton and George W. Bush, one may be shocked at how little in terms of domestic policy making has been accomplished in those 16 years. Clinton could not get his most significant domestic policy goal accomplished (health care reform), and Bush, other than his tax cuts, had a domestic policy agenda with very few successes. The current political style is "strategist politics," in which groups form temporary alliances to generally stop undesirable proposals. Although many groups have sufficient resources to block legislation successfully, few have the resources to enact legislation. Lester Thurow has studied this phenomenon in his book, appropriately titled *The Zero-Sum Society* (Thurow 1980).

Some worry that the institutions of the public sector (government) have lost real political decision-making power to the private sector, which is dominated by large corporations and powerful interest groups. Part of the concern is that the private sector faces few effective legal controls on its political activities and it is not responsible to the elected governments or the broader American society. So from the rise of interest group–representative politics, U.S. society has achieved increased representation but has also decreased accountability and responsibility. As Morris Fiorina (1980) has concluded, the U.S. political system operates superbly to articulate interests but aggregates them poorly. Does this pattern, if it is true, constitute a real political crisis for the United States? Has the United States entered into an era of a "tyranny of minorities" (Staub 1980)?

It is true that periodically throughout American political history, people have blamed interest groups and lobbyists for the troubles of their times. Robert Luce, writing in 1924, noted that "group organization is one of the perils of the time"(Luce 1924,

421). David Truman has observed that this opinion has repeated several times in U.S. history. Truman (1971) noted the common themes include alarm at the proliferation of the number of new interest groups and their domination of the governmental policy-making process.

Fear of the excessive power of interest groups has reemerged in recent years. Americans have always been suspicious of both its political parties and interest groups as dangers to its democratic practices. When pollsters asked citizens what was the main reason the U.S. system of government does not work better than it does, almost half of the respondents replied that too much influence is brought to bear on government by special interest groups and lobbies. As many as 8 of 10 Americans agree that special interests get more from government than the people do. More than half of the American public believes government is run for the benefit of a few big interests rather than for the benefit of all (Newsweek, 2003).

A student of Washington, D.C., lobbying, Lester Milbrath noted the strong American distrust of lobbying but suggested that Americans were responding to the sensational lobbying scandals they read about in the mass media (Milbrath 1963). These scandals, he argued, did not really portray the reality of what lobbying was like. Political scientists and various watchdog reform groups have studied the relationship between lobbyists' financial contributions and politicians' policy-making decisions. Evidence proving a linkage between campaign contributions and honoraria and the subsequent votes on public policy is mixed. One reason for the lack of a direct correlation is that there are too many decision-making points in the legislative and executive branch decision-making processes to pinpoint exactly when the crucial decisions were made and by whom. A good example is found in the recent controversy over the earmarking of the appropriations bill in Congress. Many of the thousands of add-ons, or earmarks, were inserted into the bill in the dark of the night—many in the last night before the final vote takes place and no one knows who put them into the bill or even that they are in the bill.

But a different sensibility is emerging surrounding this current pattern of concern about the power of interest groups and lobbyists. Interest groups are clearly better organized and have more resources than interest groups in previous eras. The pool of potential members with the needed skills and education to be effective participants in the political process is much, much larger than before. The tools of communication and persuasion are much more powerful than even a couple of decades ago. Because of these communications tools, it sometimes seems that interest groups are involved in everything that happens around us in the political environment. Additionally, groups seem more powerful because their rivals, political parties, have been in a slump for the past three or four decades. Finally, more aggressive interest groups are operating with more aggressive tactics, and they will gain media attention.

We began this chapter by posing the questions of why effective gun control seems impossible to enact despite repeated massacres and why there is a lack of effective regulation of the meatpacking industry in the United States. The answer to both questions is twofold. First, millions of voters passionately oppose these two policies despite public opinion polls that report a majority of the American people support the adoption of both. And second, groups that oppose both plans have claimed to have defeated politicians who advocated the changes. Beginning in about the 1980s, groups and their "hit lists" have claimed a number of spectacular and largely unexpected defeats of their opponents, with the NRA being just one of many such groups. Now, many single interest groups publish lists of "friends and enemies" each election, and many politicians are afraid to take the chance of getting on the wrong list. As noted earlier, the Democratic leadership in the U.S. Congress essentially dropped gun control from its list of legislative priorities in 2007–2008 after the Democrats won control of Congress in the 2006 elections. Why? Politicians fear they will lose their jobs.

Leaving the question of the role of interest groups in the United States for a moment, we consider concerns about these groups in other countries around the world. Mancur Olson, the prominent economist who has studied interest groups and their effects, wrote a book entitled *The Rise and Decline of Nations* (Olson 1982). Olson thought interest groups were the most important reason why some nations (or U.S. states, for that matter) experienced rapid growth while others went through economic decline. Olson's thesis was that the behavior of individuals and corporations in modern societies causes the formation of networks of cartels and lobbying organizations that make economies and governments less effective. In a long-term stable society, these organizations become more and more powerful and slow down economic expansion.

Are interest groups important actors in the American political process? Yes, without a doubt. Are they the most important actors in the process? Many people (including these authors) think that is the case. Arthur Bentley argued in 1908, "When groups are adequately stated, everything is stated" and "there is no political phenomena except group phenomena" (Bentley 1955). One may express doubt regarding Bentley's observations because we live in a very complicated society with many forces operating to affect politics, but there is no doubt that most of contemporary politics is based on organized, political groups (Bell 2002).

Contemporary Controversies and Political Action

Maybe Madison was right when he wrote Federalist No. 10 about how difficult it would be to control the evils of factions. An old Chinese proverb says to be careful what you wish for because it may come true and it may not have the outcomes you expected. Recent attempts to control lobbying have all had their problems. The political reforms largely enacted by the liberal Democrats in the 1970s resulted in or coincided with great changes in the interest group system. Trying to limit the role of interest group money in election politics resulted in the birth of thousands of PACs and interest groups displacing political parties as significant contributors to political campaigns. Although it seemed the reformers had won after the 1976 elections, it was clear by 2008 that the reforms had largely failed.

Consequently, one must be careful in reforming interest groups and lobbying because the results are often much different from what was anticipated. Most reforms aimed at the lobbying process seek less to regulate these activities than to disclose them to public scrutiny. Such reforms are relatively innocuous in terms of their effects on the political process. Some recommended reforms could seriously reduce the impact of long-standing interest group activities such as the use of money to create access. Federal financing of congressional elections, for example, could profoundly transform the political process. Proponents of the federal financing of congressional elections argue that it would help to protect members of Congress from the pressures and financial influence of single interest groups. Cautious observers warn that one must be careful to preserve the constitutional rights of freedom of petition, political communication, and electoral activities. They also warn that the facts regarding the danger of interest group activities in the U.S. political process are not clear, and thus one should be hesitant to embark on drastic reforms.

The interest group stalemate is not necessarily fatal to the American political system. It can continue with less-than-perfect public policy making and still survive for the foreseeable future. Conservatives would argue that when government does nothing, it is government at its best. As Ronald Reagan often said, "The best government is the least government." In fact, one wonders if one can find "normal" periods of American politics when one could prove the political process worked better than in the current era. One must keep in mind that the Founding Fathers in 1787 created a democratic republic that was designed to make changes very difficult to accomplish. Federalism, separation of powers, and all the other checks and balances of the U.S. governmental system tend to produce frustration in those who seek quick responses to the nation's problems. American government and politics have proven to be effective in periods of great crisis, such as the Great Depression, World War II, and the Cold War. Maybe we should not worry so much about the current pattern.

The current system of interest group politics in the United States is one of widespread opportunity and access. At the same time, one must admit that it has a potential for abuse. It has never been, nor will it ever be, easy to encourage people to a greater consideration of the national good rather than their own personal interests. It is easy to label someone else's political agenda as selfish. The system actually makes more sense from almost any perspective when one better understands the role of interest groups and lobbyists in what government does and does not do.

References

Bell, Lauren Cohen. 2002. *Warring Factions: Interest Groups, Money and the New Politics of Senate Confirmation.* Columbus: Ohio State University Press.

Bentley, Arthur F. 1908. *The Process of Government.* Reprint. Bloomington, IN: Principia Press, 1955, 208–209.

Burbank, Matthew J., Ronald J. Hrebenar, and Robert C. Benedict. 2008. *Parties, Interest Groups, and Political Campaigns.* Boulder, CO: Paradigm.

Campaign Legal Center. 2007. "Comparison of Lobbying Reform Legislation," June 20. Washington, DC: Campaign Legal Center.

Cato Institute. 2001. "Special Interest Reformers," July 3. [Online article; retrieved 7/11/08.] https://www.cato.org/campaignfinance/articles/.

Center for Public Integrity. 2004. "The Buying of the President." [Online article; retrieved 7/11/08.] http://projects.publicintegrity.org/bop2004.

Center for Public Integrity. 2008. "The Buying of the President 2008." [Online article; retrieved 7/11/08.] http://www.publicintegrity.org/projects/entry/277/.

Claremont Institute. 2002. "Missing the Point on Campaign Finance," March 21. [Online article; retrieved 7/11/08.] http://www.claremont.org/publications/precepts/id.171/precept_detail.asp.

Crier, Catherine. 2002. *The Case Against Lawyers.* New York: Broadway.

Etzioni, Amitai. 1982. "Making Interest Groups Work for the Public." *Public Opinion* (August–September): 53–54.

Fiorina, Morris. 1980. "The Decline of Collective Responsibility in American Politics." *Daedalus* 109 (Summer): 44.

Fukuyama, Francis. 1995. *Trust: The Social Virtues and the Creation of Prosperity.* New York: Free Press.

Hamilton, Richard F. 2006. *President McKinley.* New York: Transaction.

Herrnson, Paul S., Ronald G. Shaiko, and Clyde Wilcox. 2005. *The Interest Group Connection: Electioneering, Lobbying and Policymaking in Washington.* Boulder, CO: Westview.

Hrebenar, Ronald J. 1997. *Interest Group Politics in America.* Armonk, NY: M. E. Sharpe.

Kennedy, Edward M., and Robert T. Stafford. 1976. "Lobbying Reform Legislation." Hearings conducted by the Committee on Government Operations, U.S. Senate, 24. Washington, DC: Government Printing Office.

Ketcham, Ralph, ed. 2006. *Selected Writings of James Madison.* Indianapolis: Hackett.

Lewis, Charles. 1996. *The Buying of the President.* New York: Avon.

Loomis, Burdett A., and Allan J. Cigler. 2007. "Introduction: The Changing Nature of Interest Group Politics." In *Interest Group Politics,* edited by A. J. Cigler and B. A. Loomis, 1–36. Washington, DC: CQ Press.

Luce, Robert. 1924. *Legislative Assemblies.* Boston: Houghton Mifflin.

Milbrath, Lester. 1963. *The Washington Lobbyists.* Chicago: Rand McNally, 67.

Nelson, Michael, ed. 2005. *The Elections of 2004*. Washington, DC: CQ Press.

Newsweek. 2003. "Polls—Princeton Survey Research Associates." October 11.

Olson, Mancur. 1982. *The Rise and Decline of Nations: Economic Growth, Stagflation, and Social Rigidities*. New Haven, CT: Yale University Press.

OpenSecrets. 2007a. "Lobbying Overview." [Online article; retrieved 7/11/08.] http://www.opensecrets.org/.

OpenSecrets. 2007b. "Industry Totals: Lobbyists Long-Term Contribution Trends." [Online article; retrieved 7/11/08.] http://www.open secrets.org/.

OpenSecrets. 2007c. "Top Industries Giving to Members of Congress, 2006 Cycle." [Online article; retrieved 7/11/08.] http://www.open secrets.org/.

OpenSecrets. 2007d. "Lawyers/Law Firms: Long-Term Contribution Trends," February 17 [Online article; retrieved 7/11/08.] http://www.opensecrets.org/.

Rauch, Jonathon. 1994. *Demosclerosis: The Silent Killer of American Government*. New York: Times.

Rozell, Mark J., Clyde Wilcox, and David Madland. 2006. *Interest Groups in American Campaigns: The New Face of Electioneering*. Washington, DC: CQ Press.

Samuelson, Robert J. 1995. *The Good Life and Its Discontents*. New York: The Free Press.

Schlosser, Eric. 2002. *Fast Food Nation: The Dark Side of the All American Meal*. Boston: Houghton Mifflin.

Staub, Hans O. 1980. "The Tyranny of Minorities." *Daedalus* 109 (Summer 1980): 159–168.

Thurow, Lester. 1980. *The Zero-Sum Society*. New York: Basic.

Truman, David. 1971. *The Governmental Process: Political Interests and Public Opinion*. New York: Alfred A. Knopf.

Unruh, Jesse. 2008. Home page. [Online information; retrieved 5/13/08.] http://www.jesseunruh.com.

Wills, Garry. 2002. *A Necessary Evil: A History of American Distrust of Government*. New York: Simon & Schuster.

Yarrow, Andrew L. 2008. "Viewpoint: Toward a New American Consensus." Public Agenda Foundation. [Online article; retrieved 10/26/08]. http://www.publicagenda.org/articles-speeches-list.

3

Worldwide Perspective

When they discuss their politics and political institutions, Americans often seem to emphasize how different the American system is from those of the other nearly 200 nations in the world and how the other countries should be following the American example in developing their emerging democracies. In terms of interest group politics and lobbying, the American system is clearly on one end of the international continuum with its extreme pluralism and armies of lobbyists, lobbying firms, money politics, and the merger of interest group and electoral campaigning in recent years. But vibrant interest group politics does exist in many other nations. Lobbying is a significant part of the policy-making process in Europe and all of the advanced industrialized nations in one style or another, and it exists in more personalized and traditional forms in all of the emerging nations and in even the authoritarian states in a very undemocratic form. In this chapter, some of the other nations' lobbying patterns are examined. Special attention is paid to Canada because it offers an interesting combination of a growing American-style pluralist interest group politics within a parliamentary political system. Also, the Japanese lobbying system is profiled. Japan was the first Asian nation to industrialize, was the first Asian nation to become a "great power;" and today has the world's second-largest economy and a level of modernization that is incredible while still retaining an Asian cultural tradition and style of politics. Europe, with its dozens of nations, is examined from several perspectives.

The special style of European interest group politics is examined by looking at lobbying in two nations (Austria and Sweden) with a very different style of interest group system—they are known as "corporatist" nations. Then a brief look at the largest nations in Europe (the United Kingdom, France, and Germany) is followed by examining in more detail how the former Communist nations of Eastern and Central Europe have begun to develop their interest group systems during the nearly two decades of democratization since their emergence from the Soviet bloc in 1991. Following is a discussion of the emerging European "super state," the European Union (EU), and its exploding lobbyist community in Brussels, which presents another style of lobbying in an industrialized community. Other forms of international lobbying and nongovernmental organizations are discussed, and finally, a brief tour of the less-developed world attempts to draw some conclusions about how lobbying is depicted in Asia, Africa, and South America. Let us begin our survey in Canada.

Lobbying in Canada

Canada makes for a very interesting contrast in terms of its interest groups and lobbying patterns compared with its close and often dominant neighbor, the United States. It shares the continent with the United States, and American politics, news, and culture wash over it daily, but despite this presence, Canada has developed a different lobbying system from that of the United States. Perhaps its British-style parliamentary system makes its lobbying system appear closer to that of London than of Washington, D.C. in political style. Canada has also developed a multiparty system, unlike its two-party American neighbor. It has no nationally elected head of government like the American president, and it has carefully established and maintained a set of election laws that have effectively kept Canadian politics inexpensive to conduct and have largely eliminated the problems associated with the role of interest groups as financial sources for individual campaigns. In fact, some argue the Canadians do almost everything "right," from a reasonable universal health care system to effective gun control and reduced societal violence, as well as a low-cost and low-corruption governmental and political system.

One analysis of Canadian interest group politics noted that until just recently, the topic was largely ignored in Canada. It concluded:

in the last twenty years a vibrant, expanding and public pressure group system has taken hold in Canada.
This has happened despite the persistence of cabinet-
parliamentary institutions. Since the 1960s interest
groups have so proliferated and have become so active
in the policy process, they have aroused public concern
(Pross 1993, 67).

Pross also noted the style of lobbying had changed as well.
Before the 1960s, lobbying was done mostly behind closed doors
with very few public tactics used, such as holding demonstrations, lobbying in the American style, and creating associations
for lobbyists. Today, lobbying is open and often intense, and it
has become an established industry. The forces that promoted
these changes are not directly associated with the influence of its
neighbor to the south but with the increased complexity of
Canada's government and the decentralization of policy making
and new attitudes reflecting changes in political culture.

Although the Canadian civil service or bureaucracy still
dominates the policy-making process, changes in the nature and
role of the parliament have increased the political power of individual members to such a level as to make them important targets
for lobbies. Much more lobbying has taken place in the various
stages of the parliamentary decision-making processes than in the
past, such as in drafting legislation, committee hearings, and
question sessions. Some reforms, such as changing the committee
system in the House of Commons rules, have added to the ability
of individual members to influence the details of ongoing legislation. The bureaucracy has expanded in size and thus lost some
focus in the policy formation process, and the process has become
much more transparent, allowing fewer backroom deals and
more access by a wider range of better organized interests.

Canada's strong federal structure also provides many opportunities for interest groups to participate at the provincial
level. Many of the powerful organizations not only have offices
in Ottawa but in the provincial capitals as well. In recent years,
many of the policy issues have devolved from the federal level to
the provinces, and the lobbying has moved with them. Cultur-
ally, Canadians historically have had a much more deferential attitude toward government decision making than their American
counterparts, but that sentiment has changed since the 1970s,

when most Canadians seemed willing to accept as legitimate public challenges and demands to the political elites. In this respect, the everyday presence of American media reports on the American style of politics has certainly had some impact.

Also until recently, almost no governmental restrictions or regulations were placed on lobbying and lobbyists. Just as the Americans have become more concerned over the abuses in their lobbying system, so have the Canadians, and in the past 20 years, several relatively light lobbying laws have been enacted. The Lobbyist Registration Act was passed in 1988, and one of the interesting items revealed by the law is a view of the growth of the professional consulting firms engaged in lobbying. The professional lobbying firms moved from interest-specific small firms to a few full-service firms to firms that now offer international lobbying. The Canadian firms offer a variety of services similar to those in the United States but call them different names: mapping, dating, and representation. *Mapping* refers to gathering information and advising on a topic; *dating* involves setting up meetings between clients and governmental officials; and *representation* is what Americans would term the lobbyist representing the interest group's interests. The American perspective of representation is not generally accepted in Canada, where it is assumed that the interest's own leaders are the best communicators for the interest. One point seems to be quite clear: the Canadian interest group and lobbying system seems to be moving quickly in the American direction. Finally, the kind of "policy area systems" or "subgovernments" the American scholars such as Schattschneider and others have been describing seem to have also taken root in Canada. Now a policy area's members will include governmental agencies, interest groups, media, and interested citizens, and leadership is taken by the appropriate bureaucracy, the most powerful interest groups, and maybe some provincial governmental units. This usually takes place at the industry level but tends to be balanced by regional demands and intergovernmental conferences. All in all, the Canadian interest group system is open, competitive, and decentralized, and it is coming to look very much like the United States' system.

An Overview of Lobbying in Europe

European Corporatism

The political institutions, both formal and informal, of Europe have produced different patterns of interest groups and lobbying. Perhaps most important is the prevalence of parliamentary forms of government featuring mass membership parties, with disciplined, strong party line voting parties in the legislatures. Such a system severely reduces the independence of individual members of parliament and therefore makes them infrequent targets of lobbying. Instead, interests tend to lobby the central policy-making organs of the political parties, and especially the bureaucracies of the government that have oversight over the interests.

Whereas the American system, discussed in the previous two chapters, has been described as pluralist or neopluralist, the pluralist label can be applied to some of the European interest group systems to a certain degree, but the label *neocorporatist* seems to be the consensus choice of many of the political scientists who specialize in European politics.

Corporatism is a term that describes how interest groups, political parties, and bureaucracy interact to produce public policy; it has its roots in 19th-century European politics. Its most well-known form was found in the fascist politics of Nazi Germany and fascist Italy in the 1930s, but those states collapsed at the end of World War II. It was also present in some of the Latin American nations and Spain and Portugal. This authoritarian form of corporatism is sometimes called *state corporatism*. The most recent examples have been found in Taiwan.

The newest form of corporatism is now generally referred to as "neocorporatism," and it describes a policy-making process based on a cooperative agreement among various powerful interest groups and the government. This cooperative arrangement has as a primary objective the establishment of economic stability in the nation's economy. In other words, it seeks to create an economic political situation with very few, if any, domestic surprises. This goal can be achieved by making sure that the most important actors in the economic world, big business and labor, are deeply involved in the policy-making process with the government and any decisions thus made are consensual and are enforceable in the broad society. Schmitter (1974) is largely credited with making the concept of neocorporatism a popular description of these patterns of decision making. One of the characteristics of neocorporatism is the creation of peak associations to represent each of the major sectors of the tripartite model. Thus, a large labor confederation represents almost all, if not all, the major labor unions in the nation, and a major business confederation represents the business world in that nation. These groups then meet regularly with the governmental bureaucrats to hammer out policies such as wage settlements, inflation policies, and tax levels. Such peak associations are recognized by the government as legitimate representatives of their sector, and in exchange for admission to the decision-making process, the peak associations agree to cooperate in producing reasonable outcomes.

It is often noted that Austria and Sweden are the most purist examples of the modern neocorporative system, although they exemplify the system in different ways. So, we begin our discussion of the European interest group system with a brief example of these two models.

The Two Best Examples of Neocorporatism: Austria and Sweden

Most studies of neocorporatism in Europe point to Austria and Sweden as the two best, but somewhat competing, models. Some observers have called the two basic forms of European corporatism the Continental Europe and the Scandinavian models. The Continental group is usually considered to be Switzerland, Belgium, the Netherlands, Germany, and Austria. The Scandinavian model is best seen in Sweden, but also includes, to a greater or lesser degree, Norway and the other Scandinavian nations. What seems to separate the two models most has been the strong emphasis in the former on the use of social agreements to avoid economic and social conflict in their societies. In fragmented societies, the development of democratic governments could result in severe conflicts that might endanger the existence of the nation. The Swedish model was characterized by a coordinated set of policies to produce full employment, low levels of inflation, and a relatively equal distribution of national wealth. Sweden's long run of social democratic corporatism ran into the wall of globalization, domestic societal changes, and the entry into the European Union in the 1990s, the result of which was rising unemployment; higher levels of inflation; and severe strains on the ability of the corporatist model to keep business, labor, and the farming sector happy in a very internationalized environment.

The strength of the Austrian commitment to its so-called social partnership is what separates it from the other neocorporatist nations of Europe (Bischof and Pelinka 1996). The Austrian model goes far beyond the usual pattern of governmental bureaucracy, business, and labor consulting each other and cooperating on labor conditions or annual wage agreement. In Austria, such cooperative, institutionalized patterns of policy making are extended to nearly every aspect of Austrian society. The pattern started in the immediate post–World War II period as the nation tried to deal with the impact of severe inflation with informal cooperation; later it was extended to a broad range of social and economic policy making.

The Austrian Parity Commission for Wages and Prices is central to the establishment of an incomes policy in the nation. The commission's members are the Austrian Trade Union Federation; the Chambers of Commerce, Labor, and Agriculture; and the various appropriate ministers of the federal bureaucracy. The chancellor (prime minister) of Austria is the chairman, but the government officials have no vote in the decision making. Unanimous decision making is a requirement, and the commission has no powers to enforce its decisions, which are implemented by the government almost always without resistance. It has price and wage subcommittees as well as the Economic and Social Advisory Board, which has a wide-ranging policy focus. In addition to the Parity Commission are many more advisory boards and committees that deal with such policy areas as social security, banking, foreign labor, and immigration and industrial policy.

The neocorporatist system seems to work best in a nation such as Austria for several reasons. Austria is a small and relatively homogeneous nation with an integrated economy; its economic, social, and political leaders are accustomed to working together. It has a multiparty parliamentary system with frequent coalitions that require cooperation across a range of interests. The current government (2007–2008), based on the two biggest parties—the Conservatives and Social Democrats—is an example of politics and cooperation over ideology. Supporters of the social partnership argue that without it Austria could not have progressed from its status as a poor country in the prewar era to become one of the world's richest countries. Contributing to this success has been a consensus by all the key participants on the need to emphasize economic growth and full employment over other policies such as income redistribution.

When Communism lost its control over the nations of Eastern Europe in the early 1990s, the newly democratizing nations looked at the two competing models of Austrian and Swedish corporatism as possible paths to follow. Of course, the American pluralist model was also an option, and in the next section, we examine the development of Eastern European interest group systems since 1991.

Party Development and Weak Interest Group Lobbying Systems in the Transitioning Democracies of Eastern Europe

The collapse of the Soviet Union and its Eastern European client states in the early 1990s produced an opportunity for an examination of how nations build party and interest group/lobbying systems. These two systems of representative democracy in that region have had a very mixed record. First, both parties and interest group politics developed with difficulty in the parts of the old Soviet Union. Russia itself seemed to have slid back to its old authoritarian roots under President Vladimir Putin. The other parts of the Soviet Union have experienced little democratic development, with the possible exception of the Ukraine, in the past several years. In terms of political parties and democratic elections, the various states of the Baltics and central Eastern Europe have produced surprising patterns of elections and parties. From Lithuania, Latvia, Estonia, and Poland in the north to the Czech Republic, Slovakia, and Hungary in the south, parties and elections have been established and they seem to work quite well.

In a recent study of Lithuanian interest group politics and lobbying, Hrebenar, McBeth, and Morgan (2008) found the lobbying system to be quite primitive, with just a handful of lobbyists, a couple of small lobbying firms, and broad and strong rejection of lobbying and lobbyists as illegitimate parts of the political system. Part of the legacy from its Communist era was a rejection of labor unions as powerful political actors and direct lobbying by big business to the powerful political parties, largely skipping any interest group or lobbyist intermediaries. Although democracy within the institutions of parties and elections seems to be fairly well rooted in Lithuania, interest group politics' roots are very shallow.

Poland is the easiest interest group system in Eastern Europe to understand. Ost (2001) has described the complicated relationship among the political parties, interest groups, and social movements in Poland that has become a special type of interest articulation in which the traditional roles played by the three actors have been blurred, transformed, and institutionalized. The Polish movement Solidarity, which began as a social movement, evolved into a labor-oriented interest group, and then became a political party, demonstrates this merging of functions and roles. Movements and parties in today's Poland remain weak (Millard 1999). Recent presidential and parliamentary elections in Poland indicate that the strength of parties to dominate politics is still a reflection of the weak organizations of the parties and the need to find attractive candidates in order to win elections.

The other major Eastern European nation (after Poland and the former East German state that merged with West Germany) is Czechoslovakia. It split into two nations, the Czech Republic and the Slovak Republic, in 1995. In the Czech Republic, the political parties have sought to monopolize the policy-making process and thus have limited the roles and influence of interest groups and lobbying (Evanson and Magstadt 2001, 206). Czech political culture and its preference for centralized governmental decision making support this pattern. Also a factor is the Eastern European suspicion of interest group politics and lobbying as well as a personalism of direct person-to-person style of everyday politics that leaves interest groups on the outside in Prague (the Czech Republic capital). Finally, the legacy of Communism still lingers, with its preference for state-party decision making and the disorganized, fragmented, and poorly funded private-sector interests. The Czech Republic is the larger and more industrialized of the two nations and, in many respects, the more Westernized. In the Czech Republic, the interest groups are definitely subordinated to the stronger political parties, and Western-style lobbying and lobbyists are not common. Many of the Czech elite continue to hold the party-state model of politics that tends to exclude interests that are not channeled through either of those institutions. Most interest groups are poorly organized and poorly financed and thus at a tremendous disadvantage when they try to compete with the major parties for influence. As in Poland, corruption and lobbying scandals seem to be the nature of the game in the Czech Republic, with under the table payoffs the preferred method of influence acquisition. The peak associations of a tripartite social partnership have been established in the Czech Republic but lack the independent power base and legitimacy to operate effectively. Labor has been particularly disadvantaged in this arrangement. Business seems to be rather disorganized and unconnected to the world of politics, as are the farmers.

Some observers, such as Birgitt Haller, saw the emerging democracies in Central and Eastern Europe as having a similar situation to that in which Austria found itself in the early 1950s as it moved to democratize (Haller 1996). The need was urgent not only to establish new market economies but also to establish institutions of democratic government. Austria tried to export its model to its immediate neighboring countries, such as Hungary, the Czech and Slovak republics, and Slovenia. It met with varying degrees of success in its effort to transplant its version of corporatism. Although all four former Communist nations have developed different forms of institutional tripartite employer/labor/state interest mediation, the Slovenes and Hungarians have evolved closer to the Austrian model than have the Czechs and Slovaks.

One of the problems in these emerging countries was that capitalism had to be built without capital and without capitalists (Haller 1996, 148). All four of these nations placed a priority on social peace between labor and business, but in the economies of the 1990s, it has become much more difficult to do this in a postindustrial world economy. In fact, the centralized nature of both the Austrian political and economic systems made corporatism easy to implement, but the much more complicated (fragmented and heterogeneous) worlds of these four nations' political and economic systems have proven to be more resistant to such institutional harmony. Trade unions and employers' associations have not developed in the same way as those in Austria and thus are unable to enforce any consensual agreements to seek a social partnership.

The Lithuanian example discussed earlier and the failure to develop the necessary social partnership institutions in some of the Central European nations are evidence that the Western styles of interest group politics and lobbying simply do not exist in these developing democracies. Lobbyists in the Western sense do not operate with any significant degree of legitimacy, and they do not use the strategies and tactics found in Western Europe or North America. Interests are represented, of course. They deal directly with powerful politicians and party leaders, and much of this contact is made behind closed doors with significant exchanges of money to lubricate the decision-making processes. As noted early in this chapter, it is far easier to build a party system with free and democratic elections than it is to build an interest group and lobbying system with a low level of corruption and effective representation of interests in the democratic forums of politics. Eastern and Central Europe have made some inroads, but they have a long distance left to travel in this institution building, though their inclusion in the European Union and its exploding interest group politics and lobbying will teach them the game much quicker than if they were trying to learn it on their own.

Lobbying in Western Europe

The "Big Four" nations of Western Europe are Germany, France, the United Kingdom, and Italy. All four are long-standing parliamentary democracies but have very different political cultures and interest group systems and lobbying patterns. Here we summarize the broad patterns of interest group politics of these nations.

The United Kingdom is in many respects the mother of modern democracy, at least in the modern European context. The Magna Carta, in which the interests of the landed aristocracy and religious orders forced the English king to acknowledge that they and others in the realm had specific political rights that must be protected from the asserted absolute power of the monarch, serves as a reminder of its role in democracy. Until recently, the major economic interests of business and labor were clearly allied with one of the two major political parties in such a way that defied the continental European pattern of social partnership or corporatism. The Conservative Party represented big business in the form of the Confederation of British Industries, professions, agriculture, and the labor sector. The antiwar groups, environmentalists, and big labor were solidly in the camp of the Labour Party. Under the leadership of former prime minister Tony Blair, the Labour Party moved much closer to the center, and various Conservative Party leaders have moved that party to the center as well; thus, both are less closely tied to their traditional interest group supporters (Jordan and Maloney 2001). With a parliamentary political system, the style of lobbying is quite different from that found in the United States. Lobbying is focused on the governmental bureaucracy and the party in government rather than on any other institutions. Of these two, the bureaucracy is still the main site of access and interest influence. The United Kingdom has developed a complex system of consultation between the many interest groups and the governmental bureaucracy. The knowledge and expertise of the interest groups are made available to the bureaucrats to assist in the policy-making process. Indeed, lobbying in the United Kingdom can be characterized as truly insider lobbying using the bureaucracy.

In terms of their gross domestic product in 2007, Germany ranked first at $2.9 trillion; following were the United Kingdom at $2.3 trillion, France at $2.2 trillion, and Italy at $1.8 trillion. Germany has been and continues to be the dominant political and economic power of Western Europe. Germany remains a classic neocorporatist democracy largely governed by close relationships among several peak associations, the several large political parties, and the governmental bureaucracy (Gellner and Robertson 2001). The various new social movements representing environmentalists and antiwar and antinuclear groups are vibrant but clearly secondary to the major corporatist institutions. These institutions are the Federation of German Industry, the German Trade Union Federation, the German Farmers Association, and various other peak small business or professional associations. More than 1,000 interest groups lobby the German Parliament, and many members of parliament have close ties to one or more interest groups, but most of the influential interests have established firm ties to the relevant governmental bureaucratic units most important for their interests. When looking at the two access points, it is estimated that more than 80 percent of the "lobbying" is bureaucracy directed and less than 10 percent is parliament directed (Gellner and Robertson 2001).

France is often characterized as the ultimate bureaucratic political system, with the elite civil servants making all the decisions and the democratic institutions of government ratifying them and announcing the will of the bureaucrats to the public. Actually, there is a great deal of truth to this generalization. The French Republic seems to promote associational politics, and there are thousands of interest groups in France, but the culture and government of France seem to channel interest group participation through the governmental bureaucracy and not lobbying or other types of American-style interest group politics. Recently, many French interest groups have come to see the strong French government as a protection against the growing interventionist policies of the European Union. However, most French interest groups have not been closely allied with political parties or often participants in French electoral politics. The bureaucracy has tremendous power in French policy making and a strong disdain for popular politics or interest groups seeking to influence the policy-making process outside normal channels. This is not a classic neocorporatist pattern because the ties between the state and interests are far more ambiguous in France than in Germany or Austria. Two elements of French political culture also work against a greater role of interest groups in policy making: a deep distrust of intermediary organizations in the political process and the general public's preference for direct action (Appleton 2001). All of these factors have produced a public attitude that is decidedly anti–interest group and antilobbying.

French peak associations have been very difficult to construct, and as such, labor remains largely fragmented. Business peak associations have not been very effective lobbying organizations either. The interest group/political party system in France is one of "strong party group relations with limited policy impact" (Appleton 2001). The state or French governmental bureaucracy continues to dominate in France's unusual style of channeled corporatist politics.

If France's politics has been well channeled over the past several decades, Italian politics has been pluralist and chaotic. Italy formerly had a one-party state (Christian Democratic Party, or CDP) and close relationships between that party and major interests seeking governmental favors and policies. The Italian pattern has often been compared with that described for Japan (1955–1993) and for Mexico in the 20th century. In Italy, the pattern of *clientela* (clientelism) and corruption came crashing down in a corruption scandal during 1992–1993. Until then, the pattern of party-group relationship was one of dominant party with a collection of close interest groups seeking all types of government favors and in return providing the party with the money and other support to stay in office. Italy's extremely fragmented interest group system contributed to this pattern of corruption, and the interest groups themselves have been almost completely unable to get their desires on the political policy-making table without the support of the dominant political party.

The 1992–1993 scandal destroyed the CDP and its cozy relationships with Italian interests. What emerged was the aforementioned chaos of more corruption and ambiguous paths of influence creation, access buying, and frequent and periodic influence peddling scandals. Business, labor, and agriculture were so fragmented as to preclude effective representation of their sectors' policy preferences. When combined with the impact of Italy's membership in the European Union, the destruction of the CDP severely reduced the power of political parties to control access to Italian policy-making venues. All the old governmental parties have been destroyed, and the old opposition parties have had to cope with the rise of many new parties (Constantelos 2001). Interest groups are trying new lobbying techniques such as data and research provision to bureaucrats and new party elites. Italy has been in a period of profound political change for several decades, and it continues. Its system is neither a pluralist nor a corporatist interest group one. What seems to be emerging is some combination of these patterns, but it is still too early to make any definitive statement on contemporary interest group politics in Italy.

Non-European Patterns of Interest Group Politics

Let us now shift from Europe to Asia in the survey of how interest group politics operate in different parts of the world. Democracy came late to much of Asia compared with Europe. Almost every Asian nation except Japan can claim a pattern of democratic politics only since the 1950s, and many can claim only a few years of real democracy over that time frame. So, let us begin with the best example of democratic politics in Asia—Japan—as our frame of reference.

Japan: Pluralist, Neo-Confucian, Corporatist Pattern?

Japan, the first Asian nation to modernize, Westernize, and become a great power, continues to be one of the most difficult states to categorize in terms of its interest group and lobbying system. In many respects, it appears to be remarkably Americanized. The United States supervised the rebuilding of Japan's government, society, and economy after the end of World War II in 1945. The United States, under its supreme commander, General Douglas MacArthur, did not insist that the new Japanese gov-

ernment and so-called MacArthur Constitution of 1948 be mod-
eled exactly on the American system. It was decided to recon-
struct the parliamentary system existing before the war with a
wide range of reforms to strengthen democracy and reduce authoritarian tendencies.

The American-imposed Constitution of 1948 produced a
British-style parliamentary system with a bicameral diet and an
emperor as head of state. Like other unitary states, the Japanese
national bureaucracy is professional and dominant in its dealings
with subordinate political units and various constituent groups.

Japan developed a multiparty system during the 1955–1993
era as a powerful conservative party, the Liberal Democratic
Party (LDP), dominated a much smaller left wing consisting of
the larger Socialist Party and the smaller, but aggressive, Communist Party. The medium-size Buddhist Party; the Clean Government Party, or Komei-to; and a Socialist splinter party, the
Democratic-Socialist Party, completed the party system. The interest group ties for these parties were generally quite clear. The
LDP had ties to Japanese big and small businesses. It also represented the conservative farmers of Japan's rural sector as well as
many of the conservative religious organizations in Japan, except
the Soka Gakkai, which is the primary support organization for
the Komei-to. The three left-wing parties (Socialist, Communist,
and Democratic-Socialist) were all very closely tied to various
labor unions or labor confederations. The labor confederations
almost completely committed to the opposition left-wing parties
and thus were effectively marginalized. Because of this nearly
permanent exclusion of organized labor from political power,
some political scientists have called the Japanese interest group
system one of corporatism without labor.

Organized labor in Japan, like many of the new Asian democracies, has been organized in such a manner as to make it
much weaker than its European and even American counterparts. In the pre–World War II era and during the war years,
labor was very leftist and nearly destroyed by the militarist
regime. During the American occupation in the latter half of the
1940s, labor was encouraged to organize and participate in politics as part of the effort to democratize Japan, but MacArthur and
his staff were convinced by the conservative Japanese officials
that the Socialist- and Communist-dominated labor organizations posed a threat to the Japanese government in the dangerous
times of the Cold War. Japan's major corporations, often using

gangster (*yakuza*) muscle, crushed the labor movement and created a system of company unions in the private sector. So Toyota and Nissan labor unions emerged, and they were often led by Toyota and Nissan officials who alternated between working as company managers and union officials, coining the phrase *company unions*. The private-sector unions joined together in a labor confederation, Domei, that served as the supporting organization for the very moderate and impotent socialist splinter party, the Democratic-Socialists. The much stronger, but still constantly out of power, Socialist Party was the party of the labor confederation, Sohyo, which was largely organized by Japan's public-sector labor unions. The conservatives (LDP) controlled Japanese national-level politics without losing control of the Diet from their formation to the late 1980s; finally, after so many defeats, the two rival labor confederations merged to form a new organization, Rengo, which was truly a "peak association" in the European style, representing nearly the entire Japanese organized labor world.

In 1993, the LDP suffered a split, and over a number of years in the following decade, the various splinter parties and the old leftist parties (except for the Communists) merged together under Rengo's encouragement to form a true opposition party, the Democratic Party (DP), seemingly capable of defeating the LDP and taking control of Japan's national government. The DP won the elections of the upper house of the Diet in 2007, but it has never been able to replace the LDP in the much more powerful House of Representatives. Until it does, organized labor and the old left wing of Japan will be on the outside of the real game of Japanese politics.

Japan is closer to the European style of interest group system and lobbying than to that of the United States. American-style hordes of lobbyists do not exist in Tokyo, nor do Japan's interest groups use the American-style tools of mass media communications to put pressure on the governmental decision makers. Almost all successful lobbying in Japan takes place out of the public's eye, in the teahouses of Akasaka in Tokyo among associational leaders, powerful political brokers of the ruling party, and high-level bureaucrats.

On the other hand, Japan is also a very pluralist society, with every conceivable interest being organized in the society. The farmers' cooperatives have been especially powerful in an economy that has heavily subsidized the very high cost of rice and other agricultural products. Various professional groups, such as the Japan Medical Association, have had powerful roles to play in administering their professions and the governmental services associated with them.

The conventional wisdom model of Japanese policy making has been a tripod of the LDP, big business, and the bureaucracy. Each of the three institutions gave the others what they needed in terms of influencing the output of the Japanese government. The bureaucracy has dominated the policy process since the foundations of modern Japan in the 1860s under the Meiji oligarchs. But to keep its power in the postwar era, it allied itself with the conservatives and the LDP and then provided the bureaucratic leaders with entrance into high elected offices and high prestige, postretirement jobs.

Given the powerful role of the bureaucracy in Japanese policy making, it is not surprising to find frequent consultations between government bureaucrats and the interests they regulate or represent. The Ministry of Agriculture, for example, spends a great deal of time discussing many different issues with the farmers cooperative leadership; likewise, the Ministry of Economy Trade and Industry spends its time interacting with Japan's corporations, large and small, which export so many products to the world.

Japan's business peak organization, Nippon Keidanren, has long represented the industrial sector of Japan in the policy-making discussions with the LDP and the bureaucracy. The organization recently became even more powerful with its 2002 merger with Nikkeiren (Japanese Federation of Employers' Associations). Keidanren now represents 1,268 corporations, 128 industrial associations, and 47 regional employers' associations. Representing Japan's large corporations and being the more conservative of the various business groups in the country, Keidanren worked well with the conservative LDP during the decades of incredible economic growth (1950s–1990s). The less conservative and less powerful Japanese business groups are the Japanese Chamber of Commerce and the Japan Committee for Economic Development.

Japan's model of interest group politics is the closest to the American and European models. Japan is a Westernized, industrial democracy with a very pluralist pattern of interest group representation and a very corporatist pattern of policy making, with the huge exception of the European corporatist model of having a very weak and largely excluded organized labor sector. Japan is, as mentioned, "corporatism without labor."

Developing Democracies

Compared with the pluralist, corporatist, and mixed systems of developed democracies, almost no research has been conducted on interest groups, lobbying, and lobbyists in the developing democracies of Eastern Europe, Africa, South America, and Asia. The lack of research is not because interest group politics does not exist in those societies but is more a function of a "first things first" attitude held by most political scientists and democracy funding institutions. "First, we build a party system and hold democratic elections and then, later we will think about the other parts of a democratic political system such as a responsible media, interest group politics and civil society" (Hrebenar, McBeth, Morgan 2008). Even when interest groups are included in a study of a developing democracy, the data or interpretation is usually based on studies of other parts of the nation's political system, such as parties.

Among the transitional democracies, one can find several common patterns that will help us better understand their development (Thomas 2004). These patterns or characteristics can be viewed as guiding a system's development down several broad channels, much like a riverbed guides a body of water flowing toward the ocean. They may strongly influence the level of development and history of democracy in the state, the degree of legitimization of interest group activity in the society, the types of interests that play the political game, and the strategies and tactics that are considered to be acceptable in politics.

Clive S. Thomas (2004) has described the five patterns that guide the development of interest group systems in transitional democracies. The first is the degree of autonomy allowed to interest groups in the political system, or conversely, the degree of restriction the state places on interest group politics. The right of freedom of association, the existence of private voluntary interest groups, and particularly their role in lobbying government may be legally restricted, curtailed by the official ideology, and in some cases banned. A wide range of restrictions may be imposed by authoritarian regimes. Schmitter's (1974) state corporatism as found in World War II Germany, Vichy France, and pre–World

War II Austria is where the state determines the role of groups. Communist countries set up various organizations such as youth and labor organizations that were controlled by the party (Best, Rai, and Walsh 1986).

How interest groups are viewed by governmental and political elites as well as the general public can also strongly affect democratic development. Even in long-standing and successful democracies such as the United States, interest groups, lobbying, and lobbyists are often viewed with great suspicion. "Essential, but suspicious," as the recent American lobbying scandals involving Jack Abramoff have confirmed in many people's minds, lobbying and corruption go hand in hand. In many transitional states, interest groups and lobbying are viewed as injurious to the democratic development and are seen by many as illegitimate actors or, at best, as actors whose roles should be restricted and limited. Why are they viewed so negatively? Usually, the perception arises from some combination of being selfish about personal economic and political interests over the public interest of the larger society. This pattern can easily be seen in the research conducted on Lithuania and the Czech Republic and perceived not only in the former Communist states of Eastern Europe but also found among the elite attitudes in other developing democracies around the world. The idea that interest groups and lobbying are as essential for democratic development as political parties and elections has not been generally accepted in many nations.

Second, in developed societies the major form of interest group is the associational group based on formal membership. In transitional democracies, the interests tend to be represented by informal groups, such as political and professional elites, and broad-based interests, such as the bureaucracy and the military. Thus, one can say the developing state has more of an "interest-based politics" and less of an "interest group politics." In less Westernized societies, the major type of interest is the group based on kinship, tribe, lineage, neighborhood, religion, and so on. The difficulty of the American effort to build democratic institutions in Iraq can be seen as strong evidence to support this observation. One characteristic of successful transitional regimes is an increase in the number of associational groups.

Third, the weakly developed and numerically limited interest groups and associational system groups mean that group strategies and tactics are less formalized compared with those of advanced pluralist democracies. Informal contacts and personal relationships are important in all societies for interests to achieve their goal of influencing public policy, but they seem to be much more important in these transitional democracies. In the advanced pluralist societies, the freedom of the interest group system and the accepted roles of groups in the policy-making process have tended to produce regularized channels of lobbying for the interest groups. Interest group politics in these developed societies is found and accepted in the corridors of the government (legislative, executive, and judicial as well as regulatory agencies), the media, and political campaigns.

On the other hand, such interest group activities are seldom or never found in nonpluralist, transitional, and developing states. In these systems, personal relationships and power plays within and between government entities and other organizations, such as the ruling party or the senior officers of the military, are the most significant. It may seem impossible to many who follow politics in the mature, democratic nations, but even more politics is conducted behind closed doors in these transitional systems than in pluralist democracies.

Fourth, groups act as a major link between citizens and government by collecting numbers of people with similar views and speaking their views to government. This is particularly the case with mass membership organizations such as trade unions and public interest groups like environmental interests (Thomas 2001). Interest groups, political parties, and the media all tend to perform these functions in developed political systems. In contrast, and due to a combination of the four elements just explained, interest groups in developing societies rarely perform the role of mass representation, as they represent a very small segment of the population. Interest groups and interests in these societies perform other functions similar to those in advanced pluralist democracies—such as providing information, aiding in policy implementation, and providing political training—but this lack of a representational role gives them a much less significant place in the politics of their societies. This role absence includes the mass organizations in one-party and totalitarian regimes whose representative role is perfunctory and tightly controlled by the party and/or the regime.

Many also see issues of social class, religion, problems of economic development and poverty, the role of the military, ethnic and racial conflict, the aftermath of colonialism, and so on as the forces driving the politics of these societies. In this environment, interest groups and interest activity of advanced countries seemed much less important.

Although the states of South Asia (India, Pakistan, Bangladesh, and Sri Lanka) have been influenced by the British pluralist tradition, interest groups in the region have not been considered very important for a number of reasons. South Asian elites tend to see interest groups as illegitimate, and scholars in the region have been obsessed with social class as the most powerful explanation of political outcomes. In addition to social class, family, caste, religion, tribal identities, and language have been considered more important than interest groups. Powerful families in Pakistan, India, and Bangladesh play a political role more important than interest groups. Political parties are also thought to be much more powerful than any interest groups or combinations of interest groups, with the very important exception of the army in all of the South Asian nations.

Given India's size and importance, interest groups in India have been better studied than in the region's other nations. The powerful Indian governmental bureaucracy effectively limits interest group politics. Business simply could not match the power of the government to control the economy. It will be interesting to see if India's recent policies of opening up its economy to less governmental control will significantly change this pattern. More important forms of interest in India have been the so-called demand groups based on movements and issues groups such as students, workers, and farmers. Labor unions clearly do not have much access or influence in India, probably as a result of the powerful political parties dominating India's politics.

With regard to the interest group politics of the other South Asian nations of Pakistan, Bangladesh, and Sri Lanka, very little is known. Politics there seems to be driven by the powerful pattern of personalized politics and the significance of family ties over organizational identities. Business, labor, and other organized interests have great problems in these highly personalized political systems.

Chinese politics has become a combination of the powerful Communist Party and a growing number of associations that have sprung into existence in the decades of economic liberalism since the 1970s. Most of the studies conducted on Chinese interest groups conclude that a real civil society has not been developed yet in China, but the economic reforms have resulted in growing pluralism (Ogden 2000). Certainly within the political sector, the Communist Party is still the strongest power and has little interest in any competitors. As in all authoritarian states, the army and security forces hold extraordinary influence within the governmental decision-making processes.

Turning to the Middle East, again, very little is known about interest group politics except for studies on two countries, Egypt and Turkey (Ahmida 1997). Since most Middle Eastern states are one-party dictatorships or authoritarian states, the interest in studying group politics is very limited. The work on Egypt and Turkey (Bianchi 1984, 1986) suggests that the forces that restrict interest groups in the Middle East include an emphasis on culture, religion, family, and other personal relationships. Egypt seems to be closest to developed nations in terms of its interest group politics. Bianchi concludes that in Egypt, at least, the style of politics seems to be somewhere on the continuum between pluralism and corporatism (Bianchi 1989, 1990). Despite the history of authoritarian rule in the region, a very gradual rise has been seen in various democratic institutions that support an emerging interest group style of politics.

With the exception of a handful of countries, political scientists know very little about interest groups in African states. Research is essentially limited to South Africa and the patterns of interest groups before and after the apartheid regime (Borer 1998; Deegan 1999). The paucity of real democracies in Sub-Saharan Africa contribute to the dearth of studies of interest group politics. Without democracy, the military has, in country after country, assumed the dominant power position in almost all the countries, and business has had to deal with the military regime in order to gain influence in any given country in the region. Otherwise, the politics of family, clan, tribe, region, and religion overwhelm what Westerners think of as interest group politics.

Latin America and Central America have had a longer experience with democratic governments than the countries of Africa, the Middle East, and much of Asia, and therefore one should expect a higher level and more complex pattern of interest group politics in the region. The problem of Latin American politics, however, is the lack of continuity in democratic politics. Nations have moved toward democratic politics and then retreated back to military regimes and then moved back to democracy again. As a result, militaries have long been studied, because coups were so common in many Latin American states until just recently (Nun

1968). Organized labor has been very important in a number of the region's nations, such as Argentina and Chile, and has been a source of support for populism, revolution, and democracy (Collier and Collier 1991). The Catholic Church, religious movements, and peasants have been analyzed as sources of both conservatism and grassroots activism (Sharpe 1977). But by the early 1970s, corporatism, along with Marxian theory, has been used to describe the region's pattern.

Of the various nations of Central and Latin America, scholars know the most about interest groups in the largest, most democratic, and most industrialized nations, such as Mexico and Argentina. In Mexico, for example, the domination of the one-party state (Institutional Revolutionary Party, or PRI) for most of the 20th century produced a type of corporatism in which all the major actors were orchestrated by the dominant party leaders and their governments. Mexico is called a "party corporatist" state, or a unique form of neocorporatism. Most neocorporatist systems place relatively little emphasis on political parties as key actors in the system. But, in Mexico, the PRI is *the* key actor in orchestrating the policy-making system—at least until very recently. The PRI is really a collection of interest group confederations that join together to form the party. Central parts of the PRI include the Confederation of Mexican Workers and the National Peasant Confederation; and the National Confederation of Popular Organizations accounts for most of the rest of Mexican society. The outcome of the mediation of the various interests in Mexican society was, until the late 1990s, relative "political stability and social peace achieved through elite accommodation and governmental mediation of class conflict" (Rosenberg 2001). Note that members of the business world, who are prohibited from joining political parties, are free to negotiate directly with the government as outside actors.

Argentina, on the other hand, while having also had a history of strong parties, adds a pattern of strong organized labor movements and military intervention into its political system. One interesting Argentine characteristic is that the strong interest group system and the often strong political party system have not usually been tied too tightly together. They have often operated independently of each other (Johnson 2001). Frequently, the interest groups would target the government directly, rather than use the institutions of the party system; then, if all such direct lobbying failed, the military stood ready to intervene as a last resort.

What, then, does one make of the authoritarian or semiauthoritarian states scattered around the world in nations such as Russia, many of the former Soviet Union states in Central Asia, the military regimes in Myanmar, and remaining Communist states in Vietnam and Cuba? Each nation has a different history and different political patterns, but several generalizations can be made regarding interest group politics in such undemocratic states. First, all nations, no matter how undemocratic, have forms of interest group politics. In authoritarian states, the security forces usually hold enormous political power, including the military, the police, and any paramilitary associated with the ruling party or regime. Additionally, the ruling party (if there is one) and its supporting interest or interests usually have tremendous power as well and may dominate the security forces in terms of big political issues such as budgetary allocations or foreign policy. The governmental bureaucracy and the various "power ministries," such as industrialization, development, religion, agriculture, and revenue collection, all may function as lobbies for their own interests as well as any clientele. Interest group politics does not disappear in quasi-authoritarian or authoritarian states; it just tends to be more centralized and concentrated in the hands of relatively few organizations that are fundamental to the continuation of the regime in both a security and an economic manner. Furthermore, lobbying in this type of political system almost always takes place behind closed doors, and lobbyists are the powerful politicians who represent the key interests in the policy decision-making processes.

Lobbying in the International Community: The EU

With the rise of the European Union (EU) as a significant transnational governmental entity, it should come as no surprise that lobbying has become a major business in Brussels, Belgium, the EU headquarters, and Strasbourg, France, the seat of the EU Council of Europe. A number of excellent academic studies have been done on the nature of lobbying in Brussels, including works by Greenwood (2003), Schendelen (2005), and McGrath (2005). What started out as a very European style of bureaucratic politics evolved to add on an interesting layer of increasingly American-style lobbyists and interest group politics.

The first professional lobbyists to descend on Brussels in large numbers came from London; later, Americans came in large numbers as they began to understand that the new European government was making decisions that significantly affected American businesses, products, and marketing. French bureaucrats who filled many of the top posts in the growing EU bureaucracy saw the need and the potential of lobbying the bureaucracy, and many of the later lobbying firms were staffed by these former bureaucrats from France. With the growth in the EU in number of member nations from the original 12 to 25 and with potentially many more nations who seek entry or special relations, the necessity to represent these nations' interests effectively fueled the growth in the lobbying community of Brussels. Many of these newly admitted EU nations, such as the Baltic nations and the former Communist nations of Eastern and Central Europe, have little or no lobbying traditions or experience, not to mention few or no real domestic lobbyists. To lobby effectively in Brussels, they were forced to hire the Brussels lobbyists, and the lobbying business grew. Schendelen (2005) notes that thousands of interest groups are representing governments and nongovernmental bodies seeking to lobby in Brussels.

One of the academic debates regarding EU politics is whether its dominant style of interest group politics is pluralist as in the United States or corporatist as in many of its European member states. Greenwood and Young (2005) note that although one can find examples of cases where a specialized interest will triumph over the more bureaucratic policy-making process, a more corporatist pattern seems to dominate most issues. They do observe that Brussels is an "insider town," where effective interest representation requires a dense network of personal and organizational relationships, making it very difficult for outsiders to come in and be successful. In other words, it is a perfect environment for Brussels's lobbyists and lobbying firms.

In Brussels, as in much if not almost all of Europe, the terms *lobbyist* and *lobbying firm* are not commonly heard or seen. The preferred terms are *public affairs* and *interest representation*. Public affairs firms will often be much broader than American-style lobbying firms in terms of services and resource allocations. They will frequently be more business and product oriented, with an emphasis on representing a client in many types of venues—often not political at all. Some will be "event managers," setting up press conferences and conferences for the clients, and will devote a small part of the firm to traditional lobbying.

Some of the lobbying in the EU fits the corporatist pattern well, where the EU bureaucrats and the various peak organizations representing European business, labor, and agriculture come together to hammer out a consensus on a certain policy. Of course, the various nations will also have a role to play in the process, but if a consensus can be reached first among the major economic peak associations, the later impact of national-level politics can be reduced. But almost all the EU experts emphasize that, depending on the issue area and the type of policy being discussed (e.g., regulatory, distributive), a wide range of variations in types of interest group representation can be seen in Brussels.

The EU also has a wide range of institutions that can be targeted by interests. The EU Parliament in Strasbourg features a political system similar to those seen in most European parliaments. Additional targets of lobbying are the European Commission, the European Court of Justice, the European Council, the Council of Ministers, a wide range of consultative institutions such as the Economic and Social Committee, and sectoral institutions dealing with particular sectors or issues, such as EU-RATOM (European Atomic Energy Community).

The European Commission, which drafts the regulations for EU member states' politicians to consider, has a small staff and a huge amount of work. Therefore, it usually relies on interest groups and lobbyists for the data and information it needs for its work. Its staff is only a small fraction of the similar staff operating in Washington, D.C. Thus, the commission is an ideal place for interest groups to operate to help frame issues and draft future regulations. Experienced lobbyists argue that lobbying such as this in the bureaucracy is where crucial decisions are made in the EU.

EU interest group diversity is impressive. In a 2002 listing on EU interest groups, formal interest groups registered with the EU totaled 1,450, as did 350 companies, 170 national interest groups, and 143 commercial public affairs consultant firms in Brussels. A total of 3,400 annual passes are issued for public affairs monitoring purposes, although some have estimated the total number of lobbyists in Brussels to be near the 30,000 figure often noted in Washington, D.C. As in the United States, businesses make up more than two-thirds of interests seeking to influence the EU (Greenwood 2003, 19).

The EU supports a wide range of nongovernmental organizations (NGOs), with more than 1 billion Euros in annual support.

This tends to produce a healthy NGO representation in Brussels that seems to have more influence than similar interests have in Washington, D.C. On the other hand, labor organizations and professions seem to have less influence than the social partnerships pattern of many European nations would lead one to expect. Perhaps this is a result of the nature of policy making in Brussels that has been focused on expanding the EU powers in a liberal fashion rather than protecting specific sectors or professions.

Transnational and International Lobbying

The difference between transnational lobbying and international lobbying is a combination of actors and their targets. International lobbying refers to the nation-states as the actors or the targets of lobbying campaigns, whereas transnational lobbying refers to interest group lobbying across national boundaries. Three kinds of transnational actors operate on this stage: private economic organizations, such as corporations, unions, and business associations; international NGOs; and other transnational organizations, such as churches (e.g., the Roman Catholic Church) and other cause organizations (Morss 1991).

A great deal is known about the transnational economic organizations. Especially considering the rise of globalization, the international corporations have been the objects of many research projects. As political science has expanded its theoretical focus beyond the traditional nation-state, much greater attention has been devoted to the NGOs. Many recent observers of international politics have tried to paint a picture of an ever more interrelated and increasingly complex collection of actors, including many of these NGOs. Recent Nobel Peace Prizes have been awarded to NGOs in a variety of areas, including the International Campaign to Ban Landmines, microbanking organizations in Africa and Asia, and Doctors Without Borders.

Perhaps more than any other factor, the end of the Cold War brought many new issues and problems to the public's attention, and suddenly, the NGOs that had been laboring in relative obscurity now became the focus of media attention. Just as many domestic NGOs in the past two decades have become much more important in the domestic delivery of once exclusive governmental services, many now realize transnational NGOS are often the only effective actors in addressing problems that cross borders and even continents, such as the AIDS epidemic and environmental dangers.

As was noted, the EU has been particularly receptive to the roles played by NGOs in its various policy-making arenas. It subsidizes well over 1,000 such groups, thus making Brussels and Strasbourg "hotbeds" for NGO activity in Europe. Also noteworthy is the role the United Nations (UN) plays in nurturing and supporting the international NGOs. The UN's New York City headquarters and European satellite headquarters sites in Geneva and Vienna are also venues of great activity for transnational lobbying. Weiss and Gordenker (1996) report significant UN lobbying on HIV/AIDS, the environment, and women's and human rights issues. Some research on Southeast Asia and Central America also indicates a growth of NGO activities in the regional organizations of those areas.

Many readers are familiar with the more famous transnational environmentalist interest groups such as Greenpeace and Earth First!. Interest groups such as Greenpeace operate on the national level in many nations but also have transnational operations. Greenpeace's recent antinuclear tactics and environmental demonstrations have received enormous coverage in the world's mass media. These transnational environmentalist groups have probably had the most policy success in recent years of all the cause-oriented international groups because of the success of the Kyoto Treaty and the attention on the Nobel Peace Prize awarded to former U.S. vice president Al Gore and the UN climate panel in 2007.

Probably the second most active transnational cause-oriented interest group category involves a wide range of human rights issues. Amnesty International is perhaps the best known such organization in the world, but many other such organizations are working on all types of human rights causes. Many of them can be found in Latin America, where human rights abuses are still common and the political systems have opened up sufficiently to allow such organizations to operate more freely. Such may not be the case in many parts of Africa and Asia, and even Russia under Putin's increasingly repressive regime. One area that needs much more attention in research effort is that of the transnational religious and cultural organizations (especially Catholic, Evangelical Protestant, and Islamic organizations and movements) and to study their impact on various populations.

One can see from this survey of the world that many different types of interest group and lobbying systems are in operation. This diversity is now a key characteristic of our globalized political and business world. From American pluralism to European corporatism to personalized politics common to much of the developing world, interest group politics is everywhere, and everywhere it is different. It is impossible to understand politics anywhere in the world without an understanding of interest group politics and lobbying.

The best books in the world at this time on interest groups in the various nations are the several books edited by Clive S. Thomas, longtime coauthor and coeditor (with Ronald Hrebenar, the coauthor of this book) of respected works in this subject area. Thomas's books include *First World Interest Groups: A Comparative Perspective* (1993); *Political Parties & Interest Groups: Shaping Democratic Governance* (2001), and *Research Guide to U.S. and International Interest Groups* (2004). We express our sincere appreciation to Dr. Thomas for allowing us to use many of his findings in this book.

References

Ahmida, Ali Abdullatif. 1997. "Inventing or Recovering Civil Society in the Middle East." *Critique*. 10 (Spring) 127–134.

Appleton, Andrew. 2001. "France: Party-Group Relations in the Shadow of the State." In *Political Parties & Interest Groups: Shaping Democratic Governance*, edited by Clive S. Thomas, 45–62. Boulder, CO: Lynne Rienner.

Armingeon, Klaus. 1997. "Swiss Corporatism in Comparative Perspective." *West European Politics*. October.

Best, Paul J., Kul B. Rai, and David F. Walsh. 1986. *Politics in Three Worlds*. New York: John Wiley and Sons.

Bianchi, Robert. 1984. *Interest Groups and Political Development in Turkey*. Princeton, NJ: Princeton University Press.

Bianchi, Robert. 1986. "Interest Group Politics in the Third World." *Third World Quarterly*, 8:507–539.

Bianchi, Robert. 1989. *Unruly Corporatism: Associational Life in Twentieth-Century Egypt*. New York: Oxford University Press.

Bianchi, Robert. 1990. "Interest Groups and Politics in Mubarak's Egypt." In *The Political Economy of Contemporary Egypt*, edited by Ibrahim Oweiss. Washington, DC: Georgetown University Press.

Bischof, Gunter, and Anton Pelinka. 1996. *Austro-Corporatism: Past, Present, Future*. London: Transaction.

Borer, Tristan. 1998. *Challenging the State: Churches as Political Actors in South Africa.* Notre Dame, IN: University of Notre Dame Press.

Collier, David, and Ruth Collier. 1991. *Shaping the Political Arena: Critical Junctures, the Labor Movement and Regime Dynamics in Latin America.* Princeton, NJ: Princeton University Press.

Constantelos, John. 2001. "Italy: The Erosion and Demise of Party Dominance." In *Political Parties & Interest Groups: Shaping Democratic Governance,* edited by Clive S. Thomas, 119–137. Boulder, CO: Lynne Rienner.

Deegan, Heather. 1999. *South Africa Reborn: Building a New Democracy.* London: University College of London Press.

Evanson, Robert K., and Thomas M. Magstadt. 2001. "The Czech Republic: Party Dominance in a Transitional System." In *Political Parties & Interest Groups: Shaping Democratic Governance,* edited by Clive S. Thomas, 193–210. Boulder, CO: Lynne Rienner.

Gellner, Winand, and John D. Robertson. 2001. "Germany: The Continued Dominance of Neocorporatism." In *Political Parties & Interest Groups: Shaping Democratic Governance,* edited by Clive S. Thomas, 101–118. Boulder, CO: Lynne Rienner.

Greenwood, Justin. 2003. *Interest Representation in the European Union.* New York: Palgrave-MacMillan

Greenwood, Justin, and A. Young. 2005. "EU Interest Representation or US Lobbying." In *With US or Against US? The State of the European Union,* Vol. 7, edited by Nicholas Jabko and Craig Parsons, 275–298. Oxford, UK: Oxford University Press.

Haller, Birgitt. 1996. "Austrian Social Partnership—A Model for Central and Eastern Europe? Introduction." In *Austro-Corporatism: Past, Present, Future,* edited by Gunter Bischof and Anton Pelinka, 147–150. London: Transaction.

Hrebenar, Ronald. 2001. "Japan: Strong State, Spectator Democracy, and Modified Corporatism." In *Political Parties & Interest Groups: Shaping Democratic Governance,* edited by Clive S. Thomas, 155–174. Boulder, CO: Lynne Rienner.

Hrebenar, Ronald J., 2008. "Introduction: Interest Groups, Lobbying and Lobbyists in Developing Democracies," *Journal of Public Affairs,* Forthcoming.

Hrebenar, Ronald J., and Akira Nakamura. 1993. "Japan: Associational Politics in a Group-Oriented Society." In *First World Interest Groups,* edited by Clive S. Thomas, 199–216. Westport, CT: Greenwood Press.

Hrebenar, Ronald, Courtney McBeth, and Bryson Morgan. 2008. "Understanding Interest Group Activity in the Emergent Democracies of Eastern Europe: The Case of Lithuania," *Journal of Public Affairs.* Forthcoming.

Johnson, Diana E. 2001. "Argentina: Parties and Interests Operating Separately by Design and Practice." In *Political Parties & Interest Groups: Shaping Democratic Governance*, edited by Clive S. Thomas, 229–246. Boulder, CO: Lynne Rienner.

Jordan, Grant, and William Maloney. 2001. "Britain: Change and Continuity Within the New Realities of British Politics." In *Political Parties & Interest Groups: Shaping Democratic Governance*, edited by Clive S. Thomas, 27–44. Boulder, CO: Lynne Rienner.

Kindley, Randall. 1996. "The Evolution of Austria's Neo-Corporatist Institutions." In *Austro-Corporatism: Past, Present, Future*, edited by Gunter Bischof and Anton Pelinka, 53–93. London: Transaction.

Kunkel, Christoph, and Janos Pontusson. 1998. "Corporatism Versus Social Democracy." *West European Politics*, April.

Lewin, Leif. 1994. "The Rise and Decline of Corporatism: The Case of Sweden," *Journal of Political Research* 26:59–79.

Markovits, Andrei S. 1996. "Austrian Corporatism in Comparative Perspective." In *Austro-Corporatism: Past, Present, Future*, edited by Gunter Bischof and Anton Pelinka, 5–20. London: Transaction.

Marshall, Mike. 1996. "The Changing Face of Swedish Corporatism: The Disintegration of Consensus." *Journal of Economic Issues*. September.

McGrath, Conor. 2005. *Lobbying in Washington, London and Brussels: The Persuasive Communication of Political Issues*. Lewiston, NY: Edwin Mellen Press.

Millard, Francis. 1999. *Polish Politics and Society*. New York: Routledge.

Morss, Elliott R. 1991. "The New Global Players: How They Compete and Collaborate." *World Development* 19:55–64.

Nowotny, Ewald. 1993. "The Austrian Social Partnership and Democracy," Working Paper 93–1, Center for Austrian Studies. February.

Nun, Jose. 1968. "A Latin American Perspective: The Middle-Class Military Coup." In *Latin America: Reform or Revolution?*, edited by J. Petras and M. Zeitlin. New York: Fawcett.

Ogden, Suzanne. 2000. "China's Developing Civil Society: Interest Groups. Trade Unions and Associational Pluralism," In *Changing Workplace Relations on the Chinese Economy*, edited by Malcolm Warner. New York: St. Martin's Press.

Ost, David. 2001. "Poland: Parties, Movements and Ambiguity." In *Political Parties & Interest Groups: Shaping Democratic Governance*, edited by Clive S. Thomas, 211–228. Boulder, CO: Lynne Rienner.

Pross, A. Paul. 1993. "The Mirror of the State: Canada's Interest Group System." In *First World Interest Groups: A Comparative Perspective*, edited by Clive S. Thomas, 67–80. Westport, CT: Greenwood Press.

Richardson, J. J. 1993. "Government and Groups in Britain: Changing Styles," In *First World Interest Groups: A Comparative Perspective*, edited by Clive S. Thomas, 55–66. Westport, CT: Greenwood Press.

Rosenberg, Jonathan. 2001. "Mexico: The End of Party Corporatism?" In *Political Parties & Interest Groups: Shaping Democratic Governance*, edited by Clive S. Thomas, 247–268. Boulder, CO: Lynne Rienner.

Schendelen, Rinus van. 2005. *Machiavelli in Brussels: The Art of Lobbying in the E.U.* Amsterdam: Amsterdam University Press.

Schmitter, P. C., 1974. "Still a Century of Corporatism?" *The Review of Politics*. 36 (1): 85–131.

Schmitter, P. C. 1989. "Corporatism Is Dead! Long Live Corporatism!" *Government and Opposition*. 24:54–73.

Sharpe, Kenneth. 1977. *Peasant Politics*. Baltimore: Johns Hopkins University Press.

Thomas, Clive S. 1993. *First World Interest Groups: A Comparative Perspective*. Westport, CT: Greenwood Press.

Thomas, Clive S. 2001. *Political Parties & Interest Groups: Shaping Democratic Governance*. Boulder, CO: Lynne Rienner.

Thomas, Clive S. 2004. *Research Guide to U.S. and International Interest Groups*. Westport, CT/London: Praeger.

Wallace, Helen, and Alasdair R. Young. 1997. *Participation and Policy-Making in the European Union*. Oxford, UK: Clarendon Press, Oxford.

Wallace, Helen, and William Wallace. 2000. *Policy-Making in the European Union*. Oxford, UK: Oxford University Press.

Weiss, Thomas G., and Leon Gordenker. 1996. *NGOs, the UN and Global Governance*. Boulder, CO: Lynne Rienner.

Wilson, Frank L. 1993. "France: Group Politics in a Strong State." In *First World Interest Groups: A Comparative Perspective*, edited by Clive S. Thomas, 113–126. Westport, CT: Greenwood Press.

Woll, Cornealia. 2006. "Lobbying in the European Union: From *Sui Generis* to a Comparative Perspective," *Journal of European Public Policy*. 13(3): 456–469. April.

Zeigler, Harmon. 1993. "Switzerland: Democratic Corporatism," In *First World Interest Groups: A Comparative Perspective*, edited by Clive S. Thomas, 153–164. Westport, CT: Greenwood Press.

4

Chronology

Interest group politics and lobbying have been part of the politics of all societies in the history of humanity. In the ancient societies, the primary interests represented in the decision-making processes of government were groups of warriors, priests, and those with major economic interests, such as farmers. Interests became better organized as societies became more complex and diversified and as government gained greater control over more aspects of society, especially the economic and business sector. Modern interest group politics developed in its fullest manifestation in the politics of the new American nation beginning in the 1700s, and today, the best example of interest group politics and lobbying is, without doubt, found in the United States. The following is a selected chronology of some of the more important events in the development of interest group politics in the United States. Many sources have been used to create this chronology, but among the most important are Ronald Hrebenar's *Interest Group Politics in America* and the two-volume *Gale Encyclopedia of U.S. Economic History.* David Burner's *An American Portrait: A History of the United States* and Mary Beth Norton's *A People and a Nation* were also useful in selecting events and adding details to the chronology.

1763   *British mercantilism.* The American colonies resist nearly 30 acts of British mercantilism. Mercantilism is an economic theory arguing that government can use trade to enrich the home nation by routing the trade in the colonial empire through the home nation. The American colonies begin resisting Navigation Acts in 1651 that require

1763   trans-shipping of colonial exports and imports through
(cont.)   England. This produces a very lucrative American business of smuggling to avoid the British taxes and regulations. Enforcement of these rules is lax until Great Britain's
triumph over France in 1763. American colonists resist
British efforts to force them to pay their taxes to support
British military forces in North America. This becomes the
issue of taxation without representation—one of the major
justifications for the War of Independence.

1764   *Sugar Act.* This law is passed by the British Parliament in
an effort to cut down on smuggling between the West Indies and the 13 North American colonies and to raise tax
money to pay for British debts from the French and Indian War (1754–1763) and later expenditures related to
military security in the North American region. It is a
corrective response to the failure of the previously
passed Molasses Act of 1733 that tried to stop the trade
in molasses between the American colonies and French
and Dutch West Indies colonies. The American economic
interests strongly resist the idea of paying these taxes to
support the 10,000 British troops stationed in the North
American colonies. Various interests in Boston, New
York, and Rhode Island hold protests against the Sugar
Act, but it is the Stamp Act of 1765 that really helps organize colonial resistance to British economic control of
the colonies.

1765   *Stamp Act.* The Stamp Act is the first direct tax enacted by
the British government on the 13 American colonies. It
requires an official tax stamp to be placed on more than
50 documents, including newspapers and playing cards.
Its purpose is to raise tax revenue for the English government to retire debt and station military forces in
North America. The North American colonists are suffering through an economic depression after the French
and Indian War and strongly resist such direct taxation
for purposes they believe are unneeded or unwanted.
Mobs of Americans riot in Boston (Boston Tea Party) and
some British tax administrators are forced from their offices after other antitax demonstrations. Different American factions support the British government or the

antitax interests. Commercial interests in the colonies'
biggest cities agree to boycott British goods until the tax
is revoked. In February 1766, Parliament repeals the
Stamp Act while declaring it has the right to tax and
make laws for the American colonies.

1781   *Articles of Confederation.* The Articles of Confederation are
adopted by the 13 colonies in revolt against the British
government. The Articles provide for a loose confederation of national government for the 13 colonies and later
states after independence is gained in 1783, but it has too
many weaknesses to survive long. It has no real executive with a very weak president and provides for no way
to manage economic relations among the 13 states. Financial economic interests are especially focused on creating a national government with the power to raise
taxes and pay off the roughly $70 million in debts in-
curred during the War of Independence. James Madison
and others of the new American political elite realize that
a new stronger national government is necessary for lay-
ing the foundation for future American national military
and economic security.

1785   *Land Ordinance Act.* Congress passes three laws dealing
with land development in the Articles of Confederation
era. They are laws to manage the development of the
Northwest Territory (in general, part of today's upper
Midwest between the Mississippi and Ohio rivers). The
law provides for this land to be surveyed and readied for
sale to pioneers. This law regulates such land development until the passage of the Homestead Act of 1862.
One of the results of this law is to open these lands to
wealthy purchasers who buy the land at auctions until
1841. Small purchases of less than 640 acres on credit are
not allowed and most of the lands are bought by land
speculators and later sold to poorer farmers for profit.

1787   *Constitutional Convention.* Some of the most important
controversies fought over at the Philadelphia Constitutional Convention are battles between delegates representing special economic interests. Charles Beard's
Economic Interpretation of the Constitution (1913) argues

1787   that representatives of the merchant class and business-
(*cont.*)   oriented lawyers designed the Constitution to protect
these interests and private property. Clearly, the new
road map for politics in America deals with economic
rights and political responsibility. Several huge decisions
center on the need to keep southern slave-owning states
happy enough with the new plan to ratify it. The broad
issue of slavery is delayed until 1808, because several
southern states argue that they need a couple of decades
to import sufficient slaves to meet their economic needs.
The need for a strong central government to protect
America's emerging industries from cheap British goods,
combined with the demands for a strong national financial and currency system, frightens the economic elites
into supporting the idea of a stronger central government. Slave owners and those who hold the debt in-
curred by the government during the revolution are
protected in the Constitution.

1791   *First Bank of the United States established.* When the Constitution of 1787 is written, there is considerable conflict
over the question of the establishment of a national bank
of the United States. Alexander Hamilton supports it and
Thomas Jefferson opposes it. The bank is authorized
under the Washington administration in 1791, and it
handles some of the basic financial activities of the limited federal government. The bank's charter lapses in
1811. After its demise, federal and state money is unsta-
ble. The War of 1812 against Great Britain further desta-
bilizes the nation's money and the Second National Bank
of the United States is established in 1816. President Andrew Jackson vetoes the renewal of the bank, and its
charter expires in 1836. The banks are associated in many
people's minds with the financial panics of 1819 and
1837. Investors in state-level banks are opposed to the
national banks because they feel they limit their opportunities for large profits.

1803   *Louisiana Purchase.* President Thomas Jefferson purchases
the French-owned Louisiana Territory (827,000 square
miles) for the price of $23 million in 1803. Jefferson real-
izes that the new United States needs that land to facili-

tate its westward expansion and the sale also reduces the political complaints of American farmers and exporters who want easier access to the port of New Orleans. The purchase gives the United States the port of New Orleans and control of the Mississippi River, and that facilitates the expansion of the trade of American agricultural products from the South and Midwest.

1815   *Building of the National Road.* The National Road, or the Cumberland Road, is the first highway built by the federal government. Construction begins after the end of the War of 1812, and the purpose of the highway is to link the East Coast of the United States to the undeveloped lands of the Northwest Territory. It is the largest American road project until the building of the National Defense Highway System starts in the 1950s. The decision to build the road ends the controversy over whether the federal government can spend tax money for internal improvements. Presidents Madison and Monroe veto laws that attempt to spend such funds. The building of the road sets the precedent for future federal spending and earmarks in federal appropriation and budget bills.

1817   *American Colonization Society (ACS) founded.* The American abolitionist movement grows to a national movement from its organizational beginnings in the 1810s. The ACS is founded in 1817 and includes Chief Justice John Marshall and former president James Madison as members. Its program is to free the slaves in the United States, compensate their owners, and transport the freed slaves to Africa. The American Anti-Slavery Society, founded by Lloyd Garrison in 1833, is the most successful reform movement in American history. In 1860, it combines with the new Republican Party to elect Abraham Lincoln to the presidency and supports his decision to issue the Emancipation Proclamation in 1863 that ends slavery in the United States. The end of slavery is finally declared with the states' ratification of the 13th Amendment in December 1865.

1826   *American Temperance Society founded.* In the early 1800s, evangelical Protestants begin to crusade against the evils

1826   of alcohol in American society. Alcoholic consumption is
(*cont.*) widespread in colonial America. The American Temper-
        ance Society is formed in 1826 and quickly expands
        across the nation. Later the society changes its goal from
        "temperance" to "prohibition." By 1861, 13 of the 40
        states have passed laws prohibiting sales of alcohol. New
        prohibition organizations are formed and run John Bid-
        well, a widely supported candidate, for president in
        1892. In 1893, the Anti-Saloon League is founded as a
        lobbying arm for the movement that culminates in the
        passage of a World War I prohibition law that sets the
        stage for the 18th Amendment to the Constitution, which
        prohibits the manufacture, sale, import, and export of
        liquor in the United States. The amendment is ratified in
        1919, and Congress passes the Volstead Act over Presi-
        dent Wilson's veto that year to enforce the amendment.
        This outcome marks the success of one of the most ac-
        complished interest group movements in American his-
        tory. The failure of prohibition results in a counter
        movement that pushes for the 21st Amendment, which
        repeals the 18th Amendment in 1933.

1847   *American Medical Association (AMA) founded to represent
        medical doctors and medical students.* The AMA is the
        largest medical association in the United States. In addi-
        tion to advancing the interests of physicians and their
        patients, it also promotes public health. The AMA be-
        comes the most powerful group in the health lobby in
        the United States. Beginning in the late 1940s, the AMA
        lobbies against federal government participation in de-
        veloping a comprehensive health care insurance plan for
        all Americans.

1865   *The Ku Klux Klan (KKK) is formed in Pulaski, Tennessee, by
        former veterans of the Confederate Army.* The KKK believes in
        white supremacy over blacks and other races. The KKK is
        the main resistance of white Southerners to Republican
        occupation of the South after the Civil War and to black
        civil rights after the end of the occupation in 1876. The
        KKK is a terrorist organization that seeks to regain politi-
        cal power for white Southerners in the 1870s. It has orga-
        nizational strength throughout the South and even

spreads to northern and western states in the 20th century. It is reorganized in 1915 as a Protestant fraternal organization and broadens its agenda to oppose Catholics, Jews, and immigrants as well as blacks. The KKK declines as an organization in the interwar period, resurges in the 1960s during the peak of the civil rights movement in the South, but then sharply declines.

1867   *National Grange.* The National Grange is founded to advance the situation of American farmers. Granges are organized on the local level, and in the worsening economy of the 1870s, they quickly become sites for political action in support of the agricultural community. Granges lobby state governments for laws favorable to farmers, but they are especially concerned about the railroads and seek laws that limit the rates the railroads can charge for shipping the farmers' products to markets. Other farm advocacy groups, such as the Farmers' Alliances, have political successes in 1890 with the election of several governors and 30 congressmen and gaining control of the Kansas state legislature. Two years later, the Populist Party is created from many of these Farmers' Alliance organizations. It backs Democrat William Jennings Bryan in the 1896 presidential election, but after he decisively loses to William McKinley, the movement fades and disappears about a decade later.

1869   *National Women's Suffrage Association formed.* After the first women's rights convention is held in 1848 at Seneca Falls, New York, Elizabeth Cady Stanton joins with Susan B. Anthony in 1869 to form the National Woman Suffrage Association and another group, the American Woman Suffrage Association. They join together in 1890. Yearly from the 1870s, constitutional amendments fail in Congress, but the movement also focuses on the states. Women gradually win the vote in 11 mostly western states and territories, such as Wyoming (1869). Finally, after World War I, Congress passes the 19th Amendment and it is ratified by the states in 1920.

1871   *National Rifle Association (NRA) founded.* The organization is founded by Union Army veterans after the Civil War

1871
(*cont.*)

who voice concern over soldiers' poor shooting in the war. The NRA emphasizes gun and shooting training as well as shooting events. The NRA is often described as the single most powerful lobbying organization in the United States. It argues that gun ownership is a civil liberty protected by the Second Amendment of the Bill of Rights and claims to be the oldest continuously operating civil liberties organization in the United States. It also claims to have more than 4 million members.

1874

Congress creates the Interstate Commerce Commission. Building on the growing protests of farmers' organizations against the discriminatory prices and fees of railroads and ferries, state governments pass laws attempting to protect farmers. The U.S. Supreme Court later overturns many of these laws on the grounds that they violate the federal government's control of interstate commerce. The protestors then place political pressure on Congress, and this results in the creation of the Interstate Commerce Commission in 1887—the first of the so-called regulatory agencies that seek to regulate business in the public's interest.

1880

Reign of the robber barons. The 1880s is a period of unrestrained greed and wealth accumulation by the major actors in the new industrializing U.S. economy. This group of industrialists and bankers includes John P. Morgan, John D. Rockefeller, Andrew Carnegie, James Fisk, Jay Gould, Cornelius Vanderbilt, and Collis Huntington. These men, who control the nation's major railroads and banks, hire powerful lobbyists and obtain great concessions from state and federal government in terms of subsidies, land grants, and favorable tax laws. Eventually, their power is constrained by the rise of labor unions and political reformers.

1881

The American Federation of Labor (AFL) established. The AFL is reorganized by its president, Samuel Gompers, in 1886. The AFL grants its unions great local autonomy and decides to organize by crafts. The AFL reaches 1 million members by 1900 and survives violence and corporate union-busting tactics. The Committee for Industrial

Organizations (CIO) forms within the AFL in 1935 to represent industrial workers and leaves the AFL in 1938. The AFL merges with the CIO to form the AFL-CIO in 1955 and becomes the peak labor organization in the U.S. economy and politics.

1882   *Chinese Exclusionary Act.* Up to 100,000 Chinese male laborers provide manpower for the California gold rush in the late 1840s and much of the muscle for building the transcontinental railroad in the late 1860s. When the economy in the western states turns bad, discrimination and hostility toward the Chinese grow. Unions and other organizations as well as western political parties campaign to expel the Chinese from the United States. Congress passes the Exclusion Act of 1882, suspending the immigration of Chinese into the United States for 10 years and making Chinese immigrants ineligible for citizenship. This is the first law that seeks to prevent people from a specific nation from entering the United States and becoming citizens. Chinese immigrants protest the law, and violence ensues, but Congress extends the law indefinitely in 1902. In 1913, California prohibits immigrant Chinese from owning property. Discriminatory immigration laws against the Chinese do not end until after World War II.

1890   *United Mine Workers (UMW) forms in 1890 in reaction to the terrible working conditions found in American mines.* After Congress passes the National Recovery Act of 1933, the UMW rapidly expands across the nation in its representation of American miners. Representing the workers of an often dangerous industry, the UMW often engages in long and difficult strikes with the major mining companies. Automation and the decline of American mining sharply reduce the UMW's membership and economic influence. By 2000, the UMW's membership falls to half its 1946 peak and now represents about 40 percent of American miners.

Sherman Anti-Trust Act. Congress passes the act intending to break up corporate trusts that are designed to limit competition and create monopolies. The law is vague and the courts largely refuse to implement it against

1890
(*cont.*)

many of the existing trusts. In 1911, the government wins several legal victories by breaking up Standard Oil of New Jersey and the American Tobacco Company. In 1914, Congress creates the Federal Trade Commission to assist in the efforts to control trusts in the U.S. economy. The Sherman Act still largely remains the legal basis for American federal antitrust activities.

1892

The Sierra Club is the first environmental organization. It is founded in San Francisco in 1892 by early environmentalist John Muir, its first president. Among its various causes are protecting the nation's national forests, parks, and rivers and, later, opposing the building of nuclear power plants and dams. In recent years, it has become a major actor in the immigration debate in the United States as a part of its concerns regarding overpopulation.

1896

Plessy v. Ferguson. One of the most important Supreme Court decisions in American history allows segregation laws enacted in mostly southern states to stand until the civil rights movement of the 1950s and 1960s. Plessy is overturned by *Brown v. Board of Education of Topeka* (1954). After the Civil War, white Southerners retake political control of the former Confederacy following the 1876 elections. So-called Jim Crow laws are passed to segregate blacks from whites in nearly every aspect of Southern society. Homer Plessy, a black living in Louisiana in 1892, rides in the white car of a train and refuses to leave. Plessy is arrested and convicted, and his lawyers take the case to the Supreme Court, which rules that the separate but equal laws are constitutional. This case protects segregation in the South and many border states until the 1950s.

1907

Congress passes Tilman Act. This act makes it a crime for corporations and interstate banks to make direct campaign contributions to candidates for federal offices. President Theodore Roosevelt pushes Congress to pass this first American law to restrict interest group campaign funding in federal elections. Like many such laws, it is written in such a manner as to be easily circumvented. Corporations avoid the law by giving their employees large bonuses that can be contributed to political parties and candidates without restrictions.

1909 *The National Association for the Advancement of Colored People (NAACP) formed.* A policy of racial segregation is established by state laws in the southern states after the 1876 elections. Intimidated by the KKK and other terrorist organizations, blacks in the South and the border states suffer under Jim Crow laws that reduce them to the status of second-class citizens. The NAACP uses a lobbying and litigation strategy to counter this discrimination but fails to have any major successes until after World War II, when President Truman desegregates the armed forces in 1948. NAACP lawyers win the landmark Supreme Court case *Brown v. Board of Education* (1954), which eliminates the legal foundation for segregated America. Martin Luther King Jr. and the Southern Christian Leadership Conference lead the movement to challenge the segregation laws in the South and secure landmark civil rights legislation during the Johnson administration in the 1960s. The civil rights movement is the most successful political movement in American history.

1912 *The U.S. Chamber of Commerce is established in Washington, D.C.* America's premier business association is created after then president William Taft calls for a central organization to represent American business. It represents more than 3 million businesses, nearly 3,000 state and local chambers, 830 associations, and more than 90 American Chambers of Commerce abroad. The Chamber of Commerce is the world's largest business federation and perhaps the richest and best-staffed U.S. lobby.

Congress passes Radio Act. Following the sinking of the *Titanic,* Congress passes the Radio Act of 1912 to require that seafaring vessels maintain a 24-hour radio watch to begin the government's regulation of America's broadcast media. Among other regulations, the act calls for all broadcasters to be licensed and to use only assigned frequencies. The allocation of radio station frequencies is given to the secretary of commerce. The problems continue to mount as more and more stations in the eastern

1912   and northern regions of the nation operate and block
(*cont.*) each other's signals while the southern and western regions have very few radio stations. The Radio Act of 1927
sets up the Federal Radio Commission as the new licens-
ing agent for the government. In 1934, the Federal Communications Commission is created to regulate interstate
and international communications; its authority covers
radio, television, and cable transmissions.

1916   *The Brookings Institution is founded.* One of the United
States' oldest think tanks, the Washington, D.C.–based
Brookings specializes in research in the social sciences.
Although it sees itself as nonpartisan, Brookings is generally on the liberal side of the policy perspective. Brookings makes significant contributions to the policy-making
process with the creation of the United Nations, the Marshall Plan, and the Congressional Budget Office and to
such issues as deregulation in the 1970s and 1980s. Brookings' reputation in Washington, D.C., is as one of the three
most influential think tanks in the city and the most influential liberal think tank.

1919   *American Legion established to represent the interests of
American military veterans after World War I.* Earlier, veterans of the Spanish American War had formed veterans
groups in 1899, and these merge into the Veterans of Foreign Wars in 1914. The various veterans groups are an effective lobby for maintaining and enhancing benefit
programs for veterans, but since the Vietnam War, the
quality of education and health benefits is reduced compared with such programs offered to World War II and
Korean War veterans. The number of veterans who join
these organizations has fallen in recent decades, and the
organizations' political power has also declined as the
number of veterans in Congress has also declined.

1924   *Teapot Dome scandal.* This major financial scandal in the
Harding administration involves bribery of Secretary of
the Interior Albert Fall by oil company executives seeking special access to U.S. Navy oil reserves in Wyoming.
Fall leases oil reserves to oil magnates, getting kickbacks
equal to $4 million in 2000 dollars. After a special Senate

investigation, Fall is found guilty of bribery in 1929, fined $100,000, and sentenced to one year in prison, making him the first presidential cabinet member to go to prison for his actions in office. The Teapot Dome scandal is the first major American government corruption scandal of the 20th century. The scandal does reveal the problem of natural resource scarcity and the need to provide reserves against the future depletion of resources in a time of emergency.

1935   *Congress passes the Public Utilities Holding Company Act.* This act serves as the first federal law attempting to regulate lobbying of the electric power companies in the United States. Congress writes the law in such a way as to make enforcement nearly impossible, beginning a tradition of lobbying laws that are largely symbolic but reduce political pressures on Congress to do something after a lobbying scandal. Congress passes the Merchant Marine Act of 1936 to regulate lobbying in the shipping industry; the narrow law is designed to keep the shipping industry from bribing government officials regarding federal mail contracts.

1938   *The Foreign Agents Registration Act.* Congress passes a new law on the eve of World War II to force agents of foreign governments operating in the United States to register. This is another largely symbolic piece of legislation on the subject of lobbying. Most Washington, D.C., lawyers and many lobbyists representing foreign interests simply refuse to register as lobbyists by claiming they are doing legal work or just consulting for their foreign clients. President Jimmy Carter's brother is one of the few lobbyists for foreign interests to be caught by the law and forced to register as an agent of a foreign interest.

1943   *American Enterprise Institute (AEI) is founded.* The AEI, a conservative think tank located in Washington, D.C., is one of the leading policy sources for the George W. Bush administration's public policy. The AEI promotes limited government, private enterprise, individual liberty and responsibility, and American capitalism. The AEI has

1943 been one of the leading critics of the idea of global warm-
(*cont.*) ing and climate change.

1946 *The Federal Regulation of Lobbying Act becomes the first broad regulation of lobbying act covering the federal government lobbying process.* This law is part of a much larger general reform of federal governmental operations and regulations but is added on to the reform bill largely as an afterthought. The lobbying law is only several pages long and contains many loopholes that allow lobbying on the federal level to be largely unregulated and unreported. The huge loopholes in the 1946 law continue to exist until substantial reforms are adopted by Congress in 1995 and 2007.

1955 *The AFL-CIO (American Federation of Labor and Congress of Industrial Organizations) is formed by a merger of the two labor confederations.* The new group represents the vast majority of America's organized workers and becomes a major political force supporting the Democratic Party. The 1955 merger represents the high-water mark of American organized labor. By the late 1960s, the conservatives and antiunion forces regain political power and, when combined with significant changes in the U.S. economy, sharply reduce organized labor's political and economic power.

1958 *American Association of Retired Persons founded.* The AARP becomes the largest interest group in the United States and the most powerful group representing older Americans. Originally started to provide health insurance for retired schoolteachers, the AARP has more than 35 million members and solicits membership from potential members after their 50th birthday. The AARP's huge size is also a disadvantage because it has a great deal of trouble developing internal consensus among its membership to build an effective issue or political campaign. During the George W. Bush administration, the AARP supports expanding the Medicare program benefits to include prescription drugs. This is the most significant expansion of this senior citizen benefit program since the 1960s.

1961   *Retiring U.S. president and former general of the Armies Dwight D. Eisenhower warns of the dangers of the military-industrial complex.* The post–World War II Cold War environment produces a political atmosphere very conducive to successful lobbying of Congress for larger and larger military budgets. After the 9/11 attacks, the military budget is greatly expanded as Congress finds it difficult to say no to any military requests. By 2008, the combined military budget reaches approximately $1 trillion for normal military expenditures and the additional costs of the Iraq War.

1962   *César Chávez forms United Farm Workers (UFW), the first successful labor union to represent migrant agricultural workers in the United States.* Migrant agricultural workers in the United States are not protected by federal labor laws and are badly exploited by the farms where they work. In 1966, the UFW joins the AFL-CIO. It organizes a national boycott of grape farms that lasts five years and is followed by boycotts of lettuce and other farm products. The California state government passes legislation that requires farms to bargain collectively with the UFW. The UFW survives the death of its longtime president César Chávez in 1993 and a takeover attempt by the Teamsters Union in the 1970s.

Rachel Carson publishes Silent Spring. Carson's book, which lays the foundation for the American environmental movement, attacks the chemical industry and describes the dangers of pesticides and herbicides. The environmental movement begins in the 1960s but explodes in visibility and influence in the 1970s and 1980s. In 1969, Congress passes the National Environmental Policy Act and creates the Environmental Protection Agency, which requires government to conduct environmental impact studies. Later laws focus on occupational safety, clean air, clean water, and endangered species.

1966   *The National Organization of Women (NOW) is founded.* NOW, with more than 500,000 members, is the largest organization of feminist activists in the United States. Inspired by Betty Friedan and other NOW founders, the

1966   organization develops into a major force in interest
(cont.) group politics and political party campaigns at the na-
         tional and state levels. NOW's issue priorities include a
         constitutional amendment on gender equality, the pro-
         tection of abortion rights and lesbian rights, and the
         adoption of laws protecting women from violence.

1969   *Friends of the Earth (FOE) is founded.* FOE, part of an inter-
         national network of environmental organizations in 70
         countries, is a nongovernmental organization built up
         from the grassroots as a confederation of local groups con-
         cerned with environmental issues. FOE is founded in the
         United States by David Brower after a split from the Sierra
         Club over the issue of nuclear power development, which
         remains one of its most prominent concerns.

1970   *Common Cause is founded as a major nonpartisan lobbying
         group.* Common Cause represents a middle-class citizen
         action group seeking moderate reforms in the American
         political system. The organization is founded by John
         Gardner to hold public officials accountable to the public
         interest. Gardner's battle cry of "everybody's organized
         but the people" summarizes the organization's goal of
         citizen politics. Common Cause opposes the Vietnam
         War as well as the Iraq War and supports a strong pro-
         gram of political reforms, such as campaign finance re-
         forms and lobbying reforms.

         *Nader organizations help found state level public interest re-
         search groups to develop information on issues on the state level.*
         Public Citizen becomes a Washington, D.C.–based organi-
         zation engaged in consumer advocacy, government ac-
         countability, clean democracy and ethical government,
         access to the courts, global trade, and regulatory and sci-
         ence policy. Founded in 1971 by Ralph Nader, its policy
         includes energy concerns, campaign finance reform, con-
         sumer protection, medical malpractice, and public health.

1971   *Campaign Finance Act passed by Congress.* A comprehensive
         campaign finance law is enacted after the scandals associ-
         ated with the Nixon administration and the 1968 and 1970

federal elections. This act forms the core of federal rules governing the conduct of fund-raising for presidential and congressional elections. One of the most important parts of the act is the public campaign check-off provisions that allow citizens to contribute small amounts of money on their tax forms to finance presidential elections. The act is modified several times in the 1970s and again by the Bipartisan Campaign Reform Act of 2001.

1973   *Conservatives establish the Heritage Foundation, the premier conservative think tank and policy promoters in the United States.* Heritage's mission is to formulate and promote conservative public policies based on the principles of free enterprise, limited government, individual freedom, traditional American values, and a strong national defense. Initial funding comes from political conservative Joseph Coors, owner of the Coors Brewing Company, and billionaire Richard Mellon Scaife, who has funded several other conservative organizations. The Heritage Foundation is the conservatives' direct response to the Brookings Institution, the longtime liberal think tank in Washington, D.C.

1974   *Political Reform Act (Proposition 9) is passed by California state government.* At the time, this act is the most comprehensive state-level lobbying law. The act begins the process of significant change in the strategies and tactics of lobbying on the state governmental level. Among the many features of the law are those requiring great transparency of funding in lobbying and California state government campaigns and the reduction of the role of gifts and social events as lobbying techniques. Other states have used the successes and failures of the California law in their decision making in lobby law reforms.

1975   *Congress establishes Federal Election Commission (FEC) to regulate federal elections in the wake of the Nixon administration's Watergate scandals.* The FEC is a regulatory agency with some judicial powers and is independent of both the executive and legislative branches of the federal government. The six FEC commissioners are appointed by

1975
(cont.) the president and confirmed by the Senate. Three are Democrats and three are Republicans, and this division tends to produce lots of "no decisions" as the two parties seldom agree on election law.

1976 *Buckley v. Valeo.* Supreme Court rules that parts of the Campaign Finance Act of 1974 are constitutional. In *Buckley v. Valeo,* the U.S. Supreme Court upholds federal limits on campaign contributions and rules that spending money to influence elections is a form of constitutionally protected free speech. This ruling makes it more difficult to enact effective laws to control the influence of money on elections. The Court also rules that candidates can give unlimited amounts of money to their own campaigns.

Koreagate lobbying scandal. Tongsun Park, a Korean-born businessman, tries to influence Congress with financial favors to hand-picked congresspersons. Park is a central figure in two lobbying/political money scandals: Koreagate in the 1970s and the Oil-for-Food Program scandal of the 2000s. In 1976, Park is charged with bribing members of the U.S. Congress, using money from the South Korean government, in an unsuccessful effort to convince the U.S. government to keep troops in Vietnam. In 1977, a U.S. District Court convicts him of bribery, illegal campaign contributions, mail fraud, racketeering, and failure to register as an agent of the Korean Central Intelligence Agency. He avoids prison in exchange for immunity. In the 1990s, Park helps lobby for a UN Oil-for-Food Program for Iraq. In July 2006, Park is convicted, in a U.S. federal court, on conspiracy charges related to lobbying and efforts to avoid UN economic sanctions on Iraq.

1977 *Cato Institute is founded in Menlo Park, California.* The Cato Institute becomes the premier Libertarian think tank in the United States and a major intellectual center for opposition to campaign finance and lobbying reforms. As a libertarian think tank, the Cato Institute is a frequent advocate for limited government and provides intellectual perspective and support for conservatives seeking to limit and reduce the social welfare programs and other parts of the New Deal and Great Society programs of the liberals and Democrats.

1978   *The Ethics in Government Act is passed.* This U.S. federal law, passed after the Watergate Scandal, establishes financial disclosure requirements for public officials and restrictions on former government employees' lobbying activities. The attempts to stop the revolving door of lobbyists becoming governmental officials and policy makers and then returning to their lobbying for a period of time before returning again to government have mostly failed as provisions of this law have been largely interpreted to facilitate such moves.

1983   *Center for Responsive Politics is founded to provide information on campaigns, interest groups, lobbying, and political financing.* In 1989, the Center for Public Integrity is established to provide data research for various public policy issues, including campaign finance and lobbying reform. These two organizations provide extremely valuable data and insight into the American lobbying process.

1995   *Lobby Restrictions Act attempts to correct some of the most serious weaknesses of the 1946 Federal Regulation of Lobby Act.* Among the major changes made in this act are defining lobbying to mean more than just contact with members of Congress and requiring better reporting on lobbying expenditures and clients. Major loopholes unaddressed in the law are religious lobbying and grassroots lobbying campaigns.

2001   *Bipartisan Campaign Reform Act* passes. Congress intends BICRA, or the McCain-Feingold Act, to correct some of the weaknesses in the 1974 Federal Campaign Finance Act. It is challenged in *McConnell v. FEC;* the U.S. Supreme Court rules to uphold most of the act. BICRA tries to restrict the role of soft money in campaign financing. It also tries to limit the proliferation of issue ads by interest groups. This is the current federal law that regulates interest group financial contributions and advertising in federal election campaigns.

2005   *House Majority Leader Tom DeLay (R-TX) is indicted for illegal campaign fund-raising.* DeLay, the architect of the "K Street" strategy of extending Republican Party control in Washington, D.C., to include the lobbying and interest group world, is later forced from office. Lobbying reform rules and laws are enacted to keep such a strategy from occurring in the future. The end of DeLay's plans for a Republican domination of Washington's interest group world allows the lobbying pattern in the city to return to its normal more bipartisan pattern.

2006   *Lobbyist Jack Abramoff pleads guilty to felony charges associated with his lobbying business.* Abramoff, lobbying for Native American casino-gambling interests, amasses approximately $85 million in overbilled fees. Several congresspeople are convicted and jailed as a result of their dealings with Abramoff and other related scandals that year. The scandal becomes the symbol of lobbying excesses in Washington, D.C., serves to help the Democratic Party win control of Congress in the 2006 elections, and helps enact improved lobbying control legislation in 2007–2008.

2007   *Honest Leadership and Open Government Act.* Congress passes new lobbying and ethics laws/rules in reaction to the Abramoff lobbying scandals. Major loopholes on lobbying expenditures and reporting are closed and restrictions are placed on the Washington lobbying social events that are common on the state level but are never used on the federal level.

2008   *House of Representatives establishes an ethics office to monitor lobbying irregularities by members of the House of Representatives.* Critics of the 2007 reforms notes that Congress refuses to provide for an effective regulator to enforce the provisions of the law. This new office is a halfway step toward that goal but is essentially a monitoring office and not an enforcement office.

References

Bruner, David, et al. 1985. *An American Portrait: A History of the United States.* New York: Charles Scribner and Sons.

Carson, Thomas, ed., 1999. *Gale Encyclopedia of U.S. Economic History.* Vols. 1 and 2. Detroit: Gale Group.

Hrebenar, Ronald J. 1997. *Interest Group Politics in America.* 3rd ed. Armonk, NY: M. E. Sharpe.

Norton, Mary Beth, et al. 2001. *A People and a Nation.* 6th ed. Boston: Houghton Mifflin.

5

Biographical Sketches

This chapter presents brief biographical sketches of key interest group scholars and leaders and the nation's most influential lobbyists. The chapter highlights the leading contemporary scholars and commentators observing interest group activities and lists their most influential writings in the area. Many important interest groups were formed as an outgrowth of incredible individual activism and ambition. Such "public-interest entrepreneurs" have played significant roles in the formation of large interest groups such as AARP, Common Cause, Focus on the Family, Mothers Against Drunk Driving (MADD), and Public Citizen. Ralph Nader alone is credited with founding dozens of government and nongovernmental organizations and projects, including the Environmental Protection Agency. Founders of influential interest groups as well as select contemporary interest groups leaders are also presented herein. In addition, the chapter provides sketches of several top Washington, D.C., lobbyists. It is hard to exaggerate the power and influence of this "K-Street crowd." Pioneers such as Gerald Cassidy and Thomas Boggs established lucrative lobbying firms that served as models for many others. Other lobbyists, such as Jack Abramoff, scarred the lobbying profession by defrauding clients and attempting to purchase favorable government action. In essence, this chapter serves as a short "who's who" of the world of interest group politics.

SCHOLARS AND COMMENTATORS

Frank R. Baumgartner (1958–)

Dr. Frank R. Baumgartner (PhD, University of Michigan, 1986) is the Bruce R. Miller and Dean D. LaVigne Professor of Political Science at Pennslyvania State University. His work focuses on public policy, agenda setting, and interest groups in American politics. Baumgartner created the Policy Agendas Project (www.policy agendas.org) with Bryan D. Jones and codirects it with John Wilkerson. The project traces changes in U.S. and European policy agenda since the end of World War II by using extensive datasets that include legislative hearings and legislation, government reports, news articles, and public opinion data. In 2007, the Policy Agendas Project received the American Political Science Association's Best Instructional Web site award. Recent books from that project include *Comparative Studies of Policy Agendas,* a special issue of the *Journal of European Public Policy* (Vol. 13, no. 7, 2006, coedited with Bryan D. Jones and Christoffer Green-Pedersen); *The Politics of Attention: How Government Prioritizes Problems* (with Bryan D. Jones, University of Chicago Press, 2005); *Policy Dynamics* (coedited with Bryan D. Jones, University of Chicago Press, 2002); and *Agendas and Instability in American Politics* (with Bryan Jones, University of Chicago Press, 1993). Baumgartner's most recent book, *The Decline of the Death Penalty and the Discovery of Innocence* (with Suzanna De Boef and Amber E. Boydstun, Cambridge University Press, 2008), won the Gladys M. Kammerer Award, presented by the American Political Science Association for the best book on U.S. national policy. Baumgartner's personal Web page is http://www.personal.psu.edu/frb1/.

Jeffrey M. Berry (dates unknown)

Dr. Jeffrey M. Berry (PhD, Johns Hopkins University, 1974) is the John Richard Skuse, Class of 1941, Professor of Political Science at Tufts University. Berry specializes in the areas of interest groups, citizen participation in government and elections, nonprofits, and public policy making. Berry was one of the first to document the rise of citizen lobbying groups in Washington,

D.C., and is a leading researcher on nonprofit advocacy and grassroots-level organizing. He is the author of *Lobbying for the People* (Princeton University Press, 1977) and *The New Liberalism: The Rising Power of Citizen Groups* (Brookings Institution, 1999), which received the Aaron Wildavsky Award, given annually by the Policy Studies Organization. His most recent books on interest groups include *Surveying Nonprofits: A Methods Handbook* (Aspen Institute, 2003); *A Voice for Nonprofits* (Brookings Institution, 2003), which received the Leon D. Epstein Outstanding Book Award of the Political Organizations and Parties section of the American Political Science Association; and *The Interest Group Society* (4th ed., Longman, 2007). Berry is a recipient of the Tufts Distinguished Scholar Award.

Jeffrey Birnbaum (dates unknown)

Jeffrey Birnbaum is a man with several roles. He is an author and writer for *The Washington Post,* television commentator for Fox News Channel and PBS's *Washington Week,* radio commentator for American Public Media's *Marketplace,* and commentator and occasional guest host on the Fox News *Tony Snow Show.* Birnbaum served for several years as the chief of *Fortune* magazine's Washington bureau and for two years as a senior political correspondent for *Time.* Birnbaum also worked for *The Wall Street Journal,* where he rose to the prestigious position of White House correspondent. Birnbaum is well known for the *K Street Confidential* column he writes for *The Washington Post*—which was the first column to expose and unravel the Jack Abramoff lobbying scandal as well as the intricacies of U.S. House Majority Leader Tom Delay's strategy to place conservatives in key lobbying organizations. Birnbaum is the author of four books. His latest, *The Money Men* (2000), examines campaign fund-raising and the effects of money on the electoral and policy-making processes. His first book, *Showdown at Gucci Gulch* (1987), which he wrote with Alan Murray, won the American Political Science Association's Carey McWilliams Award in 1988 for its detailed account of the battle over the 1986 Tax Reform Act. In 1992, Birnbaum's second book, *The Lobbyists,* was a *Washington Post* best seller. Perhaps no other contemporary commentator is as familiar with the lobbyist-dominated lawmaking process on Capitol Hill.

Virginia Gray (dates unknown)

Dr. Virginia Gray (PhD, Washington University, 1972) is the University of North Carolina Robert Watson Winston Distinguished Professor of Political Science. Few political scientists know as much about lobbying and policy making in the American states as Dr. Gray. Gray and David Lowery have collaborated on numerous research projects on state interest groups. Their publications include *The Population Ecology of Interest Representation: Lobbying Communities in the American States* (University of Michigan Press, 1996) and articles in several leading political science journals. Their ongoing research has been funded by the National Science Foundation and the Robert Wood Johnson Foundation. In addition, Gray also is the coeditor of the leading textbook on state politics, *Politics in the American States* (CQ Press, 9th ed., 2007), which provides an in-depth look at each state's policy-making process as well as a comparative look at state policies in the areas of education, taxes, and corrections. Gray's personal Web page is http://www.unc.edu/depts/polisci/faculty_pages/gray.html.

Ronald J. Hrebenar (1945–)

Dr. Ronald J. Hrebenar (PhD, University of Washington–Seattle) is a professor of political science and has been a faculty member at the University of Utah since 1973. He is the former chair of the department (2000–2007) and former interim director of the Hinckley Institute of Politics (2003–2005). He was a Fulbright professor at Tohoku University in Japan in 1982–1983 and served as the Fulbright Distinguished Professor of American Studies at the University of Vienna (Austria) in 2007–2008. Hrebenar's research agenda has focused on various aspects of political behavior and political organizations and specifically on interest groups, lobbying, political campaigns, political parties, and elections in the United States and Japan. He is the author, coauthor, editor, or coeditor of 15 books and more than 50 journal articles and book chapters. His books include *Interest Group Politics in America* (M. E. Sharpe, 1997), *Political Parties, Campaigns and Interest Groups, Parties in Crisis* (Westview Press, 1999), and *Japan's New Party System* (Westview Press, 2000), as well as four books on interest-group politics in the 50 states published by four university presses. Among his recent articles and book chapters are "What Happened to the Japanese Lobby in Washington? The Decline of the Japanese Lobby and the Rise of the New China Lobby" (*Interest Group Politics*, edited by Cigler, CQ Press, 2006), "Interest Groups" (*Politics in the American States*, edited by Gray and Hanson, CQ Press, 2007), and "Patterns of Interest Group Power in the States" (*Book of the States*, 2003–2004). Hrebenar's personal Web page is http://www.poli-sci.utah.edu/hrebenar.html.

Grant Jordan (dates unknown)

Dr. Grant Jordan joined the University of Aberdeen Department of Politics and International Relations as a lecturer in September 1974 and became a senior lecturer in September 1986, personal chair in October 1990, established chair in August 1995, and head of the department in 1998. His research interests include public policy making, government design, interest group politics, and interest group membership management. Jordan has published several books, including *Shell, Greenpeace, and Brent Spar* (Palgrave, 2001); *The Protest Business? Mobilizing Campaigning Groups* (Manchester University Press, 1997); *Commercial Lobbying* (Aberdeen University Press, 1991); *British Politics and the Policy Process* (Allen and Unwin, 1987); *Government and Pressure Groups in Britain* (Clarendon Press, 1987); and *Limits of Planning: the Moray Firth Working Party and Multi-Organisational Co-ordination* (London: Economic and Social Research Council, 1984).

David Lowery (1952–)

Dr. David Lowery (PhD, Michigan State University, 1981) joined the Department of Public Administration at the University of Leiden in 2004. Lowery teaches and conducts research on the politics of interest representation (with the support of a grant from the U.S. National Science Foundation), urban politics and administration, bureaucratic politics, and tax and spending policy. He has authored a number of articles on these and other topics that have appeared in the *American Political Science Review*, the *American Journal of Political Science*, and the *Journal of Politics*. He is also the coauthor of *The Population Ecology of Interest Representation: Lobbying Communities in the American States* (University of Michigan Press, 1996) and *Organized Interests and American Politics* (McGraw-Hill, 2004).

Lowery's personal Web page is http://www.publicadministration. leidenuniv.nl/index.php3?c=186.

Andrew McFarland (dates unknown)

Dr. Andrew McFarland (PhD, University of California at Berkeley, 1966) is a professor at the University of Illinois at Chicago. McFarland's areas of research include political participation, civic reform, interest groups, public policy, and social movements. He has published several works, including *Power and Leadership in Pluralist Systems* (Stanford University Press, 1969); *Public Interest Lobbies: Decision Making on Energy* (American Enterprise Institute, 1976); *Common Cause: Lobbying in the Public Interest* (Chatham House, 1984), which won him national acclaim; *Cooperative Pluralism: The National Coal Policy Experiment* (University Press of Kansas, 1993); and *Neopluralism: The Evolution of Political Process Theory* (University Press of Kansas, 2004). He also coedited *Social Movements and American Political Institutions, a Book of Original Papers* (Rowman & Littlefield, 1997). McFarland's personal Web page is http:// www.uic.edu/depts/pols/faculty/andrewmcfarland.html.

Anthony J. Nownes (dates unknown)

Dr. Anthony J. Nownes (PhD, University of Kansas, 1993) is an associate professor of political science at the University of Tennessee, Knoxville, where he has taught since 1994. His research on interest groups has appeared in a number of journals, including the *British Journal of Political Science,* the *Journal of Politics,* and *American Politics Research.* His first book, *Pressure and Power: Organized Interests in American Politics,* was published by Houghton Mifflin in 2000. Most recently, Nownes's publications include "Interest Groups and Journalists in the States" (*State Politics and Policy Quarterly* vol. 7, 2007: 39–53); *Total Lobbying: What Lobbyists Want and How They Try to Get It* (Cambridge University Press, 2006); "Women Lobbyists: The Gender Gap and Interest Representation" (*Politics and Policy* vol. 33, 2005: 136–153); "Perceptions of Power: Interest Groups in Local Politics" (*State and Local Government Review* vol. 37, 2005: 206–216); and "The Population Ecology of Interest Group Death: Gay and Lesbian Rights Interest Groups in the United States, 1948–1998" (*British Journal of Politi-*

cal Science vol. 35, 2005: 303–319). Nownes's personal Web page is http://web.utk.edu/~anownes/.

Robert Salisbury (dates unknown)

Dr. Robert Salisbury (PhD, University of Illinois) is a Washington University (St. Louis) professor emeritus of political science. Salisbury is the author of many books on urban government and is an expert on American politics, interest groups, religion and politics, voting behavior, political participation, and how lobbyists and interest groups work in Washington, D.C. He studies how the Washington community of lawyers, congressional staffs, and interest groups interact to make national policy. Salisbury has written on how the electoral process and campaigning have been influenced by (and are contributing to) the decline in civic responsibility and the sense of community in America. His publications include *State Politics and the Public Schools* (edited by Masters and Eliot, Knopf, 1964); *Citizen Participation in the Public Schools* (Lexington Books, 1980); *Interests and Institutions: Substance and Structure in American Politics* (University of Pittsburgh Press, 1992); and *The Hollow Core: Private Interests in National Policy Making* (edited by Heinz, Laumann, and Nelson, Harvard University Press, 1993). Salisbury's personal Web page is http://news-info.wustl.edu/sb/page/normal/453.html

Kay Lehman Schlozman (dates unknown)

Dr. Kay Lehman Schlozman (PhD, University of Chicago, 1973) is the J. Joseph Moakley Professor in the Boston College Department of Political Science. Schlozman was awarded the Frank J. Goodnow Award for Distinguished Service to the Profession of Political Science and the American Political Science Association. In 2006, Schlozman was made a senior research fellow at the Ash Institute and later, in 2006–2007, was made a senior research fellow at the John F. Kennedy School of Government at Harvard University. Schlozman's recent publications include *The Private Roots of Public Action: Gender, Equality and Political Participation* (Harvard University Press, 2001); *Voice and Equality: Civic Voluntarism and American Politics* (Harvard University Press, 1995); *Organized Interests and American Democracy* (Harper and Row, 1986);

and *Injury to Insult: Unemployment, Class and Political Response* (Harvard University Press, 1979). Schlozman's personal Web page is http://www.bc.edu/schools/cas/polisci/meta-elements/pdf/schlozman.pdf.

Philippe C. Schmitter (dates unknown)

Dr. Philippe C. Schmitter (PhD, University of California at Berkeley, 1967) served as an assistant professor, an associate professor, and a professor in the Politics Department of the University of Chicago (1967–1982). Schmitter then held teaching positions at the European University Institute (1982–1986) and at Stanford University (1986–1996). Most recently, Schmitter returned to serve as a professor of political science at the European University Institute in Florence, Italy, Department of Political and Social Sciences, where he then became a professorial fellow. Schmitter's publications include books and articles on comparative politics; regional integration in Western Europe and Latin America; the transition from authoritarian rule in southern Europe and Latin America; and the intermediation of class, sectoral, and professional interests. Schmitter's most recent publications include "The Renaissance of National Corporatism: Unintended Side-Effect of European Economic and Monetary Union, or Calculated Response to the Absence of European Social Policy?" in *Renegotiating the Welfare State* (edited by Grote, van Waarden, and Lehmbruch, Routledge, 2003, 279–302); "Democracy in Europe and Europe's Democratization" (*Journal of Democracy* 2003, 14 (4):71–85); and *Neo-Neofunctionalism* in *Europen Integration Theory* (edited by Wiener and Diez, Oxford University Press, 2004, 45–74). Schmitter's personal Web page is http://www.iue.it/SPS/People/Faculty/CurrentProfessors/bioSchmitter.shtml.

Wolfgang Streeck (dates unknown)

Dr. Wolfgang Streeck (PhD, Johann Wolfgang Goethe University, 1980) currently serves as the director of the Max Planck Institute for the Study of Societies in Cologne, Germany. He previously served as a professor of sociology and industrial relations at the University of Wisconsin–Madison (1988–1995), a senior fellow with Wissenschaftszentrum in Berlin (1980–1988), an assistant professor of sociology with the University of Münster Department of Economics and Social Sciences (1974–1976), and a research fellow with the International Institute of Management in Berlin (1976–1980). Streeck's most recent work focuses on German welfare policies, interest groups, and labor unions. Streeck's recent publications include *The Diversity of Democracy: Corporatism, Social Order and Political Conflict* (Edward Elgar, 2006); *Governing Interests: Business Associations Facing Internationalization* (Routledge, 2006); and *Beyond Continuity: Institutional Change in Advanced Political Economies* (Oxford University Press, 2005). Streeck's personal Web page is http://www.mpifg.de/people/ws/index_en.asp.

Clive S. Thomas (1945–)

Dr. Clive S. Thomas (PhD, London School of Economics, 1979) is a University of Alaska Southeast professor of political science. His teaching and research interests include American politics and state politics, Western European politics, and special interest groups. He has published 10 books and more than 40 articles and chapters in books mainly in the fields of interest groups, state politics, legislative process, and intergovernmental relations. Thomas's publications include *Interest Group Politics in the American West* (University of Utah Press, 1987); *Politics and Public Policy in the Contemporary American West* (University of New Mexico Press, 1991); *Interest Group Politics in the Southern States* (University of Alabama Press, 1992); *Interest Group Politics in the Northeastern States* (Pennsylvania State University Press, 1993); *Interest Group Politics in the Midwestern States* (Iowa State University Press, 1993); *First World Interest Groups: A Comparative Perspective* (Greenwood Press, 1993); *Political Parties and Interest Groups: Shaping Democratic Governance* (Lynne Rienner Publishers, 2001); and *Research Guide to U.S. and International Interest Groups* (Praeger Publishers, 2004). Thomas's personal Web page is http://www.uas.alaska.edu/faculty_staff/organization/provost/arts-sciences/social-sciences/social-science-faculty/thomas.html.

James Q. Wilson (1931–)

Dr. James Q. Wilson (PhD, University of Chicago, 1959) is the Ronald Reagan Professor of Public Policy at Pepperdine University.

From 1961 to 1987, he taught political science at Harvard University, where he was the Shattuck Professor of Government. He was the James Collins Professor of Management and Public Policy at UCLA from 1985 until 1997. Wilson is the author or coauthor of 14 books, including *American Government* (Houghton Mifflin, 2004), *Bureaucracy* (Basic Books, 1991), *Thinking About Crime* (Vintage, 1985), and *Political Organizations* (Princeton University Press, 1995). In addition, he has edited or contributed to books on urban problems, government regulation of business, and the prevention of delinquency among children. Many of his writings on morality and human character have been collected in *On Character: Essays by James Q. Wilson* (American Enterprise Institute Press, 1995). Wilson's personal Web page is http://publicpolicy. pepperdine.edu/academics/faculty/default.htm?faculty=james_ wilson.

INTEREST GROUP FOUNDERS AND LEADERS

Ethel Percy Andrus (1884–1967)

Born in 1884, Dr. Ethel Percy Andrus founded the National Retired Teachers Association (NRTA) and the American Association of Retired Persons (AARP). As an educator driven by a desire to help others organize and use their strengths, Andrus sought to provide support to thousands of retired teachers who were struggling on meager pensions and had no access to affordable health insurance. The NRTA, founded in 1947, organized former educators to obtain low-cost insurance programs and, in 1956, created the first health insurance program for educators over age 65. In 1958, Andrus, expanding the scope of the NRTA to include all retirees, founded and became president of AARP. AARP still maintains her motto: "To serve, not to be served." AARP grew rapidly, developing programs to help older and retiring Americans with health insurance, travel discounts, job placement assistance, and several other membership benefits. Under Andrus's leadership, AARP quickly grew to become a powerful lobbying organization for older Americans—providing expertise to the executive branch, Congress, and state legislators on many issues related to aging and retirement. Andrus also pioneered *AARP: The Maga-*

zine (originally *Modern Maturity)*, which boasts the largest circulation of any periodical in the United States. Andrus died in 1967.

Glynn R. Birch (dates unknown)

Glynn R. Birch joined Mothers Against Drunk Driving (MADD) in 1988 after his son Courtney was killed by a drunk driver with three prior DUI (driving under the influence) convictions and a revoked license. After the offender was convicted, Birch began serving as a volunteer speaker for the Central Florida Chapter of MADD and was elected to the chapter's board of directors in 1998 and to its presidency in 1999. In this role, Birch was a featured speaker at several MADD conferences, trained new victim advocates, and represented MADD in numerous capacities on the national level. In 2000 and 2003, Birch was elected and reelected to the MADD national board of directors and named the national vice president of victim issues. In 2005, Glynn's election as the national president of MADD made him the first male and minority president in the history of the organization. While serving as president from 2005 to 2008, Birch appeared on CNN, the *Today Show,* E! Entertainment, CMT Total Access, C-Span, National Public Radio, and various other networks and programs and has been featured in publications such as *Southern Living, Ebony,* and *Town and Country.*

Carrie Chapman Catt (1859–1947)

Born Carrie Clinton Lane in Wisconsin in 1859, Catt graduated from Iowa State College. In 1883, she was selected superintendent of schools in Mason City, Iowa. After the death of her husband, Leo Chapman, in 1885, she began working in California as a newspaper reporter. Shortly thereafter she returned to Iowa, joined the Iowa Woman Suffrage Association, and became a delegate to the National American Woman Suffrage Association (NAWSA) in 1890. That same year, she married George W. Catt. Her superb organizing abilities were quickly recognized, and she was selected as the head of field organizing for NAWSA. In 1900, Catt was elected to succeed Susan B. Anthony as NAWSA president but resigned in 1905 to care for her husband. Catt was also a founder and president of the International Woman Suffrage Association—serving as the organization's honorary president from 1904 to 1923. In 1915,

Catt returned to the presidency of NAWSA and led efforts to increase the number of states allowing women to participate in primary and general elections. Catt's efforts were instrumental in the passage of the 19th Amendment to the U.S. Constitution in 1920, which gave women the right to vote. Her tenure as president of NAWSA coincided with the climax of the women's suffrage movement. After the passage of the 19th Amendment, Catt helped form the League of Women Voters in 1920, serving as its honorary president until her death in 1947.

César Chávez (1927–1993)

Born in Arizona in 1927, César Chávez became part of the migrant community at a young age—traveling with his family from farm to farm picking fruits and vegetables. In 1944, Chávez joined the U.S. Navy and served during World War II. Returning to California, he married Helen Fabela in 1948 and rejoined the migrant farmworker community. That same year, Chávez participated in his first strike to protest low pay and inferior working conditions. In 1952, Chávez joined the Community Service Organization (CSO) and began traveling throughout California urging Mexican Americans to vote. In 1958, Chávez became the national director of CSO, and in 1962, he cofounded the National Farm Workers Association (NFWA), which later became known as the United Farm Workers (UFW). In 1965, Chávez and the NFWA organized the five-year grape strike that drew national attention as Chávez and his supporters marched from Delano to Sacramento, California. This effort led to a major victory for U.S. farmworkers. Three years later, in 1968, Chávez fasted to call attention to his cause—increasing public awareness of migrant issues. When the Teamsters attempted to take power from the UFW, an agreement was reached in 1977 that gave the UFW sole organizing power over field workers. In this capacity, the UFW organized several successful strikes and boycotts for higher wages, for improved working conditions, and against the use of toxic pesticides. Chávez died in 1993.

Joan Claybrook (1937–)

Born in 1937, Joan Claybrook was raised in Baltimore and graduated from Goucher College in 1959. While working in Washington, D.C., Claybrook became close friends with Ralph Nader as they worked for automobile and highway safety improvements. In 1966, Claybrook and Nader were instrumental in the passage of the National Traffic and Motor Vehicle Safety Act and the Highway Safety Act, the nation's first auto safety laws that empowered the federal government to set safety standards for vehicles. After the passage of these laws, Claybrook directed Public Citizen's Congress Watch, an organization founded by Nader, and worked for the Public Interest Research Group, the National Traffic Safety Bureau, the Social Security Administration, and the Department of Heath, Education, and Welfare. She earned her JD from Georgetown University Law Center in 1973 and in 1977 was selected to head the National Highway Traffic Safety Administration during the administration of President Jimmy Carter. Claybrook began her tenure as president of Public Citizen in 1982 where she continues to advocate for consumer protection, environmentalism, and good governance practices.

Christopher C. DeMuth (1946–)

Christopher C. DeMuth was born in 1946 and raised in Kenilworth, Illinois. He graduated from Harvard College in 1968. In 1969, DeMuth began serving as a staff assistant to President Richard Nixon under Daniel P. Moynihan, Nixon's assistant for urban affairs. DeMuth's work on urban policy issues led him to be appointed chairman of the White House Task Force on Environmental Policy in 1970. After returning to his studies and graduating from the University of Chicago Law School in 1973, DeMuth began practicing in the areas of regulatory, antitrust, and corporate law with the Chicago firm Sidley and Austin. In 1976, he served as general counsel to the Consolidated Rail Corporation in Philadelphia and went on to teach public policy, economics, law, and regulatory policy at the Kennedy School of Government at Harvard University. From 1981 to 1984, DeMuth served as an administrator for information and regulatory affairs in the U.S. Office of Management and Budget and as the executive director of the Presidential Task Force on Regulatory Relief. In 1986, the same year in which he became managing director of the consulting firm Lexecon Inc., DeMuth was elected president of the American Enterprise Institute, a prominent conservative think tank that plays a leading role in articulating conservative thought on social, economic, and foreign policies.

James C. Dobson (1936–)

Dr. James C. Dobson was born in 1936 in Shreveport, Louisiana. Dobson graduated from Pasadena College and earned a PhD in child development from the University of Southern California in 1967. For 14 years Dobson served as an associate clinical professor of pediatrics at the University of Southern California School of Medicine, and he served as a psychiatrist for 17 years at the Children's Hospital of Los Angeles. In 1977, Dobson founded Focus on the Family, a nonprofit American evangelical organization based in Colorado Springs, Colorado, and dedicated to advancing conservative Christian policies at the state and national levels. In 1981, Dobson founded the Family Research Council as a way to achieve greater power for Christian values in politics and society, which led to the fight against the appointment of Sen. Arlen Specter to the chairmanship of the Senate Judiciary Committee because of his pro-choice views and opposition to a 2006 constitutional amendment to ban gay marriage. As the chairman of the board of Focus on the Family, Dobson produces the daily radio and television program *Focus on the Family*, which is broadcast on more than 7,000 radio stations and 60 television stations throughout the world. More than 220 million people in 164 countries hear the *Focus on the Family* radio program each day. Dobson has authored or coauthored more than 30 books, including *Dare to Discipline* (Bantam, 1977).

Jerry L. Falwell (1933–2007)

Jerry L. Falwell was born in 1933 in Lynchburg, Virginia. He attended Lynchburg College for more than a year and then transferred to the Baptist Bible College in Springfield, Missouri, where he graduated in 1956. That same year, Falwell founded the Thomas Road Baptist Church in Lynchburg, leading services at the young age of 22 and airing his *Old Time Gospel Hour* on radio and television. In 1971, he founded Lynchburg Bible College, now Liberty University, a Christian liberal arts university in Lynchburg. Seeking to advance traditional family policies, in 1979 Falwell founded the Moral Majority, which soon became the nation's largest evangelical Christian political organization and exerted considerable influence in the 1980 presidential election in support of Ronald Reagan. The Moral Majority's areas of interest include pornography, abortion, drugs, and welfare. In 2001, Falwell was widely criticized for describing the 9/11 terrorist attacks as a judgment of God on America for "throwing God out of the public square" and indicating that feminists, homosexuals, and secularists were to blame. Falwell quickly retracted the statements and apologized. Falwell passed away in 2007.

Edwin J. Feulner Jr. (1941–)

Edwin J. Feulner Jr. was born in 1941 in Chicago. He graduated from Regis University and received an MBA from the University of Pennsylvania's Wharton School of Business in 1964 and a doctorate from the University of Edinburgh. He began his career in Washington, D.C., as an analyst for the Center for Strategic Studies. Feulner became a special assistant to Rep. Melvin Laird (R-WI), who later became defense secretary, and then Feulner became the executive director of the Republican Study Committee. He joined the Heritage Foundation in 1973 and became the group's fourth president in 1977. As president of the Heritage Foundation, Feulner has presided over the transition of the organization from a small think tank to a powerful conservative voice. Feulner served as the chairman of the U.S. Advisory Commission on Public Diplomacy in 1982, as vice chairman of the National Commission on Economic Growth and Tax Reform in 1995, on the Congressional Commission on International Finance Institutions in 1999, and on the Gingrich-Mitchell Congressional United Nations Reform Task Force in 2005. Heralded by President Ronald Reagan as "a voice for reason and values," Feulner was awarded the Presidential Citizens Medal by Reagan in 1989. In 2007, *GQ* magazine recognized Feulner as one of "Washington's 50 most powerful," and the London *Telegraph* named him one of the 100 most influential conservatives in the United States.

Sandra S. Froman (1949–)

Sandra S. Froman was born in 1949 and raised in San Francisco. She graduated from Stanford University in 1971 and Harvard Law School in 1974. A longtime gun ownership activist, Froman was elected to the National Rifle Association (NRA) Board of Trustees in 1992 and served on the Legislative Policy, Legal Affairs, and Action Shooting committees, and as chair of the Ways and Means Committee and as a trustee of the NRA Civil Rights Defense Fund. Froman served under former NRA president Charlton Heston for two years as first vice president, and in 2005 she became NRA's first female president. As president, Froman founded the Friends of NRA dinner program and placed the organization on a firm financial foundation by establishing the NRA's permanent endowment, which now exceeds $20 million. She also spoke out frequently on the right to keep and bear arms, called for the appointment of conservative judges to federal courts, and fought tirelessly to portray the NRA as a civil rights organization and to emphasize the importance of guns as a tool of self-defense, especially for women. Froman currently sits on the NRA Board of Directors and serves on the board of the University of Arizona Rogers College of Law and the George Mason University School of Law.

John W. Gardner (1912–2002)

John W. Gardner was born in 1912 and received a BA and MA in psychology from Stanford University and a PhD from the University of California, Berkeley. In 1946, Gardner joined the Carnegie Corporation as a staff member, and by 1955 he had become the organization's president. In this role, Gardner served frequently as a consultant to federal agencies. In 1964, Gardner received the Presidential Medal of Freedom, the nation's highest civil honor. That same year, Gardner was appointed to serve as President Lyndon Johnson's secretary of health. He pioneered the Medicare program, implemented the landmark Elementary and Secondary Education Act of 1965, and helped establish the Corporation for Public Broadcasting. In 1970, Gardner created Common Cause, the first nonprofit public interest group in the United States, which quickly grew to more than 20,000 members. In 1979, Gardner founded Independent Sector, a coalition of corporations, foundations, and private voluntary organizations that work to improve nonprofit organizations. Gardner wrote several books on leadership, national renewal, and public service. He was most widely known for his book *Excellence: Can We Be Equal and Excellent Too?* (W.W. Norton & Company, 1961).

Candace Lynne "Candy" Lightner (1946–)

Candace Lynne Lightner was born in 1946 in Pasadena, California, and attended American River College in Sacramento. In 1980, Lightner's daughter Cari was killed by a drunk driver in a hit-and-run accident. When the person who hit and killed her daughter received a lenient sentence despite having four previous drunk driving convictions, Lightner channeled her frustration into organizing Mothers Against Drunk Drivers. The name was later changed to Mothers Against Drunk Driving (MADD). As the founding MADD president, Lightner testified before Congress and worked to raise public awareness about drunk driving. She fought for the formation of a California state commission to study drunk driving and was appointed to the commission by Gov. Jerry Brown. In 1982, President Ronald Reagan selected Lightner to serve on the National Commission on Drunk Driving. In 1984, MADD was successful in convincing Congress to raise the legal drinking age to 21—saving an estimated 800 lives each year. MADD would continue to grow to become the largest anti–drunk-driving organization in the world with more than 3 million members. Lightner received the President's Volunteer Action Award and was the subject of the film *Mothers Against Drunk Drivers: The Candy Lightner Story* (1983).

George Meany (1894–1980)

George Meany was born in 1894 in the Bronx, New York. Meany never completed high school, but instead followed in his father's footsteps and served a five-year apprenticeship to become a plumber. He completed his apprenticeship in 1915 and in 1922 became the manager of his union—Local 463. Meany soon rose to national prominence, serving as president of the New York State Federation of Labor from 1934 to 1939 and serving on the National Labor Relations Board during World War II. In 1952, Meany was elected president of the American Federation of Labor (AFL). After Meany's extensive negotiations with leaders of the Congress of Industrial Organizations, he orchestrated the merger of the two groups to form the powerful AFL-CIO and, in 1955, was unanimously elected to be its first president, a position he held until 1979. During Meany's tenure, the AFL-CIO created the Labor Studies Center and advocated for the creation of the

Medicare program. Under Meany's leadership, the AFL-CIO gained unprecedented benefits for working Americans, strongly supported the civil rights movement, and helped women and minorities organize and form training programs. Meany was a staunch advocate for cooperation between labor and capital. He supported the Vietnam War and detested communism in all forms, expelling leftist unions such as the United Electrical Workers and the Retail Wholesale and Department Store Employees of America in the 1950s. Meany died in Washington, D.C., on January 10, 1980.

Ralph Nader (1934–)

Ralph Nader, the son of Lebanese immigrants, was born in 1934 in Winsted, Connecticut. In 1955, Nader graduated from Princeton University and went on to graduate from Harvard Law School in 1958. After a short stint in the U.S. Army in 1959, Nader moved to Washington, D.C., in 1964 to work for Daniel Patrick Moynihan, then serving as assistant secretary of labor. In 1965, Nader wrote the book *Unsafe at Any Speed*, which documented the poor safety records of American automobiles. In 1966, Nader's book and advocacy led to the unanimous passage of the National Traffic and Motor Vehicle Safety Act and the creation of the National Highway Traffic Safety Administration. In 1971, Nader founded Public Citizen, a nongovernmental organization dedicated to consumer rights, humanitarianism, environmentalism, health care, and democracy. Public Citizen now boasts more than 140,000 members and is credited with passing the Safe Drinking Water Act and the Freedom of Information Act as well as successfully advocating for the creation of the Occupational Safety and Health Administration, the U.S. Environmental Protection Agency, and the Consumer Product Safety Commission. A staunch critic of corporations, Nader ran for president of the United States in 1992, 1996, 2000, and 2004. His campaigns were controversial, as many viewed his role in the 2000 election as aiding Republican candidate George W. Bush. In February 2008, Nader surprised many by announcing his 2008 candidacy for president on NBC's *Meet the Press*. *Life* and *Time* magazines named Nader one of the 100 most influential Americans of the 20th century.

Cecile Richards (dates unknown)

Cecile Richards, the daughter of former Texas governor Ann Richards, attended Saint Stephen's Episcopal School in Austin, Texas, and graduated from Brown University in 1980. She began her career organizing garment workers along the Rio Grande and, in 1995, founded the Texas Freedom Network, an organization dedicated to combating the antiabortion movement that was then rising to power in Texas. Richards went on to spearhead a national grassroots mobilization project for the Turner Foundation and then formed and served as president of Pro-Choice Vote, the largest 527 political organization active in the 2000 election cycle. In 2004, then serving as deputy chief of staff for Democrat Nancy Pelosi, Richards founded and led America Votes, a coalition of 30 national organizations that spent more than $350 million to increase voter turnout in the 2004 elections. In 2006, Richards was chosen to serve as the president of Planned Parenthood Federation of America and Planned Parenthood Action Fund. In this role she has been instrumental in ensuring U.S. Food and Drug Administration approval of over-the-counter status for emergency contraception and has launched a nationwide campaign to advocate for sex education for all young people in the United States.

John Sweeney (1934–)

John Sweeney was born in 1934 in the Bronx, New York. Working as a gravedigger and building porter, Sweeney graduated from Iona College in New Rochelle, New York, in 1956. Starting his career as a clerk at IBM, Sweeney quickly returned to his labor roots, taking a job as a researcher for the International Ladies Garment Workers Union. In 1960, he became a contract director for the Building Service Employees International Union (BSEIU) and then assistant to the president of Local 32B in 1972. In 1973, Sweeney was elected to the executive board and then to be vice president of Local 32B. In 1976, Sweeney was elected president of Local 32B, and later that year he led a 45,000-member strike against the New York Realty Advisory Board, which won significant wage and benefit increases. In 1980, he was elected president of the national Service Employees International Union (SEIU). Under his tenure, the SEIU expanded its membership from 600,000 to more than 1 million, joined with the National Association of Working Women and the United Food and Commercial Workers, and absorbed the National Association of Government Employees. In 1995, he was elected president of the AFL-CIO, where he has advocated for increased minimum wage laws, affordable health care, and workers' rights and has opposed job outsourcing.

Nelson Strobridge "Strobe" Talbott III (1946–)

Nelson Strobridge "Strobe" Talbott III was born in 1946 in Dayton, Ohio. He graduated from Yale University in 1968. As a Rhodes scholar at Oxford University, Talbott became acquainted with fellow Rhodes scholar Bill Clinton and translated Nikita Khrushchev's memoirs into English. During the 1980s, Talbott served as *Time* magazine's correspondent on Soviet-American relations and wrote several books on disarmament. When Bill Clinton was elected president in 1992, Talbott served as an ambassador-at-large and special advisor to the secretary of state and as deputy secretary of state from 1994 to 2001. Upon leaving government, he served as the director of the Yale Center for the Study of Globalization. In 2002, Talbott was selected to be the president of the Brookings Institution in Washington, D.C. In this role, he oversees the research of the Brookings Institution, formulates institution policies, and testifies frequently before the U.S. House of Representatives Committee on Foreign Affairs. He has written for several leading journals and periodicals, including *Foreign Affairs* and *The Economist*. Talbott's books include *Engaging India: Diplomacy, Democracy and the Bomb* (Brookings Institution Press, 2004); *The Russia Hand* (Random House, 2003); *At the Highest Levels* (Back Bay Books, 1994); *The Master of the Game* (Vintage, 1989); and *Reagan and Gorbachev* (Vintage, 1987).

Wilbert Joseph "Billy" Tauzin II (1943–2003)

Wilbert Joseph "Billy" Tauzin II was born in 1943 in Chackbay, Louisiana, and graduated from Nicholls State University in 1964 and earned a law degree from Louisiana State University in 1967. In 1972, Tauzin was elected to the Louisiana House of Representatives as a Democrat. In 1980, Tauzin won a special election to fill the U.S. House of Representatives seat of David Treen, who became governor of Louisiana. Later that year, Tauzin cemented his place in the U.S. House by winning his seat with 85 percent of the vote. As a conservative Democrat in Congress, Tauzin eventually became assistant majority whip and cofounded the House Blue Dog Coalition—a group of fiscally conservative Democrats in the U.S. House of Representatives. In a controversial move in 1995, Tauzin left the Democratic Party to become a Republican. Soon, he was elected deputy majority whip for the Republican-controlled Congress—becoming the first person to serve in the House leadership of both parties. He went on to serve as chairman of the Energy and Commerce Committee from 2001 to 2004. After retiring in January 2005, Tauzin immediately began working as the head of the Pharmaceutical Research and Manufacturers of America (PhRMA). His quick transition from congressman to head of PhRMA was the subject of much controversy and speculation, as Tauzin had played a major role in shaping the Medicare Prescription Drug Bill passed in 2003.

Jack Joseph Valenti (1921–2007)

Jack Joseph Valenti was born in Houston, Texas, in 1921. The son of Italian immigrants, Valenti served as a lieutenant in the U.S. Army Air Corps during World War II, flying 51 combat missions as a B-25 pilot. He graduated from the University of Houston and received an MBA from Harvard University. In charge of the press during President John F. Kennedy's visit to Houston in 1963, Valenti was present at Lyndon Johnson's swearing in aboard Air Force One and became a special assistant to President Johnson. In 1968, Valenti became the president of the Motion Picture Association of America (MPAA). As president, Valenti created the MPAA film-rating system that still stands today and advocated for strict enforcement of copyright laws in the United States and throughout the world. In 1998, Valenti lobbied for the Digital Millennium Copyright Act, and in 2003, led a controversial move to ban studios from sending screener copies of films to critics and reviewers in order to prevent the early release of pirated copies of films. He served as president of the MPAA until 2004, when he was replaced by Dan Glickman, former member of Congress and secretary of agriculture. Valenti died in 2007.

Fredric Michael "Fred" Wertheimer (1939–)

Fredric Michael "Fred" Wertheimer was born in 1939. He served as legislative counsel to Rep. Silvio Conte (R-MA) and to the House Small Business Committee and as an attorney with the Securities and Exchange Commission. Joining Common Cause, a citizen lobbying organization that promotes government accountability, in 1971, Wertheimer served as legislative director and vice president for program operations and was responsible for the organization's legislative and grassroots activities, policy development, finances, and public communications. Wertheimer served as the president of Common Cause from 1981 to 1995 and has been a fellow at the Shorenstein Center on the Press, Politics and Public Policy at Harvard University, a visiting lecturer at Yale Law School, and a political analyst for CBS News, ABC News, and ABC's *Nightline*. In 1997, Wertheimer founded Democracy 21 and Democracy 21 Education Fund, which are dedicated to working in the areas of money in politics, government accountability, and governmental reform. *The New York Times* has described Wertheimer as "the country's leading proponent of campaign finance reform" and as "the lobbyist most closely associated with pressing to change the system." Wertheimer played a key role in the passage of the Bipartisan Campaign Reform Act of 2002, as well as its subsequent and continuing defense before the U.S. Supreme Court and its implementation by the Federal Election Commission.

INFLUENTIAL LOBBYISTS

Jack Abramoff (1959–)

Jack Abramoff was born in 1959. From 1981 to 1985 he was the national chairman of the College Republican National Committee. Abramoff was a leading lobbyist for Preston Gates and Ellis (1994–2001), Greenberg Traurig (2001–2004), and Cassidy and Associates (2004–2006), and was director of the National Center for Public Policy Research, a conservative think tank. As a "Bush Pioneer" (a designation for raising more than $100,000 for the reelection campaign of President George W. Bush) and Republican "superlobbyist," Abramoff became a central figure in the corruption scandals that rocked Washington, D.C., in 2005. On January 3, 2006, he pleaded guilty to three criminal felony counts in federal court for defrauding American Indian tribes and attempting to illegally influence public officials. Abramoff, with help from prominent Republicans Ralph E. Reed Jr., Grover Norquist, and Michael Scanlon, collected tens of millions of dollars from Indian tribe gambling operations that was used to buy influence from prominent White House and congressional officials and staffers and to enrich himself. By overbilling the Indian tribes, Abramoff was able to secretly amass millions in profits. The ensuing investigation, which is ongoing, has led to the conviction of White House official Steven Griles, Rep. Bob Ney (R-OH), and nine other congressional staffers and lobbyists, some of whom worked for House Majority Leader Tom DeLay.

Thomas Hale "Tommy" Boggs Jr. (1940–)

Thomas Hale "Tommy" Boggs Jr., the son of former Democratic House majority leader Hale Boggs (D-LA), has consistently been ranked by such publications as *National Journal* and *Washingtonian* as one of the top lobbyists in Washington, D.C. He served as an economist for the Joint Economic Committee and in the Executive Office of the president as a coordinator for the National Defense Executive Reserve. In 1966, he joined Patton Boggs LLP and has helped build what has traditionally been considered to be the nation's leading lobbying firm—bringing in more than $22 million in 2007 alone. Known for taking lawmakers on weekend hunting trips to his Eastern Shore estate, Boggs boasts of his leading role in securing congressional approval of a $1.5 billion federal bailout of Chrysler Corporation in 1979. When the Republicans took control of Congress in 1994, many thought Boggs's influence would diminish. However, Boggs has surprised his critics by remaining incredibly influential. For instance, one of his largest clients, Mars, pays him more than $2 million to maintain the presence of their Snickers candy bars and M&M's in military rations. Boggs currently serves as the chairman of the Patton Boggs Executive Committee and continues to advise clients in the areas of tax, health care, trade, and telecommunications.

Gerald Cassidy (1940–)

Gerald Cassidy, a graduate of Villanova University in 1963 and Cornell University Law School in 1967, has gained widespread attention for creating one of Washington, D.C.'s top governmental affairs and public relations firms, Cassidy and Associates. A former executive director and general counsel of the Democratic National Committee's Party Reform Commission and general counsel to the U.S. Senate Select Committee on Nutrition and Human Needs, Cassidy has been named to several lists of the top Washington, D.C., lobbyists and was named by *Forbes* magazine as No. 52 on the national "Power 100" list. In 2007, Cassidy was named a member of the "cast of characters" in *The Washington Post* "Citizen K Street" series by Robert Kaiser. Cassidy and Associates boasts expertise in gaining federal funding for local governments and universities. It brought in more than $12 million in lobbying fees in 2007 and has long been considered one of the most profitable and influential lobbying firms in Washington, D.C. Currently, Cassidy and Associates stands near the top in lobbying fees, behind firms such as Patton Boggs, Akin Gump, and Van Scoyoc Associates.

Linda Daschle (1955–)

Linda Daschle, wife of former Democratic Senate majority leader Tom Daschle (D-SD), joined Baker, Donelson, Bearman, Caldwell, and Berkowitz in 2004 to lead the firm's Federal Public Policy practice group. As an avid aviation enthusiast and the second woman ever to serve as deputy administrator of the Federal Aviation Administration (FAA) and the first to serve as FAA acting administrator, Daschle has been ranked as one of the nation's most effective lobbyists by such publications as *National Journal, The Hill,* and *Washingtonian.* In 2003, she was awarded the Amelia Earhart Pioneering Achievement Award, given annually to an individual who reinforces self-confidence and self-worth in women. Her knowledge of the intricacies of aviation policy has led the nation's largest airlines, airports, and airplane manufacturers to turn to her to represent them in Washington, D.C. Her clients include American Airlines, Boeing, and Lockheed Martin. Her practice also includes the areas of homeland security, transportation, and communications. Daschle brings in more than $1 million each year in lobbying fees—having become wealthier since her husband left the U.S. Senate, which enabled her to lift her self-imposed ban on lobbying the upper house.

Robert Joseph "Bob" Dole (1923–)

Robert Joseph "Bob" Dole was born in 1923 in Russell, Kansas, and graduated from the University of Kansas. He received a law degree from Washburn University after being injured while serving in the U.S. Army during World War II. Dole was elected to the U.S. House of Representatives in 1960 and to the U.S. Senate in 1968. Dole ran as President Gerald Ford's vice presidential candidate in 1976, chaired the Senate Finance Committee from 1981 to 1985, served as the majority leader from 1985 to 1987, and served as minority leader from 1987 to 1995. In 1996, Dole failed to beat incumbent president Bill Clinton. Upon leaving the Senate, Dole announced that he was willing to lobby for anything—"Viagra to Dunkin' Donuts"—and the companies came running. Joining Alston and Bird, Dole represented the Arab-owned company Dubai Ports World in a controversial attempted takeover of U.S. seaports that attracted extensive media attention. Dole received more than $300,000 in lobbying fees for his work. In another controversial role, Dole received more than $500,000 to help a Russian billionaire obtain a visa to the United States. Dole stands at the top of the senators-turned-lobbyists crowd and, at age 85, shows no sign of slowing down anytime soon.

Edward W. Gillespie (1962–)

Edward W. Gillespie was born in 1962 in Browns Mills, New Jersey. He graduated from the Catholic University of America in Washington, D.C., in 1983, and began his Washington career as a U.S. Senate parking lot attendant and later a telephone solicitor for the Republican National Committee. Gillespie worked as a top aide for U.S. House Majority Leader Dick Armey (R-TX) and was an influential contributor to the Republican "Contract with America" and takeover of Congress in 1994. In 1996, Gillespie became the director of communications and congressional affairs for the Republican National Committee, and in 2003, he was chosen by President George W. Bush to chair the Republican National Committee, where he served until 2005. Gillespie joined with Jack Quinn to form Quinn Gillespie and Associates in 2000, a bipartisan lobbying and public relations firm that took in more than $8 million in lobbying fees in 2007 alone. His clients include AT&T, Sony, and several large pharmaceutical companies. Gillespie remained close to the White House, shepherding John Roberts and Samuel Alito through the Senate confirmation process for the Supreme Court. In June 2007, he replaced Dan Bartlett and Karl Rove in serving as a special counselor to President Bush.

Joel Jankowsky (dates unknown)

Joel Jankowsky, a graduate of the University of Oklahoma in 1965 and the University of Oklahoma College of Law in 1968, served as a legislative assistant to Rep. Carl Albert (D-OK), speaker of the U.S. House of Representatives from 1972 to 1977. Jankowsky also served as a captain in the U.S. Army Judge Advocate General Corps from 1968 to 1972. Jankowsky helped form Akin Gump Strauss Hauer and Feld in 1977 and currently heads the firm's policy department and serves on its management committee. As the most profitable lobbying firm in the first six months of 2008, according to OpenSecrets.org, Akin Gump brought in more than $17 million in lobbying fees. Jankowsky specializes in entertainment, telecommunications, and technology and has recently been noted for his unsuccessful efforts to gain approval for China's National Offshore Oil Company to buy California-based giant Unocal. China ultimately lost out to Chevron, but for his efforts Jankowsky received $2.2 million.

Tony Podesta (dates unknown)

Tony Podesta, founder of Podesta Group, a top Washington, D.C., lobbying firm, was named by *Wired* magazine as one of Washington's "canniest and best-connected dealmakers" and was selected as one of the "Power 50" by *Washingtonian* magazine. A devoted Democrat, Podesta arrived in Washington, D.C., in 1970 to work for Common Cause, a citizen lobbying organization that promotes government accountability. Podesta boasts extensive personal connections in Congress and in the White House. In fact, Podesta's brother, John, served as the White House chief of staff to President Bill Clinton. The Podesta Group brought in more than $6 million in lobbying fees in 2007, specializing in technology and greasing the wheels of government for the nation's top high-tech firms, such as IBM and Genentech, as well as such major corporations as MCI, Universal, CBS, and the National Association of Broadcasters. Podesta gained national attention when in 2008 he represented BP in congressional hearings as they sought to mitigate the regulatory problems created by pipeline problems and refinery fires.

Jack Quinn (1949–)

Jack Quinn is a founder and cochair of Quinn Gillespie and Associates, a strategic consulting company he formed in January 2000 with Ed Gillespie (see above). Born in New York and a graduate of Georgetown University in 1971 and the Georgetown University Law Center in 1975, Quinn served as a staff member on the U.S. Senate Select Committee on Nutrition and Human Needs and practiced for 20 years as a partner in the Washington, D.C., law firm Arnold and Porter. At just 26 he managed Morris "Mo" Udall's (D-AZ) presidential campaign in 1976. He served as Vice President Al Gore's chief of staff and counselor from 1993 to 1995, and then as counsel to President Bill Clinton from 1995 to 1997. The formation of Quinn Gillespie and Associates propelled Quinn to the top of field of Democratic lobbyists—allowing him to charge an estimated $500,000 per lobbying contract. His clients include the Alliance for Quality Nursing Home Care, pharmaceutical companies, banks, and telecommunications companies. Quinn's most notorious and controversial lobbying contract was for securing a presidential pardon for international fugitive Marc Rich as President Clinton was leaving the White House.

6

Data and Documents

Classical Writings

Federalist No. 10 (1787)
James Madison

James Madison's writing in Federalist No. 10 continues and elaborates on Alexander Hamilton's discussion of "factions" and "insurrections" in Federalist No. 9. Madison's writing addresses the role of factions in American democracy and the prospect that the interests of a few concentrated citizens may overpower the public interest. According to Madison, a "well constructed Union" provides the best safeguard against factions gaining undue influence over the public interest.

The Utility of the Union as a Safeguard Against Domestic Faction and Insurrection To the People of the State of New York:

Among the numerous advantages promised by a well constructed Union, none deserves to be more accurately developed than its tendency to break and control the violence of faction. The friend of popular governments never finds himself so much alarmed for their character and fate, as when he contemplates their propensity to this dangerous vice. He will not fail, therefore, to set a due value on any plan which, without violating the principles to which he is attached, provides a proper cure for it. The instability, injustice, and confusion introduced into the public councils, have, in truth, been the mortal diseases under which popular governments have everywhere perished; as they continue to be the favorite and fruitful topics from which the adversaries to liberty derive their most specious declamations. The valuable improvements made by the American constitutions on the popular models, both ancient and modern, cannot certainly be too much admired; but it would be an unwarrantable partiality, to contend that they have as effectually obviated the danger on this side, as was wished and expected . . .

By a faction, I understand a number of citizens, whether amounting to a majority or a minority of the whole, who are united and actuated by some common impulse of passion, or of interest, adverse to the rights of other citizens, or to the permanent and aggregate interests of the community. There are two methods of curing the mischiefs of faction: the one, by removing its causes; the other, by controlling its effects. There are again two methods of removing the causes of faction: the one, by destroying the liberty which is essential to its existence; the other, by giving to every citizen the same opinions, the same passions, and the same interests. It could never be more truly said than of the first remedy, that it was worse than the disease. Liberty is to faction what air is to fire, an aliment without which it instantly expires. But it could not be less folly to abolish liberty, which is essential to political life, because it nourishes faction, than it would be to wish the annihilation of air, which is essential to animal life, because it imparts to fire its destructive agency. . . .

The diversity in the faculties of men, from which the rights of property originate, is not less an insuperable obstacle to a uniformity of interests. The protection of these faculties is the first object of government. From the protection of different and unequal faculties of acquiring property, the possession of different degrees and kinds of property immediately results; and from the influence of these on the sentiments and views of the respective proprietors, ensues a division of the society into different interests and parties. The latent causes of faction are thus sown in the nature of man; and we see them everywhere brought into different degrees of activity, according to the different circumstances of civil society. A zeal for different opinions concerning religion, concerning government, and many other points, as well of speculation as of practice; an attachment to different leaders ambitiously contending for pre-eminence and power; or to persons of other descriptions whose fortunes have been interesting to the human passions, have, in turn, divided mankind into parties, inflamed them with mutual animosity, and rendered them much more disposed to vex and oppress each other than to co-operate for their common good. So strong is this propensity of mankind to fall into mutual animosities, that where no substantial occasion presents itself, the most frivolous and fanciful distinctions have been sufficient to kindle their unfriendly passions and excite their most violent conflicts. . . .

It is in vain to say that enlightened statesmen will be able to adjust these clashing interests, and render them all subservient to the public good. Enlightened statesmen will not always be at the helm. Nor, in many cases, can such an adjustment be made at all without taking into view indirect and remote considerations, which will rarely prevail over the immediate interest which one party may find in disregarding the rights of another or the good of the whole. The inference to which we are brought is, that the causes of faction cannot be removed, and that relief is only to be sought in the means of controlling its effects. If a faction consists of less than a majority, relief is supplied by the republican principle, which enables the majority to defeat its sinister views by regular vote. It may clog the administration, it may convulse the society; but it will be unable to execute and mask its violence under the forms of the Constitution. When a majority is included in a faction, the form of popular government, on the other hand, enables it to sacrifice to its ruling passion or interest both the public good and the rights of other citizens. To secure the public good and private rights against the danger of such a faction, and at the same time to preserve the spirit and the form of popular government, is then the great object to which our inquiries are directed. Let me add that it is the great desideratum by which this form of government can be rescued from the opprobrium under which it has so long labored, and be recommended to the esteem and adoption of mankind. By what means is this object attainable? Evidently by one of two only. Either the existence of the same passion or interest in a majority at the same time must be prevented, or the majority, having such coexistent passion or interest, must be rendered, by their number and local situation, unable to concert and carry into effect schemes of oppression. If the impulse and the opportunity be suffered to coincide, we well know that neither moral nor religious motives can be relied on as an adequate control. They are not found to be such on the injustice and violence of individuals, and lose their efficacy in proportion to the number combined together, that is, in proportion as their efficacy becomes needful. From this view of the subject it may be concluded that a pure democracy, by which I mean a society consisting of a small number of citizens, who assemble and administer the government in person, can admit of no cure for the mischiefs of faction. A common passion or interest will, in almost every case, be felt by a majority of the whole; a communication and concert result from the form of government itself; and there is nothing to check the inducements to sacrifice the weaker party or an obnoxious individual. Hence it is that such democracies have ever been spectacles of turbulence and contention; have ever been found incompatible with personal security or the rights of property; and have in general been as short in their lives as they have been violent in their deaths. Theoretic politicians, who have patronized this species of government, have erroneously supposed that by reducing mankind to a perfect equality in their political rights, they would, at the same time, be perfectly equalized and assimilated in their possessions, their opinions, and their passions. A republic, by which I mean a government in which the scheme of representation takes place, opens a different prospect, and promises the cure for which we are seeking. Let us examine the points in which it varies from pure democracy, and we shall comprehend both the nature of the cure and the efficacy which it must derive from the Union. The two great points of difference between a democracy and a republic are: first, the delegation of the government, in the latter, to a small number of citizens elected by the rest; secondly, the greater number of citizens, and greater sphere of country, over which the latter may be extended. The effect of the first difference is, on the one hand, to refine and enlarge the public views, by passing them through the medium of a chosen body of citizens, whose wisdom may best discern the true interest of their country, and whose patriotism and love of justice will be least likely to sacrifice it to temporary or partial considerations. Under such a regulation, it may well happen that the public voice, pronounced by the representatives of the people, will be more consonant to the public good than if pronounced by the people themselves, convened for the purpose. On the other hand, the effect may be inverted. Men of factious tempers, of local prejudices, or of sinister designs, may, by intrigue, by corruption, or by other means, first obtain the suffrages, and then betray the interests, of the people. The question resulting is, whether small or extensive republics are more favorable to the election of proper guardians of the public weal; and it is clearly decided in favor of the latter by two obvious considerations. . . .

The influence of factious leaders may kindle a flame within their particular States, but will be unable to spread a general conflagration through the other States. A religious sect may degenerate into a political faction in a part of the Confederacy; but the variety of sects dispersed over the entire face of it must secure the national councils against any danger from that source. A rage for paper money, for an abolition of debts, for an equal division of property, or for any other improper or wicked project, will be less apt to pervade the whole body of the Union than a particular member of it; in the same proportion as such a malady is more likely to taint a particular county or district, than an entire State (Madison 1787).

Democracy in America (1835)
Alexis de Tocqueville

French aristocrat Alexis de Tocqueville's travels throughout the United States in the early 1830s documented the remarkable ability of Americans to organize into political associations. Among other observations, Tocqueville noted that "In the United States associations are established to promote the public safety, commerce, industry, morality, and religion. There is no end which the human will despairs of attaining through the combined power of individuals united into a society."

Book 1, Chapter 12. Political Associations in the United States

. . . In no country in the world has the principle of association been more successfully used or applied to a greater multitude of objects than in America. Besides the permanent associations which are established by law under the names of townships, cities, and counties, a vast number of others are formed and maintained by the agency of private individuals.

The citizen of the United States is taught from infancy to rely upon his own exertions in order to resist the evils and the difficulties of life; he looks upon the social authority with an eye of mistrust and anxiety, and he claims its assistance only when he is unable to do without it. This habit may be traced even in the schools, where the children in their games are wont to submit to rules which they have themselves established, and to punish misdemeanors which they have themselves defined. The same spirit pervades every act of social life. If a stoppage occurs in a thoroughfare and the circulation of vehicles is hindered, the neighbors immediately form themselves into a deliberative body; and this extemporaneous assembly gives rise to an executive power which remedies the inconvenience before anybody has thought of recurring to a pre-existing authority superior to that of the persons immediately concerned. If some public pleasure is concerned, an association is formed to give more splendor and regularity to the entertainment. Societies are formed to resist evils that are exclusively of a moral nature, as to diminish the vice of intemperance. In the United States associations are established to promote the public safety, commerce, industry, morality, and religion. There is no end which the human will despairs of attaining through the combined power of individuals united into a society. . . .

If, among a people who are imperfectly accustomed to the exercise of freedom, or are exposed to violent political passions, by the side of the majority which makes the laws is placed a minority which only deliberates and gets laws ready for adoption, I cannot but believe that public tranquility would there incur very great risks. There is doubtless a wide difference between proving that one law is in itself better than another and proving that the former ought to be substituted for the latter. But the imagination of the multitude is very apt to overlook this difference, which is so apparent to the minds of thinking men. It sometimes happens that a nation is divided into two nearly equal parties, each of which affects to represent the majority. If, near the directing power, another power is established which exercises almost as much moral authority as the former, we are not to believe that it will long be content to speak without acting; or that it will always be restrained by the abstract consideration that associations are meant to direct opinions, but not to enforce them, to suggest but not to make the laws. . . .

It must be acknowledged that the unrestrained liberty of political association has not hitherto produced in the United States the fatal results that might perhaps be expected from it elsewhere. The right of association was imported from England, and it has always existed in America; the exercise of this privilege is now incorporated with the manners and customs of the people. At the present time the liberty of association has become a necessary guarantee against the tyranny of the majority. In the United States, as soon as a party has become dominant, all public authority passes into its hands; its private supporters occupy all the offices and have all the force of the administration at their disposal. As the most distinguished members of the opposite party cannot surmount the barrier that excludes them from power, they must establish themselves outside of it and oppose the whole moral authority of the minority to the physical power that domineers over it. Thus a dangerous expedient is used to obviate a still more formidable danger.

The omnipotence of the majority appears to me to be so full of peril to the American republics that the dangerous means used to bridle it seem to be more advantageous than prejudicial. And here I will express an opinion that may remind the reader of what I said when speaking of the freedom of townships. There are no countries in which associations are more needed to prevent the despotism of faction or the arbitrary power of a prince than those which are democratically constituted. In aristocratic nations the body of the nobles and the wealthy are in themselves natural associations which check the abuses of power. In countries where such associations do not exist, if private individuals cannot create an artificial and temporary substitute for them I can see no permanent protection against the most galling tyranny; and a great people may be oppressed with impunity by a small faction or by a single individual. . . .

The most natural privilege of man, next to the right of acting for himself, is that of combining his exertions with those of his fellow creatures and of acting in common with them. The right of association therefore appears to me almost as inalienable in its nature as the right of personal liberty. No legislator can attack it without impairing the foundations of society. Nevertheless, if the liberty of association is only a source of advantage and prosperity to some nations, it may be perverted or carried to excess by others, and from an element of life may be changed into a cause of destruction. A comparison of the different methods that associations pursue in those countries in which liberty is well understood and in those where liberty degenerates into license may be useful both to governments and to parties. . . .

Most Europeans look upon association as a weapon which is to be hastily fashioned and immediately tried in the conflict. A society is formed for discussion, but the idea of impending action prevails in the minds of all those who constitute it. It is, in fact, an army; and the time given to speech serves to reckon up the strength and to animate the courage of the host, after which they march against the enemy. To the persons who compose it, resources which lie within the bounds of law may suggest themselves as means of success, but never as the only means.

Such, however, is not the manner in which the right of association is understood in the United States. In America the citizens who form the minority associate in order, first, to show their numerical strength and so to diminish the moral power of the majority; and, secondly, to stimulate competition and thus to discover those arguments that are most fitted to act upon the majority; for they always entertain hopes of drawing over the majority to their own side, and then controlling the supreme power in its name. Political associations in the United States are therefore peaceable in their intentions and strictly legal in the means which they employ; and they assert with perfect truth that they aim at success only by lawful expedients.

Book 2, Chapter 5. Of the Use Which the Americans Make of Public Associations in Civic Life

. . . The political associations that exist in the United States are only a single feature in the midst of the immense assemblage of associations in that country. Americans of all ages, all conditions, and all dispositions constantly form associations. They have not only commercial and manufacturing companies, in which all take part, but associations of a thousand other kinds, religious, moral, serious, futile, general or restricted, enormous or diminutive. The Americans make associations to give entertainments, to found seminaries, to build inns, to construct churches, to diffuse books, to send missionaries to the antipodes; in this manner they found hospitals, prisons, and schools. If it is proposed to inculcate some truth or to foster some feeling by the encouragement of a great example, they form a society. Wherever at the head of some new undertaking you see the government in France, or a man of rank in England, in the United States you will be sure to find an association.

I met with several kinds of associations in America of which I confess I had no previous notion; and I have often admired the extreme skill with which the inhabitants of the United States succeed in proposing a common object for the exertions of a great many men and in inducing them voluntarily to pursue it.

I have since traveled over England, from which the Americans have taken some of their laws and many of their customs; and it seemed to me that the principle of association was by no means so constantly or adroitly used in that country. The English often perform great things singly, whereas the Americans form associations for the smallest undertakings. It is evident that the former people consider association as a powerful means of action, but the latter seem to regard it as the only means they have of acting.

Thus the most democratic country on the face of the earth is that in which men have, in our time, carried to the highest perfection the art of pursuing in common the object of their common desires and have applied this new science to the greatest number of purposes. Is this the result of accident, or is there in reality any necessary connection between the principle of association and that of equality?

Aristocratic communities always contain, among a multitude of persons who by themselves are powerless, a small number of powerful and wealthy citizens, each of whom can achieve great undertakings single-handed. In aristocratic societies men do not need to combine in order to act, because they are strongly held together. Every wealthy and powerful citizen constitutes the head of a permanent and compulsory association, composed of all those who are dependent upon him or whom he makes subservient to the execution of his designs.

Among democratic nations, on the contrary, all the citizens are independent and feeble; they can do hardly anything by themselves, and none of them can oblige his fellow men to lend him their assistance. They all, therefore, become powerless if they do not learn voluntarily to help one another. If men living in democratic countries had no right and no inclination to associate for political purposes, their independence would be in great jeopardy, but they might long preserve their wealth and their cultivation: whereas if they never acquired the habit of forming associations in ordinary life, civilization itself would be endangered. A people among whom individuals lost the power of achieving great things single-handed, without acquiring the means of producing them by united exertions, would soon relapse into barbarism.

Unhappily, the same social condition that renders associations so necessary to democratic nations renders their formation more difficult among those nations than among all others. When several members of an aristocracy agree to combine, they easily succeed in doing so; as each of them brings great strength to the partnership, the number of its members may be very limited; and when the members of an association are limited in number, they may easily become mutually acquainted, understand each other, and establish fixed regulations. The same opportunities do not occur among democratic nations, where the associated members must always be very numerous for their association to have any power. . . .

As soon as several of the inhabitants of the United States have taken up an opinion or a feeling which they wish to promote in the world, they look out for mutual assistance; and as soon as they have found one another out, they combine. From that moment they are no longer isolated men, but a power seen from afar, whose actions serve for an example and whose language is listened to. The first time I heard in the United States that a hundred thousand men had bound themselves publicly to abstain from spirituous liquors, it appeared to me more like a joke than a serious engagement, and I did not at once perceive why these temperate citizens could not content themselves with drinking water by their own firesides. I at last understood that these hundred thousand Americans, alarmed by the progress of drunkenness around them, had made up their minds to patronize temperance. . . .

Nothing, in my opinion, is more deserving of our attention than the intellectual and moral associations of America. The political and industrial associations of that country strike us forcibly; but the others elude our observation, or if we discover them, we understand them imperfectly because we have hardly ever seen anything of the kind. It must be acknowledged, however, that they are as necessary to the American people as the former, and perhaps more so. In democratic countries the science of association is the mother of science; the progress of all the rest depends upon the progress it has made.

Among the laws that rule human societies there is one which seems to be more precise and clear than all others. If men are to remain civilized or to become so, the art of associating together must grow and improve in the same ratio in which the equality of conditions is increased (Tocqueville 1956).

The Process of Government (1908)
Arthur Bentley

Arthur Bentley was the first political scientist to depart from traditional study on political institutions and power structures and use the concept of interest groups to develop and articulate a modern approach to understanding the American governmental process. His 1908 work, The Process of Government, *articulated the view—then considered controversial—that understanding the composition and activities of interest groups was necessary to understanding government decision making and could stand alone as a comprehensive analytical tool.*

Chapter 7. Group Activities
The whole social life in all its phases can be stated in such groups of active men . . . What a man states to himself as his argument or reasoning or thinking about a national issue is, from the more exact point of view, just the conflict of the crossed groups to which he belongs . . .

The great task in the study of any form of social life is the analysis of these groups. It is much more than classification, as that term is ordinarily used. When the groups are adequately stated, everything is stated. When I say everything I mean everything. . . .

. . . There is no group without its interest. An interest, as the term will be used in this work, is the equivalent of a group . . . If we try to take the group without the interest, we have simply nothing at all.

There is no way to get hold of one group interest except in terms of others . . . When we succeed in isolating an interest group the only way to find out what it is going to do, indeed the only way to be sure we have isolated an interest group, is to watch its progress. . . .

First of all, the number of men who belong to the group attracts attention. Number alone may secure dominance. Such is the case in the ordinary American election. . . .

Intensity is a word that will serve as well as any other to denote the concentration of interest which gives a group effectiveness in its activity in the face of opposition of other groups. This intensity, like interest, is only to be discovered by observation. . . .

Besides the number and intensity, there is a technique of group activities which must be taken into account. Blows, bribes, allurements of one kind and another, and arguments also, are characteristic, and to these must be added organization. A group will differentiate under fitting circumstances a special set of activities for carrying on its work. . . .

We shall always find that the political interests and activities of any given group . . . are directed against other activities of men, who appear in other groups, political or other. The phenomena of political life which we study will always divide the society in which they occur, along lines which are very real, though of varying degrees of definiteness. The society itself is nothing other than the complex of the groups that compose it (Bentley 1935).

The Governmental Process: Political Interests and Public Opinion (1951) David B. Truman

Although Bentley's The Process of Government *was the first work to articulate an interest group model of political analysis, David Truman's 1951 work,* The Governmental Process, *established the credibility of interest group theory. Truman not only reinterpreted Bentley's earlier work, but he also offered a comprehensive definition of an interest group, described the conditions under which groups emerge, conducted a comprehensive group-based analysis of American politics, and argued that groups should be viewed as serving an important and laudable role in American democracy.*

Chapter 2. Groups and Society
As used here "interest group" refers to any group that, on the basis of one or more shared attitudes, makes certain claims upon other groups in the society for the establishment, maintenance, or enhancement of forms of behavior that are implied by shared attitudes . . .

. . . There is one type of group, which almost invariably operates as an interest group, that has become of such importance in our culture that it deserves special treatment. This type may be called the association. . . .

When a disturbance occurs within two or more of these tangent groups, or subdivisions, the affected individuals are likely to seek an adjustment through interaction with others in the tangent group with whom they have "something in common." . . .

An association is said to emerge when a considerable number of people have established tangent relations of the same sort and then they interact with one another regularly on that basis. It is a group, a continuing pattern of interactions, that functions as a "bridge" between persons in two or more institutionalized groups or subdivisions thereof. . . .

. . . the function of an association is to stabilize the relations of individuals in tangent groups. This stability it may create at the expense of disturbing the accustomed behavior of those through whom the participant individuals are tangent. . . .

Chapter 3. Groups and Government

The evolution of associations does not necessarily proceed at a uniform rate. When a single association is formed, it serves to stabilize the relations among the participants in the institutionalized groups involved. At the same time, however, in the performance of its function it may cause disturbances in the equilibriums of the other groups or accentuate cleavages among them. These are likely to evoke associations in turn to correct the secondary disturbances. The formation of associations, therefore, tends to occur in waves . . . (Truman 1951).

The Semisovereign People (1960)
E. E. Schattschneider

E. E. Schattschneider's The Semisovereign People *(1960) was one of many prominent works to describe American politics as a system dominated by powerful groups and individuals. This theory has become known as "elitism." Schattschneider argued that powerful interests worked to discourage widespread participation in policy making. Schattschneider viewed interest groups as having undemocratic organizational structures or an "upper-class bias" (he preferred to refer to such groups as pressure groups) and believed the sovereign but oppressed majority needed to balance pressure group dominance by participating in powerful political parties.*

When lists of these organizations are examined, the fact that strikes the student most forcibly is that the system is very small. The range of organized, identifiable, known groups is amazingly narrow; there is nothing remotely universal about it. There is a tendency on the part of the publishers of directories of associations to place an undue emphasis on business organizations, an emphasis that is almost inevitable because the business community is by a wide margin the most highly organized segment of society. Publishers doubtless tend also to reflect public demand for information. Nevertheless, the dominance of business groups in the pressure system is so marked that it probably cannot be explained away as an accident of the publishing industry. . . .

The business or upper-class bias of the pressure system shows up everywhere. Businessmen are four or five times as likely to write their congressmen as manual laborers are. College graduates are far more apt to write their congressmen than people in the lowest educational category are. . . .

Broadly, the pressure system has an upper-class bias. There is overwhelming evidence that participation in voluntary organizations is related to upper social and economic status; the rate of participation is much higher in the upper strata than it is elsewhere. . . .

The bias of the system is shown by the fact that even nonbusiness organizations reflect an upper-class tendency. . . .

The vice of the groupist theory is that it conceals the most significant aspects of the system. The flaw in the pluralist heaven is that the heavenly chorus sings with a strong upper-class accent. Probably about 90 per cent of the people cannot get into the pressure system.

The notion that the pressure system is automatically representative of the whole community is a myth fostered by the universalizing tendency of modern group theories. Pressure politics is a selective process ill designed to serve diffuse interests. The system is skewed, loaded and unbalanced in favor of a fraction of a minority . . . (Schattschneider 1960).

Who Governs? (1961)
Robert A. Dahl

One year after Schattschneider published The Semisovereign People, *Yale political scientist Robert Dahl countered Schattschneider's elitism theory in his 1961 work* Who Governs? *Dahl argued that rather than power being concentrated in the hands of the power elite, continuously changing and shifting groups and governmental structures aggregate, disaggregate, and reaggregate to form governing coalitions. His theory became known as "pluralism."*

If we ask, "Who Governs?" the answer is not the mass nor its leaders but both together; the leaders cater to mass tastes and in return use the strength provided by the loyalty and obedience of the masses to weaken and perhaps even to annihilate all opposition to their rule. . . .

Viewed from one position, leaders are enormously influential—so influential that if they are seen only in this perspective they might well be considered a kind of ruling elite. Viewed from another position, however, many influential leaders seem to be captives of their constituents. Like blind men with the elephant, different analysts have meticulously examined different aspects of the body politic and arrived at radically different conclusions. . . .

. . . the relationship between leaders and citizens in a pluralistic democracy is frequently reciprocal: leaders influence the decisions of constituents, but the decisions of leaders are also determined in part by what they think are, will be, or have been the preferences of their constituents. . . .

In many pluralistic systems, however, the political stratum is far from being a closed or static group. In the United States the political stratum does not constitute a homogeneous class with well-defined class interests. In New Haven, in fact, the political stratum is easily penetrated by anyone whose interests and concerns attract him to the distinctive political culture of the stratum. It is easily penetrated because (among other reasons) elections and competitive parties give politicians a powerful motive for expanding their coalitions and increasing their electoral followings.

In an open and pluralistic system, where movement into the political stratum is easy, the stratum embodies many of the most widely shared values and goals in the society . . . The apolitical strata can be said to "govern" as much through the sharing of common values and goals with members of the political stratum as by other means. . . .

We shall discover that in each of a number of key sectors of public policy, a few persons have great direct influence on the choices that are made; most citizens, by contrast, seem to have rather little direct influence. Yet it would be unwise to underestimate the extent to which voters may exert indirect influence on the decisions of leaders by means of elections. . . . (Dahl 1961)

The Logic of Collective Action: Public Goods and the Theory of Groups (1965)
Mancur Olson

Mancur Olson's The Logic of Collective Action *(1965) provided an alternative to Truman's disturbance theory model of group behavior. Rather than focus on an equilibrium-based notion of group emergence, Olson showed that the goals of interest groups are what he calls "public goods," the acquisition of which present a free-rider dilemma. This dilemma can only be overcome by providing "selective" benefits to those who participate in attaining the public good.*

The analog to atomistic competition in the nonmarket situation is the very large group, which will here be called the "latent" group. It is distinguished by the fact that, if one member does or does not help provide the collective good, no other one member will be significantly affected and therefore none has any reason to react. Thus an individual in a "latent" group, by definition, cannot make a noticeable contribution to any group effort, and since no one in the group will react if he makes no contribution, he has no incentive to contribute. Accordingly, large or "latent" groups have no incentive to act to obtain a collective good because, however valuable the collective good might be to the group as a whole, it does not offer the individual any incentive to pay dues to any organization working in the patent group's interest, or to bear in any other way any of the costs of the necessary collective action.

Only a separate and "selective" incentive will stimulate a rational individual in a latent group to act in a group-oriented way. In such circumstances group action can be obtained only through an incentive that operates, not indiscriminately, like the collective good, upon the group as a whole, but rather selectively toward the individuals in the group. The incentive must be "selective" so that those who do not join the organization working for the group's interest, or in other ways to contribute to the attainment of the group's interest, can be treated differently from those who do . . . (Olson 1965).

Political Organizations (1973)
James Q. Wilson

James Q. Wilson's Political Organizations *(1973) provided a critique of Olson's* The Logic of Collective Action. *Wilson argued that economic self-interest is only one of several factors leading to individual participation in interest group activities. In addition to the quantifiable material benefits elaborated by Olson, Wilson adds purposive and solidary benefits. Solidary benefits are those received from the action of interacting and creating social relationships with other group members and purposive benefits are the good feelings people receive from working toward a cause they believe in.*

For organizations to maintain themselves as systems of cooperative activity, they must find and distribute incentives so as to induce various contributors (members, donors, supporters) to perform certain acts. . . .

Four general kinds of incentives can be distinguished: Material incentives. These are tangible rewards: money, or things and services readily priced in monetary terms. They include wages and salaries, fringe benefits, reductions in taxes, changes in tariff levels, improvements in property values, discounts on various commodities and services, and personal services and gifts for which one would otherwise have to pay (and for which one could pay in a market).

Specific solidary incentives. These are intangible rewards arising out of the act of associating that can be given to, or withheld from, specific individuals. Indeed, their value usually depends on the fact that some persons are excluded from their enjoyment. They include offices, honors, and deference. Some of these intangible rewards can on occasion be purchased, as in buying an office or honor from a corrupt regime, but they are not ordinarily exchanged on a regular market and they typically have little resale value; for all practical purposes they can be regarded as nonmaterial. . . .

Collective solidary incentives. These are intangible rewards created by the act of associating that must be enjoyed by a group if they are to be enjoyed by anyone. They have some of the characteristics of what economists call a "public good" in that particular individuals within the organization cannot feasibly be excluded from their benefit. They involve the fun and conviviality of coming together, the sense of group membership and inclusiveness, and such collective status or esteem as the group as a whole may enjoy. . . .

Purposive incentives. There are intangible rewards that derive from the sense of satisfaction of having contributed to the attainment of a worthwhile cause. They depend crucially on the stated objectives of the organizations and are general in that any member of such a group can derive some satisfaction from group efforts even if he himself contributed nothing but his name . . . (Wilson 1973).

Still the Century of Corporatism? (1974)
Philippe C. Schmitter

Philippe C. Schmitter's 1974 essay, "Still the Century of Corporatism?," is largely regarded as having given rise to the neocorporatism theory. Schmitter argues that democratic and nondemocratic nations share such key characteristics as the organization of interests into a small number of elite groups for each sector of society. These peak organizations, one for business, one for labor, and so on are granted broad powers in controlling government regulation of their respective areas.

To this I would simply add another: the more the modern state comes to serve as the dispensable and authoritative guarantor of capitalism by expanding its regulative and integrative tasks, the more it finds that it needs the professional expertise, specialized information, prior aggregation of opinion, contractual capability and deferred participatory legitimacy which only singular, hierarchically ordered, consensually led representative monopolies, can provide. To obtain these, the state will agree to devolve upon or share with these associations much of its newly acquired decisional authority, subject, as Keynes noted, "in the last resort to the sovereignty of democracy expressed through Parliament." This osmotic process whereby the modern state and modern interest associations seek each other out leads, on the one hand, to even further extensions of public guarantees and equilibrations and, on the other, to even further concentration and hierarchic control within these private governments. The modalities are varied and range from direct government subsidies for associations, to official recognition of bona fide interlocuteurs, to devolved responsibilities for such public tasks as unemployment or accident insurance, to permanent membership in specialized advisory councils, to positions of control in joint public-private corporations, to informal, quasi-cabinet status, and finally to direct participation in authoritative decision-making through national economic and social councils . . . (Schmitter 1979).

Lobbying

Congress has attempted to regulate lobbying activities since the House of Representatives first required lobbyists to register with the clerk of the House in 1876. However, such registration provisions were seldom enforced by Congress until 1935, when Alabama senator Hugo Black pushed Congress to rein in the corrupting practices of lobbyists by requiring public utility and certain industry agents to disclose their names, expenses, salaries, and lobbying activities in the Public Utilities Holding Company Act of 1935 and the Merchant Marine Act of 1936. During World War II, Congress expanded its regulation of lobbying activities with the passage of the Foreign Agents Registration Act of 1938, which sought to minimize the influence of foreign propaganda and the Nazi movement in the United States by requiring all "foreign agents" to register their names, addresses, and foreign clients; label all materials as being provided by foreign governments or organizations; and disclose all lobbying receipts, expenditures, and activities.

After World War II, Congress expanded regulations governing domestic lobbyists with the adoption of the Federal Regulation of Lobbying Act (FRLA) of 1946. The 1946 act established registration and quarterly disclosure requirements for all those whose "principal purpose" was to influence Congress. Violation of these requirements was punishable by a fine of up to $5,000 and one year's imprisonment. FRLA is now understood to have been woefully weak; few lobbyists registered and few were prosecuted for noncompliance. In *United States v. Harriss* (1954) the U.S. Supreme Court would further weaken the FRLA by ruling that it only applied to "paid lobbyists" who "directly communicate" with members of Congress on "pending legislation."

Forty years after the passage of the FRLA, Congress, motivated by scandal, attempted again to enact comprehensive regulation of lobbying activities by approving the Lobbying Disclosure Act (LDA) of 1995. The LDA, as amended by the Lobbying Disclosure Technical Amendments Act of 1998, requires lobbyists to register with the clerk of the House and secretary of the Senate and make semiannual reports of their lobbying activities and the policy areas they are seeking to influence.

"Gimme Five"—Investigation of Tribal Lobbying Matters. Final Report Before the Committee on Indian Affairs. One Hundred and Ninth Congress, Second Session. June 22, 2006

In 2006, Washington, D.C., was rocked by the news that prominent Republican lobbyist Jack Abramoff, whoses connections included House Majority Leader Tom DeLay, Ralph Reed Jr., Grover Norquist, and Michael Scanlon, had defrauded several Indian tribes into paying his firm more than $85 million in overpriced lobbying fees to open and maintain gambling casinos. A report of the Senate Committee on Indian Affairs reveals that Abramoff and his associates were secretly orchestrating against their own clients to force them to pay for lobbying services and illegal donations, gifts, and lavish golf vacations to several executive branch and congressional officials over Indian affairs.

After (or at the same time when) several Tribes hired Abramoff as their federal lobbyist, Abramoff urged some of them to hire Scanlon to provide grassroots support. Abramoff, however, failed to disclose that he and Scanlon were partners. Evidence obtained over the course of a two-year investigation indicates that Abramoff and Scanlon had agreed to secretly split, between themselves, fees that the Tribes paid Scanlon from 2001 through 2003. Abramoff and Scanlon referred to this arrangement as "gimme five."

In total, six tribes paid Scanlon's companies, in particular a company called Capitol Campaign Services ("CCS") (which also did business as Scanlon Gould Public Affairs and Scanlon Public Affairs), at least $66,000,000 over the three-year period. . . . The $66,000,000 figure includes only those payments made by the Tribes to Scanlon for grassroots activities. The total cost of doing business with Abramoff and Scanlon was actually much higher. (Committee on Indian Affairs 2006)

Lobbying Reform: Accountability through Transparency.
House Committee on Rules, March 2, 2006
Thomas E. Mann, Brookings Institution

In March 2006, the House Committee on Rules convened hearings regarding the Abramoff scandal and possibilities for reforming existing lobbying laws. Tom Mann testified before the committee, offering his views on needed reforms.

Mr. Chairman and other members of the Committee, thank you for inviting me to share my views on lobbying reform with you this morning. The revelations from the prosecution and guilty pleas of lobbyist Jack Abramoff and Rep. Randy "Duke" Cunningham have understandably brought to public attention the laws, congressional rules, and enforcement mechanisms regulating the interactions between lobbyists and Members of Congress and their staff. Congress is under enormous pressure to act quickly to deal with the perceived inadequacy of that regulatory system. The good news is that these scandals could provide the boost required to enact long-needed changes in that system. The bad news is that whenever Congress acts quickly to deal with a politically embarrassing situation and without sufficient deliberation, it runs the risk of producing a flawed product, one that fails to deal with the problems identified and possibly even does more harm than good. I hope you and your colleagues are able to take the time necessary to fully plumb the issues at hand and to enact reforms that offer more than a cosmetic response to them.

Lobbying has changed dramatically in recent years. The number of registered lobbyists has tripled. Budgets for Washington representation and grassroots lobbying have risen exponentially. Retiring or defeated Members of Congress are now more likely to stay in Washington and join their ranks. Congressional staff routinely move from Capitol Hill to lobbying shops around town. Some Members of Congress have been actively involved in placing their staff and those of their colleagues in key positions within the lobbying community. Many Members of Congress enlist lobbyists to help raise campaign funds for their re-election campaigns, leadership PACs, endangered colleagues, and political party committees. The escalating cost of campaigns has put intense pressure on Members of Congress, even those with safe seats, and lobbyists to raise and contribute substantial sums of money. At the same time, more opportunities exist for members of Congress and their leaders to deliver benefits to lobbyists and their clients. These include earmarks, in appropriations and authorization bills; invitations to participate in informal mark-up sessions in party task forces, standing committees, and conference committees; amendments added late in the legislative process under the veil of secrecy; and letters and calls to executive branch officials. These conditions foster practices that risk conflicts of interest and unethical or illegal behavior.

The Abramoff case is appalling in many dimensions, not least the brazenness and financial ambitions of the man and his close associates. From the perspective of those looking for appropriate reforms, I would point to his cultivation and recruitment for well-paid lobbying positions of staff in key congressional offices; the market among some members and staff for privately-financed, first-class travel with tenuous connections to official responsibilities or public policy education; the reality that the abuses of Abramoff (and Cunningham) were initially detected by journalists in spite of, not thanks to the official reporting and disclosure systems; and the fact some private groups and individuals apparently believe that hiring well-connected lobbyists and showering campaign and other funds on members of Congress as directed by those lobbyists is essential to protecting or advancing their interests. These lessons suggest dealing more effectively with the revolving door (for Members and staff); ensuring that privately-financed travel is legitimate and consistent with chamber rules and guidelines; setting up more effective reporting and disclosure systems; and reducing the opportunities available to members to deliver (or appear to deliver) special benefits for narrow interests.

Transparency is key to lobbying reform, in my view more important than a ban or further restrictions on gifts and travel. Electronic filing and Internet posting of more frequent (quarterly) and detailed (with information on member and staff contacts) lobbying reports would be a good first step, but only a first step. Members and staff should routinely report in the same fashion on privately-financed travel, gifts, and meals. More luminous transparency will increase Members' incentives to heed the spirit as well as the letter of ethics' rules. They should also be required to obtain from the trip's sponsor a certification that the trip is not funded, directly or indirectly, by a lobbyist or foreign agent.

But to be effective, that transparency must extend to the legislative process as well. Earmarks in appropriations and authorizing bills should be clearly listed in the bills along with the Members who proposed them and their public policy purpose. No additions or deletions should be allowed in conference reports after the full conference committee has voted to approve the report in a public session. Conference committee reports should routinely be made available well in advance of their consideration on the floor, so that Members and the public know what is being voted on. That means no more special rules waiving the layover requirements in House rules (but how can it be enforced?). Procedural means ought to be provided for votes on individual earmarks in conference reports.

Lobbying reform also requires a greatly strengthened enforcement process. The House Ethics Committee has been emasculated. At times it has functioned in the requisite bipartisan fashion but there is no sign of a return to those days. Now the House and Senate need some melding of an Independent Ethics Commission (including former Members) and an Office of Public Integrity to work alongside the standing ethics committees to investigate or dismiss charges of unethical behavior, provide staff continuity for managing a strengthened reporting and disclosure system, advise Members and staff on appropriate behavior, and assist the Commission in its investigations. I believe it is possible for Congress to establish such a new ethics apparatus without shirking its constitutional responsibility to discipline its Members or suffering the horrors of single-minded independent or special counsels. The United Kingdom might well provide the best model.

All professional groups, including lobbyists, can benefit from higher ethical standards and self-regulation. But I think it is a mistake to assume the broader problem is one of their own making. The Congress would be well advised to focus on its own Members and staff, for its leaders to articulate and champion high ethical standards in dealing with lobbyists and to set up educational programs whereby those inside Congress are assisted in meeting those standards, and to establish effective systems of transparency and enforcement. Lobbyists will respond to the fallout from Abramoff with some form of education and self-regulation. Inquiring minds at the DOJ Office of Public Integrity will focus their attention.

Given the relatively narrow focus of this hearing and the nature of the specific questions posed to those of us invited to testify today, I won't burden you with my further thoughts on needed reforms in Congress generally, and the House specifically. They are elaborated in a book Norm Ornstein and I recently completed, which will be published this summer under the title, *The Broken Branch.* Suffice it to say that the issues we are discussing today are integrally connected to the weakening of institutional identity and loyalty among Members of Congress, the decline of deliberation and regular order, and the special problems associated with money and politics. But those are for another discussion (Mann 2006).

The Honest Leadership and Open Government Act of 2007

When Democrats retook the House and Senate in the 2006 elections, public interest advocacy groups urged Democratic leaders to quickly pass comprehensive lobbying and ethics reforms. Less than one year later the House and Senate passed, and President George W. Bush signed, the Honest Leadership and Open Government Act of 2007. Table 6.1 is taken from a chart produced by the Campaign Legal Center, which shows the significant areas of lobbying and ethics regulations that were altered with the enactment of the 2006 reforms. Tables 6.2 through 6.7 present additional data about lobbying from the Center for Responsive Politics.

TABLE 6.1
Honest Leadership and Open Government Act of 2007

Area of Regulation	Previous Law	Honest Leadership and Open Government Act of 2007
Changes to Lobbying Disclosure 2 U.S.C. 1601 (P.L.104-65)	Requires semiannual filing of lobbying reports, which are made publicly available	Requires quarterly electronic filing of lobbying reports in a publicly searchable database on the Internet. Requires lobbyists to certify on reports that they did not provide or direct gifts or travel to members of Congress or staff that would violate Senate or House rules
Penalties for failure to comply with lobbying laws	Provides penalties up to $50,000 for failure to comply with all rules and regulations	Increases civil penalty for failure to comply with lobbying laws to $200,000 and adds a criminal penalty for whoever knowingly and corruptly fails to comply with any provision including possible imprisonment for up to 5 years
Disclosure of organizations involved in lobbying activities	Requires disclosure of an organization, other than the client, that contributes more than $10,000 to fund lobbying activities, and that "in whole or part, plans, supervises or controls" lobbying activities	Requires disclosure of organizations, other than the client, that contribute more than $5,000 per quarter to the client or lobbyist to fund lobbying activities, and that "actively participate in the planning, supervision or control of such lobbying activities"
Disclosure of lobbyists' campaign contributions	Does not require lobbyists to disclose their campaign contributions or campaign activities by lobbyists	Requires lobbyists to file semiannual reports with the secretary of the Senate and the clerk of the House, disclosing contributions made to a Member of Congress, federal candidate, leadership political action committee (PAC), or political party by the lobbyist, the lobbyist's employer, or an affiliated PAC, which in the aggregate exceed $200
Bundling disclosure	Does not require lobbyists to disclose bundled contributions	Requires candidate committees, political party committees, and leadership PACs to disclose semiannually to the Federal Election Commission (FEC) their receipt of contributions bundled by a lobbyist that in the aggregate exceed $15,000 in a 6-month period; Requires disclosure reports to include name, address, and employer of the bundling lobbyist, and aggregate amount bundled. Requires the FEC to ensure that the information is publicly available on the Internet in a manner that is searchable, sortable, and downloadable

continues

TABLE 6.1   continued

Area of Regulation	Previous Law	Honest Leadership and Open Government Act of 2007
Post-Employment/ Revolving Door 18 U.S.C. 207	Provides for a one-year cooling-off period before former members of Congress can lobby the legislative branch; Senior congressional staff may not lobby former office or committee for one year	Increases cooling-off period from one to two years before former Senators and senior executive personnel can engage in lobbying. Prohibits Senate officers and senior employees from lobbying the entire Senate for one year after they leave Senate employment; retains the one-year cooling off period for House staff under current law. Prohibits a member of Congress's spouse and immediate family who are lobbyists from engaging in lobbying contacts with a member of Congress's staff (Senate rule exempts a spouse who was serving as a registered lobbyists at least one year before a senator's election)
K Street Project: Influencing hiring decisions of private entities on a partisan basis	Does not prohibit members of Congress from influencing the hiring decisions of private entities	Members of the House and Senate and congressional staff are prohibited from influencing hiring decisions of private entities on the sole basis of "partisan political affiliation"; violations are subject to criminal penalty, including imprisonment for up to 15 years
Congressional Ethics Rules	Does not require mandatory ethics training for members of Congress or staff	Requires Senate Ethics Committee to provide mandatory ethics training to senators and staff
Floor privileges for former members of Congress	Former senators have floor, gym, and parking privileges	Revokes floor, gym, and parking privileges for former senators who are lobbyists
Lobbyist gifts to members of Congress and staff	Does not allow members of Congress to solicit or accept anything of value unless the gift is pursuant to rules or regulations established by the supervising ethics office; No gift may be accepted in return for being influenced in the performance of any official act; members of Congress and staff may accept gifts valued up to $50; $100 aggregate gift limit from same source in one year	Bans all gifts to members of Congress and staff from lobbyists and entities that retain lobbyists, subject to existing gift rules. Requires entertainment and sports tickets given to senators and staff to be valued at market rates; Senate and House members may not participate in events honoring the member at national party conventions if the event is paid for by a lobbyist (unless the member is the party's presidential or vice presidential nominee)

continues

TABLE 6.1   continued

Area of Regulation	Previous Law	Honest Leadership and Open Government Act of 2007
Privately Funded Travel	Allows members of Congress to go on privately funded trips, but they must disclose each trip; lobbyists are not permitted to fund travel	Prohibits senators or staff from accepting privately financed travel from lobbyists or an entity that employs or retains lobbyists or a trip organized or attended by lobbyists; provides exception for travel funded by an entity that employs lobbyists if travel is connected to an event of one day or less, or sponsored by a 501(c)(3) organization that has been preapproved by the Ethics Committee; requires senators and staff to provide the Ethics Committee, before travel, with certification from the trip organizer that privately funded travel is (1) not funded in any part by a lobbyist or an organization that employs lobbyists, (2) not planned, organized, or arranged by a lobbyist, and (3) not attended by lobbyists; requires senators and staff to file with the secretary of the Senate a description of meetings and events, and any contact with lobbyists during travel, no later than 30 days after completion of travel. Allows senators and staff to accept free attendance at a conference or other event in their home state if it is sponsored and attended by constituents, provided there are no registered lobbyists in attendance, and that the cost of any meal served is less than $50. Requires that travel by Senate members financed by outside groups be posted on a searchable, sortable, and downloadable Web site by January 1, 2008, and by August 1, 2008, for the House
Corporate jets	Allows members of Congress to take flights on corporate jets with lobbyists, reimbursing the corporation at the price of a first-class ticket	Requires candidates, other than those running for a seat in the House, and senators to pay charter rates for travel on privately owned jets; Allows the committee or leadership PAC of a candidate for the House to make expenditures only for travel on commercial jets, unless the jet is owned by a governmental entity; provides exception to these requirements for jets owned or leased by a candidate or by his or her immediate family members

continues

TABLE 6.1   continued

Area of Regulation	Previous Law	Honest Leadership and Open Government Act of 2007
Lobbyist attendance on privately funded trips	Permits lobbyists to attend privately funded trips	Prohibits lobbyists from attending privately funded trips
Other Provisions *Earmarks*	None	Requires chairman of committee of jurisdiction or majority leader to certify that all earmarks and their sponsors have been identified in Senate bills, joint resolutions, committee reports, conference reports, and managers' statements, and that this information has been posted on the Internet at least 48 hours before consideration of the measure; requires earmarks contained in any amendments to a bill or resolution to be disclosed as soon as practicable. Requires senators to disclose to the committee chairman and ranking member the intended recipients of proposed earmarks and the purpose of the earmarks and to certify that the senator and the senator's immediate family will not derive pecuniary benefit from the earmarks. Requires Senate committees to disclose, to the extent practicable, in unclassified language, the funding level and the name of the sponsor of any earmark contained in the classified portion of a report. Provides for a point of order against any new earmarks added for the first time to a conference report; earmark will be eliminated unless 60 senators vote in favor of keeping the provision. Prohibits senators from introducing an earmark if its "principal" purpose is to further the pecuniary interest of the senator, the senator's immediate family, or a limited class of persons to which the senator and/or his or her immediate family belongs

Source: Campaign Legal Center. *Lobbying Reform Bills Side by Side Comparison Chart as of August 20, 2007.* [On-line information; retrieved 11/2/07.] http://www.campaignlegalcenter.org/press-2845.html.

TABLE 6.2

Top-Spending Lobbying Organizations: 1998–2008

Organization	Total Spent
U.S. Chamber of Commerce	$398,224,680
American Medical Association	$190,662,500
General Electric	$173,052,000
American Hospital Association	$152,947,280
AARP	$140,492,064
Pharmaceutical Research and Manufacturers of America	$135,663,400
Edison Electric Institute	$120,195,999
Northrop Grumman	$118,315,253
Business Roundtable	$101,660,000
National Association of Realtors	$107,960,380

Source: Center for Responsive Politics. *Lobbying Overview. Top Spenders: 1998–2008.* [Online information; retrieved 10/ 4/08.] http://www.opensecrets.org/lobby/top.php?indexType=s.

TABLE 6.3

Top Lobbying Firms: 1998–2008

Lobbying Firm	Total Income
Patton Boggs LLP	$289,172,000
Cassidy and Associates	$271,055,000
Akin, Gump, Strauss, Hauer, and Feld LLP	$237,585,000
Van Scoyoc Associates	$192,098,000
Williams and Jensen	$141,509,000
Hogan and Hartson	$128,763,907
Ernst & Young	$126,636,780
Barbour, Griffith and Rogers	$114,430,500
Quinn, Gillespie and Associates	$111,493,500
PMA Group	$107,495,132

Source: Center for Responsive Politics. *Lobbying Overview. Top Lobbying Firms: 1998–2008.* [Online information; retrieved 10/4/08.] http://www.opensecrets.org/lobby/top.php?indexType=l.

TABLE 6.4

Top-Spending Lobbying Sectors: 1998–2008

Lobbying Sector	Total Spent
Finance, insurance, and real estate	$3,210,888,755
Health	$3,040,457,664
Miscellaneous business	$2,860,453,867
Communications/electronics	$2,600,546,542
Energy and natural resources	$2,144,035,408
Transportation	$1,696,171,991
Other	$1,653,640,930
Ideological/single issue	$1,100,268,444
Agribusiness	$974,673,144
Defense	$904,688,489

Source: Center for Responsive Politics. *Lobbying Overview. Ranked Sectors: 1998–2007.* [Online information; retrieved 10/4/08.] http://www.opensecrets.org/lobby/top.php?indexType=c

TABLE 6.5

Top-Spending Lobbying Industries: 1998–2008

Industry	Total Spent
Pharmaceuticals/health products	$1,437,033,781
Insurance	$1,096,036,248
Electric utilities	$985,593,737
Computers/Internet	$809,103,734
Business associations	$742,485,001
Education	$711,329,278
Real estate	$684,395,914
Oil and Gas	$666,122,779
Hospitals/nursing homes	$636,064,978
Miscellaneous manufacturing and distributing	$601,413,630

Source: Center for Responsive Politics. *Lobbying Overview. Top Industries: 1998–2008.* [Online information; retrieved 10/4/08.] http://www.opensecrets.org/lobby/top.php?indexType=il.

TABLE 6.6

Highest-Paying Lobbying Contracts: 1998–2008

Firm	Client	Total Spent
Swidler BerlinSheriff Friedman LLP	Asbestos Study Group	$30,020,000
Dickstein Shapiro LLP	Loews Corporation	$16,790,000
Patton Boggs LLP	Mars Inc.	$16,440,000
Canfield and Associates	Consumer Mortgage Coalition	$12,960,000
Akin Gump Strauss Hauer and Feld LLP	Gila River Indian Community	$12,210,000
Alcade and Fay	International Council of Cruise Lines	$8,930,660
Cassidy and Associates	Boston University	$8,820,000
Hogan and Hartson	FM Policy Focus	$8,660,000
Mayer Brown	U.S. Chamber of Commerce	$8,438,159

Source: Center for Responsive Politics. *Lobbying Overview. Top Contracts: 1998–2008.* [Online information; retrieved 10/4/08.] http://www.opensecrets.org/lobby/top.php?indexType=f

TABLE 6.7

Top Lobbying Issues by Number of Quarterly Reports: 1998–2008

Issue	Number of Registered Lobbyists
Federal budget and appropriations	33,535
Health Issues	15,286
Defense	14,602
Taxes	13,878
Transportation	12,257
Trade	9,382
Education	9,337
Environment and Superfund	9,217
Energy and Nuclear Power	8,897
Medicare and Medicaid	7,960

Source: Center for Responsive Politics. *Lobbying Overview. Top Issues: 1998–2008.* [Online information; retrieved 10/5/08.] http://www.opensecrets.org/lobby/top.php?indexType=u

The Role of Money in American Politics: The Tillman Act (1907)

The first major attempt by Congress to limit the funds available to political candidates was the Tillman Act of 1907. In response to allegations by Democratic presidential nominee Alton B. Parker that President Theodore Roosevelt had received large contributions from corporations during the 1904 presidential election, Roosevelt, who also called for public financing of federal campaigns, urged Congress to ban corporate federal campaign contributions and gifts to federal candidates. After a subsequent congressional investigation revealed that large contributions had been given from insurance companies to candidates and elected officials in preceding elections, Congress passed the Tillman Act, which banned corporate contributions and gifts to federal candidates. What follows is the original wording of the Tillman Act of 1907.

It is unlawful for any national bank, or any corporation organized by authority of any law of Congress, to make a contribution or expenditure in connection with any election to any political office, or in connection with any primary election or political convention or caucus held to select candidates for any political office, or for any corporation whatever, or any labor organization, to make a contribution or expenditure in connection with any election at which presidential and vice presidential electors or a Senator or Representative in, or a Delegate or Resident Commissioner to, Congress are to be voted for, or in connection with any primary election or political convention or caucus held to select candidates for any of the foregoing offices, or for any candidate, political committee, or other person knowingly to accept or receive any contribution prohibited by this section, or any officer or any director of any corporation or any national bank or any officer of any labor organization to consent to any contribution or expenditure by the corporation, national bank, or labor organization, as the case may be, prohibited by this section . . . (Tillman Act of 1907).

Federal Corrupt Practices Act (1910, 1911, and 1925)

For many reformers the Tillman Act—detailed in Table 6.8—did not go far enough. Cries for limiting the influence of wealthy individuals in federal campaigns were frequent and intense, and in 1910 Congress reacted by passing the Federal Corrupt Practices Act, also known as the Publicity Act of 1910. The act required national party committees and congressional campaign committees to file postelection reports that dis-

closed campaign receipts and expenditures. The 1911 amendments to the Federal Corrupt Practices Act enhanced disclosure rules by requiring Senate and House campaigns to disclose receipts and expenditures and requiring pre-election reports and established the first campaign spending limits for federal campaigns ($5,000 for House and $10,000 for Senate campaigns), which were later struck down by the Supreme Court in Newberry v. United States *(1921).*

In response to the Teapot Dome scandal, which involved the gift of large sums of money to federal officials in return for oil leases, Congress passed the Federal Corrupt Practices Act of 1925, which required all multistate political committees and all congressional candidates to file quarterly disclosure reports that divulged all contributions of more than $100 and revised and increased the spending limits ($5,000 for House and $25,000 for Senate campaigns) to address the concerns of the Supreme Court expressed in Newberry (Mann, Ortiz, and Potter 2005).

Hatch Act (1939 and 1940)

The increase of the federal workforce due to programs of President Franklin Roosevelt's New Deal was a cause of great concern to many who worried that employees in federal public works programs would be pressured by political parties to donate to and campaign for their candidates. The Hatch Act of 1939—detailed in Table 6.8—responded to these concerns by banning political activity by federal workers who were not included in the provisions of the 1883 Pendleton Act. The Hatch Act also prohibited political committees from soliciting contributions from federal government employees, including those employed by public works programs. The 1940 amendments to the Hatch Act banned political contributions by federal contractors, placed a $5,000 annual limit on the amount that individuals could contribute to any federal candidate or national party committee, and limited the total receipts of national party committees to $3 million per year (Mann, Ortiz, and Potter 2005).

Federal Election Campaign Act (1971, 1974, 1976, and 1979)

The rising power of labor unions and their growth as a source of funds for Democratic Party candidates aroused concerns regarding the undue influence of labor unions and their leaders on lawmakers. In response to these concerns, Congress overrode a veto by President Truman and amended the National Labor Relations Act by passing the Taft-Hartley

Act of 1947, which extended the Tillman Act's ban on corporate contributions to labor unions. The act also prohibited corporations and labor unions from independently spending funds to support or oppose federal candidates.

To circumvent the ban on corporate and labor union contributions to federal political campaigns, unions and corporations began to form what are known as political action committees, or PACs, from which corporations and unions could contribute unlimited amounts to political parties and campaigns as long as the funds donated were voluntary contributions to the PAC and not from the corporation's or union's treasury. In response to the growing influence of PACs, the rising costs of federal campaigns, and concerns that wealthy individuals and interests were gaining undue influence over the policy-making process, Congress acted by passing the Federal Election Campaign Act of 1971 (FECA)—detailed in Table 6.8. FECA attempted to address the rise of PACs, the undue influence of the wealthy on officeholders, and the lack of enforcement of federal election laws.

FECA limited money that candidates could donate to their own campaigns, limited total campaign spending, and enhanced disclosure provisions. FECA also limited individual contributions (an aggregate of which was not to exceed $25,000 per year) to candidates to $1,000 per candidate per election, $5,000 per year to PACs, and $20,000 per year to national political party committees, and it limited PAC contributions to candidates and national political party committees to $5,000 per election. FECA also limited the amount of funds that national party committees could give to candidates, created the presidential public funding system, established a federal subsidy for national political party conventions, and created the Federal Election Commission to enforce federal campaign finance laws.

In 1976, the U.S. Supreme Court ruled on the constitutionality of several of FECA's provisions in the landmark case Buckley v. Valeo *(424 U.S. 1, 1976). The Supreme Court's ruling struck down the campaign spending limits, except in the case of presidential candidates who accept spending limits as a means of qualifying for the presidential public funding system, and eliminated the limits on the amount a candidate could donate to his or her own campaign (Mann, Ortiz, and Potter 2005).*

Bipartisan Campaign Reform Act (2002)

The limits imposed on individuals, PACs, and national political party committees by FECA gave rise to what is known as "soft money," that is, unregulated money, including corporate and labor union contributions raised and spent by national political party committees on behalf of candidates. Beginning in 1988, political parties concentrated heavily on raising large sums of soft money to support federal candidates, including the airing of candidate-supporting "issue ads" that evaded federal campaign finance laws as long as the ads did not contain specific "express advocacy" phrases. In response, Congress passed the Bipartisan Campaign Reform Act of 2002 (BCRA). BCRA closed the soft money loophole by prohibiting national party committees from receiving or spending unregulated funds and established electioneering communications provisions that regulated funds used to pay for advertising. BCRA required ads that refer to federal candidates, appear within 60 days of a primary or 30 days of a general election, and are targeted to the candidate's constituency to be paid for by regulated funds or "hard money."

Upon BCRA's passage, Sen. Mitch McConnell (R-KY) and several organizations challenged the constitutionality of several of BCRA's provisions. After granting four hours for oral argument and receiving briefs supporting both sides from several interest groups, the U.S. Supreme Court upheld virtually all of BCRA's provisions. Excerpts from the Court's ruling in McConnell v. Federal Election Commission *regarding the rationale for upholding BCRAs provisions follow* (Mann, Ortiz, and Potter 2005).

McConnell v. Federal Election Commission.
540 U.S. 93 (2003).
Argued September 8, 2003.
Decided December 10, 2003.
Governmental Interests Underlying New FECA

The question for present purposes is whether large soft-money contributions to national party committees have a corrupting influence or give rise to the appearance of corruption. Both common sense and the ample record in these cases confirm Congress' belief that they do. . . . Under this system, corporate, union, and wealthy individual donors have been free to contribute substantial sums of soft money to the national parties, which the parties can spend for the specific purpose of influencing a particular candidate's federal election. It is not only plausible, but likely, that candidates would feel grateful for such donations and that donors would seek to exploit that gratitude. . . .

For their part, lobbyists, CEOs, and wealthy individuals alike all have candidly admitted donating substantial sums of soft money to national committees not on ideological grounds, but for the express purpose of securing influence over federal officials. For example, a former lobbyist and partner at a lobbying firm in Washington, D.C., stated in his declaration:

"You are doing a favor for somebody by making a large [soft-money] donation and they appreciate it. Ordinarily, people feel inclined to reciprocate favors. Do a bigger favor for someone—that is, write a larger check—and they feel even more compelled to reciprocate. In my experience, overt words are rarely exchanged about contributions, but people do have understandings.' " Id., at 493 (Kollar-Kotelly, J.) (quoting declaration of Robert Rozen, partner, Ernst & Young ¶ ;14; see 8-R Defs. Exhs., Tab 33). Particularly telling is the fact that, in 1996 and 2000, more than half of the top 50 soft-money donors gave substantial sums to both major national parties, leaving room for no other conclusion but that these donors were seeking influence, or avoiding retaliation, rather than promoting any particular ideology. See, e.g., 251 F. Supp. 2d, at 508–510 (Kollar-Kotelly, J.) (citing Mann Expert Report Tbls. 5–6); 251 F. Supp. 2d, at 509 (" 'Giving soft money to both parties, the Republicans and the Democrats, makes no sense at all unless the donor feels that he or she is buying access.' " (quoting declaration of former Sen. Dale Bumpers ¶ ;15, App. 175)).

The evidence from the federal officeholders' perspective is similar. For example, one former Senator described the influence purchased by nonfederal donations as follows:

"Too often, Members' first thought is not what is right or what they believe, but how it will affect fundraising. Who, after all, can seriously contend that a $100,000 donation does not alter the way one thinks about—and quite possibly votes on—an issue? . . . When you don't pay the piper that finances your campaigns, you will never get any more money from that piper. Since money is the mother's milk of politics, you never want to be in that situation.' " 251 F. Supp. 2d, at 481 (Kollar-Kotelly, J.) (quoting declaration of former Sen. Alan Simpson ¶ ;10 (hereinafter Simpson Decl.), App. 811); 251 F. Supp. 2d, at 851 (Leon, J.) (same). See also id., at 489 (Kollar-Kotelly, J.) ("The majority of those who contribute to political parties do so for business reasons, to gain access to influential Members of Congress and to get to know new Members." (quoting Hickmott Decl., Exh. A, ¶ ;46). . . .

The record in the present case is replete with similar examples of national party committees peddling access to federal candidates and officeholders in exchange for large soft-money donations. See 251 F. Supp. 2d, at 492–506 (Kollar-Kotelly, J.). As one former Senator put it: " 'Special interests who give large amounts of soft money to political parties do in fact achieve their objectives. They do get special access. Sitting Senators and House Members have limited amounts of time, but they make time available in their schedules to meet with representatives of business and unions and wealthy individuals who gave large sums to their parties. These are not idle chit-chats about the philosophy of democracy. . . . Senators are pressed by their benefactors to introduce legislation, to amend legislation, to block legislation, and to vote on legislation in a certain way.'" Id., at 496 (Kollar-Kotelly, J.) (quoting declaration of former Sen. Warren Rudman ¶ ;7 (hereinafter Rudman Decl.), App. 742); 251 F. Supp. 2d, at 858 (Leon, J.) (same).

So pervasive is this practice that the six national party committees actually furnish their own menus of opportunities for access to would-be soft-money donors, with increased prices reflecting an increased level of access. For example, the DCCC offers a range of donor options, starting with the $10,000-per-year Business Forum program, and going up to the $100,000-per-year National Finance Board program. The latter entitles the donor to bimonthly conference calls with the Democratic House leadership and chair of the DCCC, complimentary invitations to all DCCC fundraising events, two private dinners with the Democratic House leadership and ranking members, and two retreats with the Democratic House leader and DCCC chair in Telluride, Colorado, and Hyannisport, Massachusetts. Id., at 504–505 (Kollar-Kotelly, J.); see also id., at 506 (describing records indicating that DNC offered meetings with President in return for large donations); id., at 502–503 (describing RNC's various donor programs); id., at 503–504 (same for NRSC); id., at 500–503 (same for DSCC); id., at 504 (same for NRCC). Similarly, "the RNC's donor programs offer greater access to federal office holders as the donations grow larger, with the highest level and most personal access offered to the largest soft money donors." Id., at 500–503 (finding, further, that the RNC holds out the prospect of access to officeholders to attract soft-money donations and encourages officeholders to meet with large soft-money donors); accord, id., at 860–861 (Leon, J.).

In sum, there is substantial evidence to support Congress' determination that large soft-money contributions to national political parties give rise to corruption and the appearance of corruption. . . .

Tables 6.9 to 6.14 provide data on the activities of fund-raisers, interest groups, industries, and so-called 527 organizations in the 2006 Congressional elections. Tables 6.9 and 6.10 detail the donations of the top-spending organizations broken down by House and Senate candidates and by major political party. Tables 6.11 and 6.12 show the 10 political action committees and interest group sectors that donated the most money in 2006 and also how their donations were allotted to Republican and Democratic candidates. Table 6.13 demonstrates the relatively recent trend of industries to donate heavily to incumbents by showing how their donations were allotted to incumbents, challengers, and open-seat candidates. Finally, Table 6.14 provides figures on the receipts and expenditures of all 527 organizations that spent more than one million dollars influencing 2006 Congressional elections.

TABLE 6.8
A Brief History of Campaign Finance Laws in the United States

The Tillman Act (1907)	• Outlawed corporate political contributions and gifts to federal candidates.
Federal Corrupt Practices Act (1910) As amended in 1911 and 1925 and upheld by the U.S. Supreme Court.	• Required national party, congressional campaign, and House and Senate campaign committees to file quarterly reports disclosing campaign contributions of more than $100 and expenditures. • Established campaign spending limits for federal campaigns ($5,000 for House and $25,000 for Senate campaigns).
Hatch Act (1939)	• Prohibited federal employees not covered by the Pendleton Act from participating in political activities. • Prohibited the solicitation of political contributions from federal government employees. • Prohibited political contributions by federal contractors. • Limited individual contributions to federal candidates and national party committees to $5,000 annually. • Limited total receipts of national party committees to $3 million annually.
Taft-Hartley Act (1947)	• Prohibited political campaign contributions and independent expenditures by labor unions. • Prohibited independent expenditures by corporations.
Federal Election Campaign Act (1971) As amended in 1974, 1976, and 1979 and upheld by the U.S. Supreme Court.	• Required disclosure of contributions and expenditures for federal candidates, PACs, and political parties. • Limited individual contributions to federal elections to $1,000 per candidate per election, $5,000 per year to a political committee, and $20,000 per year to political committees. Limited annual aggregate individual contributions to $25,000. • Limited PAC contributions to candidates to $5,000 per candidate per election and to $15,000 per year to national party committees. • Established the Federal Election Commission. • Established the presidential public funding system. • Established a federal subsidy for national political party conventions.

continues

TABLE 6.8   continued

Bipartisan Campaign Reform Act (2002) As upheld by the U.S. Supreme Court.	• Prohibited national political party committees from receiving or spending "soft money."
	• Regulated the federal "electioneering communications" of labor unions and corporations.
	• Increased individual contribution limits to federal elections to $2,000 per candidate per election and $25,000 per year to political committees. Increased the limits on aggregate individual contributions to $95,000 every two years.

Sources:

Federal Election Commission, *Bipartisan Campaign Reform Act of 2002.* [Online information; retrieved 11/28/07.] http://www.fec.gov/pages/bcra/bcra_update.shtml.

Mann, Thomas E., Daniel R. Ortiz, and Trevor Potter. 2005. *The New Campaign Finance Sourcebook.* Washington, DC: Brookings Institution Press.

Potter, Trevor, Daniel R. Ortiz, and Anthony Corrado. 2004. *The Campaign Finance Guide.* Washington, DC: The Campaign Legal Center.

TABLE 6.9
2006 Congressional Elections Bundling Organizations and Recipients

House Candidates		
Organization	**Recipient**	**Amount Bundled**
ActBlue	Joe Sestak (D-PA)	$565,479
ActBlue	Tim Mahoney (D-FL)	$400,016
ActBlue	Daniel Seals (D-IL, defeated)	$387,615
EMILY's List	Tammy Duckworth (D-IL, defeated)	$269,450
Democratic Congressional Campaign Committee	Michael Arcuri (D-NY)	$262,411
Democratic Congressional Campaign Committee	Chris Murphy (D-CT)	$258,695
Club for Growth	Adrian Smith (R-NE)	$249,455
Club for Growth	Tim Walberg (R-MI)	$241,995
ActBlue	Judith Feder (D-VA, defeated)	$228,049
Democratic Congressional Campaign Committee	Bruce Braley (D-IA)	$224,086

continues

TABLE 6.9   continued

Senate Candidates		
Organization	Recipient	Amount Bundled
EMILY's List	Claire McCaskill (D-MO)	$523,538
Club for Growth	Stephen Laffey (R-RI, defeated)	$443,918
ActBlue	James Webb (D-VA)	$419,075
EMILY's List	Amy Klobuchar (D-MN)	$359,700
ActBlue	John Morrison (D-MT, defeated)	$313,527
Moveon.org	Ned Lamont (D-CT, defeated)	$251,126
Club for Growth	Michael Steele (R-MD, defeated)	$242,831
EMILY's List	Debbie Stabenow (D-MI)	$189,375
Club for Growth	Michael Bouchard (R-MI, defeated)	$187,005
Club for Growth	Michael McGavick (R-WA, defeated)	$176,352

Source: Center for Responsive Politics. *2006 Cycle. The Big Picture: Bundles of Money.* [Online information; retrieved 10/5/08.] http://www.opensecrets.org/bigpicture/bundles.asp?cycle=2006.

TABLE 6.10
2006 Congressional Elections Contributing Organizations and Political Ideology

Organization	Amount Contributed	To Democrats	To Republicans
ActBlue	$4,713,402	100%	0%
National Association of Realtors	$3,840,782	49%	51%
EMILY's List	$3,571,426	100%	0%
Goldman Sachs	$3,561,116	64%	36%
National Beer Wholesalers Association	$2,967,250	31%	69%
Club for Growth	$2,931,628	4%	96%
National Association of Home Builders	$2,910,150	26%	73%
International Brotherhood of Electrical Workers	$2,836,838	98%	3%
National Auto Dealers Association	$2,823,100	30%	70%
American Bankers Association	$2,798,975	36%	64%

Source: Center for Responsive Politics. *2006 Cycle. The Big Picture: Top Overall Donors.* [Online information; retrieved 10/5/07.] http://www.opensecrets.org/bigpicture/topcontribs.asp?Bkdn=DemRep&Cycle=2006.

TABLE 6.11

2005–2006 Congressional Elections Nonparty PAC Contributors

PAC	Total Amount	To Democrats	To Republicans
National Association of Realtors	$3,752,005	49%	51%
National Beer Wholesalers Association	$2,946,500	31%	69%
National Association of Home Builders	$2,900,000	26%	73%
National Auto Dealers Association	$2,821,600	30%	70%
International Brotherhood of Electrical Workers	$2,796,875	97%	3%
Operating Engineers Union	$2,784,435	78%	21%
American Bankers Association	$2,748,299	36%	64%
Laborers Union	$2,687,150	85%	15%
American Association for Justice	$2,558,000	96%	3%
Credit Union National Association	$2,412,853	45%	54%

Source: Center for Responsive Politics. *2006 Cycle. The Big Picture: Top PACs.* [Online information; retrieved 10/5/08.] http://www.opensecrets.org/bigpicture/toppacs.php?cycle=2006.

TABLE 6.12

2006 Congressional Elections Interest Group Sector Contributors by Political Ideology

Interest Group Sector	Amount	To Democrats	To Republicans
Finance, insurance, and real estate	$258,802,407	44%	54%
Ideology and single-issue	$227,007,611	55%	44%
Other	$165,693,954	51%	47%
Lawyers and lobbyists	$144,865,605	66%	33%
Miscellaneous business	$140,756,780	40%	59%
Health	$99,747,428	37%	62%
Communications and electronics	$70,515,326	55%	44%
Labor	$66,414,243	87%	12%
Construction	$54,438,261	29%	70%
Energy and natural resource	$47,802,472	25%	74%

Source: Center for Responsive Politics, *2006 Cycle. The Big Picture: Totals by Sector.* [Online information; retrieved 10/5/07.] http://www.opensecrets.org/bigpicture/sectors.asp?Cycle=2006&Bkdn=DemRep&Sortby=Rank.

TABLE 6.13

2006 Congressional Elections PAC Industry Contributors by Donations to Incumbents, Challengers, and Candidates in Open Seats

Industry	Total (in millions)	To Incumbents	To Challengers	Open Seats
Ideology and single issue	$60.9	57%	24%	19%
Labor	$59.4	68%	21%	12%
Finance, insurance, and real estate	$58.5	91%	2%	6%
Health	$39.8	91%	3%	6%
Miscellaneous business	$29.3	89%	3%	8%
Energy and natural resource	$22.1	92%	2%	6%
Communications and electronics	$21.1	95%	1%	3%
Agribusiness	$19.9	91%	3%	6%
Transportation	$19.5	93%	2%	6%
Lawyers and lobbyists	$14.4	85%	8%	7%
Construction	$14.3	90%	3%	7%
Defense	$10.6	97%	1%	2%

Source: Center for Responsive Politics. *2006 Cycle. The Big Picture: PAC Dollars to Incumbents, Challengers, and Open Seats.* [Online information; retrieved 10/5/07.] http://www.opensecrets.org/bigpicture/pac2cands.asp?cycle=2006.

TABLE 6.14

2006 Congressional Elections 527 Committee Expenditures

527 Committee	Receipts	Expenditures
Service Employees International Union	$25,053,546	$28,212,510
America Votes	$14,391,893	$14,106,236
Progress for America	$6,175,025	$13,000,574
EMILY's List	$11,776,201	$11,128,005
College Republican National Committee	$3,720,110	$10,260,343
GOPAC	$2,936,890	$8,394,833
Club for Growth	$7,217,080	$8,157,383
Citizens United	$707,485	$7,256,082
America Coming Together	$4,494,107	$6,998,238
International Brotherhood of Electrical Workers	$5,538,113	$5,529,067
September Fund	$5,230,500	$4,950,861
Economic Freedom Fund	$5,050,450	$4,835,805
Laborers Union	$3,688,250	$3,762,110
National Education Association	$38,201	$3,576,428
National Federation of Republican Women	$1,518,658	$3,028,197
Gay and Lesbian Victory Fund	$2,247,467	$2,962,060
Americans for Honesty on Issues	$3,030,221	$2,830,148
Grassroots Democrats	$2,039,648	$2,584,756

continues

TABLE 6.14   continued

527 Committee	Receipts	Expenditures
Sheet Metal Workers Union	$1,998,623	$2,134,586
Majority Action	$2,157,250	$1,995,692
Media Fund	$725,000	$1,985,044
United Food and Commercial Workers Union	$2,235,000	$1,927,431
Illinois Hospital and Health Systems Association	$1,415,144	$1,818,023
Lantern Project	$1,700,900	$1,633,502
Young Democrats of America	$1,632,929	$1,576,603
Coloradans For Life	$1,375,021	$1,524,654
League of Conservation Voters	$1,923,000	$1,512,585
International Association of Fire Fighters	$0	$1,511,787
Floridians for a Better/Brighter Future	$1,411,000	$1,411,000
Softer Voices	$1,403,300	$1,266,000
New Democrat Network	$1,774,204	$1,256,434
New West Fellowship Group	$1,189,940	$1,246,049
Free Enterprise Fund Committee	$1,239,003	$1,231,630
Senate Majority Fund	$1,144,184	$1,186,675
Patriot Majority Fund	$1,145,000	$1,148,047
Sierra Club	$60,000	$1,121,016
Colorado Leadership Fund	$1,270,485	$1,096,087
Swift Vets and POWs for Truth	$2,300	$1,092,373
Operating Engineers Union	$1,601,192	$1,091,798
Ironworkers Union	$1,054,332	$1,020,080

Source: Center for Responsive Politics, *527 Committee Activity.* [Online information; retrieved 10/5/07.] http://www.opensecrets.org/527s/527cmtes.asp?level=C&cycle=2006.

References

Bentley, Arthur. 1935. *The Process of Government.* Evanston: The Principia Press of Illinois.

Committee on Indian Affairs. 2006. "Gimme Five"—Investigation of Tribal Lobbying Matters: Final Report Before the Committee on Indian Affairs. 109th Congress, Second Session. June 22, 2006. [Online information; retrieved August 23, 2007.] http://indian.senate.gov/public/_files/Report.pdf.

Dahl, Robert A. 1961. *Who Governs?* New Haven, CT: Yale University Press.

Federal Election Commission. *Bipartisan Campaign Reform Act of 2002.* [Online information; retrieved November 28, 2007.] http://www.fec.gov/pages/bcra/bcra_update.shtml.

The Hatch Act of 1939. 53 Stat. 1147.

Madison, James. "Federalist Number 10: The Same Subject Continued: The Utility of the Union as a Safeguard Against Domestic Faction and Insurrection." *The New York Packet,* Friday, November 23, 1787. [Online information; retrieved March 3, 2008.] http://thomas.loc.gov/home/histdox/fed_10.html.

Mann, Thomas E. *Accountability Through Transparency.* House Committee on Rules. March 2, 2006. [Online information; retrieved September 17, 2007.] http://www.brookings.edu/testimony/2006/0302governance_mann.aspx

Mann, Thomas E., Daniel R. Ortiz, and Trevor Potter. 2005. *The New Campaign Finance Sourcebook.* Washington, DC: Brookings Institution Press.

McConnell v. Federal Election Commission. 540 U.S. 93 (2003).

Olson, Mancur. 1965. *The Logic of Collective Action: Public Goods and the Theory of Groups.* Cambridge, MA: Harvard University Press.

Potter, Trevor, Daniel R. Ortiz, and Anthony Corrado. 2004. *The Campaign Finance Guide.* Washington, DC: The Campaign Legal Center.

Schattschneider, E. E. 1960. *The Semisovereign People.* New York: Holt, Rinehart and Winston.

Schmitter, Philippe C. 1979. "Still the Century of Corporatism." *Review of Politics* 36 (1): 85–131.

The Tillman Act of 1907. 34 Stat. 864.

Tocqueville, Alexis de. 1956. *Democracy in America.* New York: Mentor.

Truman, David B. 1951. *The Governmental Process: Political Interests and Public Opinion.* New York: Alfred A. Knopf.

Wilson, James Q. 1973. *Political Organizations.* New York: Basic Books.

7

Directory of Organizations, Associations, and Agencies

A s the nation approached the 2008 presidential election, hundreds and perhaps thousands of new interest groups entered the political arena for the first time. Millions of dollars were spent on donations to local, state, and federal candidates and for independent expenditures on such things as television advertisements and voter registration drives. More than 20,000 organizations are active in American politics on the national level. Just keeping track of the large number of organizations that form and dissolve each year is a daunting task. This chapter presents a select list of interest groups and think tanks based on their power (i.e., ability to influence public opinion and policy), size, membership distribution, and level of activity. Many organizations operate affiliated political action committees (PACs), foundations, and charities. These are listed herein when such information was available. It is important to note that it is the goal of many interest groups to disguise certain activities they engage in, and many national organizations operate local and state-level chapters and affiliated organizations that often form their own separate PACs and foundations.

AARP
601 E Street NW
Washington, DC 20049
Telephone: Toll-free: 888-OUR-AARP (888-687-2277)
Washington, D.C.: (202) 434-2277
Web site: www.aarp.org

Information on Web site: Biographical information, policy positions, health and wellness information, research, *AARP The Magazine, AARP Segunda Juventud, AARP Bulletin,* and membership information.

Overview: AARP is a nonprofit membership organization of persons age 50 and older. It is dedicated to advancing the interests and well-being of the 50 and older population. AARP seeks to advance the quality of life for aging Americans by leading the drive for positive social change and delivering value to its members through information, advocacy, and services. AARP provides its members with a wide variety of benefits, products, and services, including access to publications, discounts at thousands of locations, volunteer opportunities, financial services, and counseling.

Membership: More than 38 million members nationwide.

Current Concerns: Economic security, Social Security, health care, health and wellness, long-term care and family caregiving, and personal enrichment.

Accuracy in Media (AIM)
4455 Connecticut Avenue NW, Suite 330
Washington, DC 20008
Telephone: (202) 364-4401
Web site: www.aim.org

Information on Web site: Biographical information, publications and reports, blogs, merchandise, multimedia, RSS feeds (automatically updating summaries of news headlines that can be added to a blog or Web page), issue information, and membership information.

Overview: Accuracy in Media (AIM) is a nonprofit, grassroots citizens watchdog of the news media that critiques news stories and seeks to publish accurate information on important issues that have received slanted coverage. It accomplishes this mission by convening conferences and seminars and producing films, videos, and television and radio programs.

Membership: 3,000 members nationwide.

Current Concerns: Accurate news reporting and statements of public officials.

American Bankers Association (ABA)
1120 Connecticut Avenue NW

Washington, DC 20036
Telephone: 800-BANKERS
Web site: www.aba.com

Information on Web site: Biographical information, ABA products and services, ABA-related news and announcements, consumer resources, research, surveys and reports, and banking statistics.

Overview: Founded in 1875, the American Bankers Association (ABA) is the largest banking trade association in the United States. The ABA represents banks, holding companies, savings associations, trust companies, and savings banks. The ABA is dedicated to enhancing the role of financial services institutions through pursuing favorable federal legislation and regulation, legal action, consumer education, and research and through products and services distributed to consumers and its members. The ABA has consistently been ranked as one of the most powerful interest groups in the nation, in part because of its use of its PAC, BankPac, which donated more than $2 million to the U.S. Senate and House of Representatives candidates in the 2006 election cycle.

Membership: Member institutions in all 50 states, including banks, holding companies, savings associations, and trust companies.

Current Concerns: Accounting, bankruptcy, credit union competition, data security, credit reporting, mergers and acquisitions, money laundering, predatory lending, Social Security, and wealth management.

American Civil Liberties Union (ACLU)
125 Broad Street, 18th Floor
New York, NY 10004
Telephone: (212) 549-2500
Web site: www.aclu.org

Information on Web site: Biographical information, Supreme Court case information, legislative updates, "action center" with issues of interest, media, and membership/donation information.

Overview: The mission of the American Civil Liberties Union (ACLU) is to preserve the constitutional rights of freedom of speech, religion, association, and assembly as well as freedom of the press, equal protection under the law, due process, and privacy. Founded in 1920, the ACLU is a nonprofit and nonpartisan organization that currently handles nearly 6,000 court cases each year from its state offices. The ACLU is supported by annual member dues and contributions, grants from private foundations, and donations from individuals.

Membership: More than 500,000 members.

Current Concerns: Civil rights, death penalty, gay rights, immigrant rights, racial equality, religious liberty, reproductive rights, voting access and rights, and workplace discrimination.

American Enterprise Institute for Public Policy Research (AEI)
1150 17th Street NW
Washington, DC 20036
Telephone: (202) 862-5800
Web site: www.aei.org

Information on Web site: Biographical information, events, research and publications, issue information, and donation information. Individuals may also sign up to create a personalized AEI Web page and receive e-newsletters.

Overview: The American Enterprise Institute for Public Policy Research (AEI) is a nonpartisan, nonprofit institution dedicated to research and education on issues of government, politics, economics, and social welfare. Founded in 1943, AEI sponsors research and conferences and publishes books, monographs, and periodicals. AEI's purpose is to defend the principles and improve the institutions of American freedom and democratic capitalism by focusing on limited government, private enterprise, individual liberty and responsibility, vigilant and effective defense and foreign policies, political accountability, and open debate. AEI research is conducted through three research divisions: Economic Policy Studies, Social and Political Studies, and Defense and Foreign Policy Studies.

Membership: None.

Current Concerns: Economics and trade, tax policy, international relations, regulatory policies, national defense and homeland security, and political accountability.

American Farm Bureau Federation (AFBF)
600 Maryland Avenue SW, Suite 1000W
Washington, DC 20024
Telephone: (202) 406-3600
Web site: www.fb.org

Information on Web site: Biographical information, listings of state farm bureaus, farm bureau–related news, press releases, links to agricultural organizations, blog, issues of interest to the Farm Bureau, updates on legislative activities, and agriculture-related research and statistics.

Overview: The American Farm Bureau Federation (AFBF) is the largest and most influential agricultural organization in the United States representing farmers and ranchers in all 50 states. Founded in 1919, the AFBF is dedicated to improving the farming and ranching industries by making farming more profitable and strengthening farming communities. The AFBF's mission ranges from improving education quality to increasing economic opportunities for farmers at all levels—local, county, state, national, and international. Members receive benefits ranging from farming advice and research to banking services through the Farm Bureau Bank. The AFBF conducts grassroots lobbying through its Farm Bureau Agricultural Contact Team (FBACT) network that gives the AFBF the ability to mobilize its membership through e-mail and Internet alerts. Each year, the AFBF awards the Golden Plow Award to members of Congress who support the AFBF's legislative goals. Each state Farm Bureau also operates its own PAC, giving campaign contributions to agriculture-friendly candidates and officeholders.

Membership: State Farm Bureaus have been established in all 50 states.

Current Concerns: Animal identification implementation, domestic energy production, water resource development, land use regulations, immigration, rural development, and the estate and alternative minimum taxes.

American Federation of Labor-Congress of Industrial Organizations (AFL-CIO)
815 16th Street NW
Washington, DC 20006
Telephone: (202) 637-3907
Web site: www.aflcio.org

Information on Web site: Biographical information, research and statistics, publications, press releases and AFL-CIO-related news and announcements, games, legislative issues, and links to affiliated unions.

Overview: The AFL-CIO is a voluntary federation of 55 national and international unions that was created in 1995 by the merger of the American Federation of Labor and the Congress of Industrial Organizations. Representing more than 10 million working men and women, the AFL-CIO seeks to improve the lives of workers through economic and social justice and by organizing and training union members throughout the United States and the world. With many member and affiliated organizations, the AFL-CIO is largely a grassroots-based organization that seeks to influence legislative policy by training and mobilizing its membership. AFL-CIO voter guides instruct members how candidates stand on key positions, and members are strongly encouraged to run for political office themselves. Through the AFL-CIO Committee on Political Education Political Contributions Committee, the AFL-CIO's PAC, the organization donated more than $1.4 million during the 2006 election cycle.

Membership: The AFL-CIO has approximately 10 million members in the United States that are affiliated with the organization through its 55 national unions.

Current Concerns: Work-related issues, including minimum wage laws, health care, job outsourcing, unemployment assistance, workers' rights, Social Security, immigration, civil and women's rights, and education.

American Israel Public Affairs Committee (AIPAC)
440 First Street NW, Suite 600
Washington, DC 20001
Telephone: (202) 639-5200
Web site: www.aipac.org

Information on Web site: Biographical information, action center, membership information, legislation and policy, upcoming events, publications, and press center.

Overview: The American Israel Public Affairs Committee (AIPAC) works to make Israel more secure by ensuring that American support of Israel remains strong. As a national grassroots movement, AIPAC works with both Democratic and Republican political leaders to enact public policy that strengthens the U.S.–Israel relationship. AIPAC holds conferences and seminars, testifies at congressional hearings, produces pro-Israel research and publications, conducts public education campaigns, and engages in direct and indirect lobbying.

Membership: 100,000 members nationwide.

Current Concerns: Supporting and defending Israel, preparing and supporting pro-Israel leaders and policy makers, nuclear weapons in Iran, Hamas's control of Gaza, relations with Syria, and terrorism.

Americans United for Separation of Church and State
518 C Street NE
Washington, DC 20002
Telephone: (202) 466-3234
Web site: www.au.org

Information on Web site: Biographical information, blog, issues of interest, membership information, media, publications, and research.

Overview: Americans United for Separation of Church and State seeks to advocate the separation of church and state in order to preserve the constitutional guarantee of religious freedom for all Americans. Founded in 1947 by religious and civic organizations, Americans United is a nonsectarian, nonpartisan organization that seeks to educate legislators, the media, and the public about the importance of religious freedom. Americans United does not contribute to federal or state election campaigns.

Membership: More than 75,000 members in all 50 states.

Current Concerns: Church political activities, faith-based initiatives, freedom of religion, marriage rights, religion in public schools, and religious school vouchers.

Anti-Defamation League (ADL)
823 United Nations Plaza
New York, NY 10017
Telephone: (212) 885-7700
Web site: www.adl.org

Information on Web site: Biographical information, regional office information, press center, and research and publications.

Overview: Founded in 1913, the Anti-Defamation League (ADL) seeks to stop, by appeals to reason and conscience and, if necessary, by appeals to law, the defamation of the Jewish people. It seeks to secure justice and fair treatment for all citizens and to end the unfair discrimination against and ridicule of any sect or body or citizens. The ADL accomplishes this mission by conducting media outreach programs, giving awards, forming coalitions, convening conferences and seminars, monitoring extremist group activities, and conducting and disseminating research and publications.

Membership: None.

Current Concerns: Anti-Semitism, civil rights, Holocaust education, interfaith alliances, international affairs, Israel support and defense, separation of church and state, and terrorism.

The Brookings Institution
1775 Massachusetts Avenue NW
Washington, DC 20036
Telephone: (202) 797-6404
Web site: www.brookings.edu

Information on Web site: Biographical information, research, programs, multimedia, publications, merchandise, and bookstore.

Overview: The Brookings Institution is a private nonprofit organization devoted to independent research and innovative policy solutions. With more than 140 resident and nonresident scholars, Brookings is able to research issues; write books, papers, articles, and opinion pieces; testify before congressional committees; and participate in seminars and conferences each year. For more than 90 years, Brookings has analyzed current and emerging issues and produced new ideas that matter—for the nation and the world. Brookings's goal is to provide high-quality analysis and recommendations for decision makers in the United States and abroad on the full range of challenges facing an increasingly interdependent world.

Membership: None.

Current Concerns: Antitrust policy, fiscal policy, campaign finance reform, education, foreign affairs, homeland security, immigration, economic policy, Social Security, tax policy, transportation, and welfare reform.

Business Industry Political Action Committee (BIPAC)
888 16th Street NW, Suite 305
Washington, DC 20006
Telephone: (202) 833-1880
Web site: www.bipac.net

Information on Web site: Biographical information, press releases, and a listing of BIPAC-supported candidates.

Overview: The Business Industry Political Action Committee (BIPAC) is dedicated to championing free enterprise through the election of business-friendly candidates to Congress. BIPAC combines grassroots advocacy with targeted contributions through the use of the Prosperity Fund, the Prosperity Project, affiliated PACs, and its own PAC, the Action Fund, which donated to several U.S. Senate candidates and dozens of U.S. House of Representatives candidates in 2006. BIPAC relies exclusively on its political analysis (available for purchase or to members) in choosing which candidates receive financial support. Through its *Elections Insight* weekly e-mail newsletter, BIPAC is able to keep its membership updated on issues of interest as well as election developments.

Membership: More than 400 corporations and approximately 300 individuals.

Current Concerns: Economic development, global competitiveness, sustainable growth, technology, tax policy, regulatory reform, education, infrastructure, energy, health care, immigration, and Social Security.

Business Roundtable

1717 Rhode Island Avenue NW, Suite 800
Washington, DC 20036
Telephone: (202) 872-1260
Web site: www.businessroundtable.org

Information on Web site: Biographical information, issues, publications, press releases, and news.

Overview: The Business Roundtable is an association of chief executive officers of leading U.S. corporations and is dedicated to advocating for policies that advance economic growth, expand the global economy, and provide for a well-trained and productive U.S. labor force. The Business Roundtable seeks to influence public policy through the use of issue task forces that conduct research, produce position papers, and recommend policies to Congress and the executive branch.

Membership: More than 150 corporations with an estimated workforce of more than 10 million employees.

Current Concerns: Corporate governance, education, energy, environment, technology, economic development, fiscal policy, international trade, and Social Security.

Cato Institute

1000 Massachusetts Avenue NW
Washington, DC 20001

Telephone: (202) 842-0200
Web site: www.cato.org

Information on Web site: Biographical information, newsroom, events, publications, bookstore, blog, and membership information.

Overview: The Cato Institute was founded in 1977 by Edward H. Crane and is a nonprofit public policy research foundation. The institute is named for Cato's Letters, a series of libertarian pamphlets that helped establish the philosophical foundation for the American Revolution. The Cato Institute seeks to broaden the parameters of public policy debate to allow consideration of the traditional American principles of limited government, individual liberty, free markets, and peace. To accomplish this goal, the Cato Institute strives to achieve greater involvement of the intelligent, concerned lay public in policy and the proper role of government.

Membership: 14,000 members, 75 corporate sponsors, and 50 foundation sponsors.

Current Concerns: Civil liberties, constitutional law, national security policy, free markets, health and welfare reform, international economic development, monetary policy, Social Security, and taxation.

Center for Media and Public Affairs (CMPA)
2100 L Street NW, Suite 300
Washington, DC 20037
Telephone: (202) 223-2942
Web site: www.cmpa.com

Information on Web site: Biographical information, press releases, media monitor, research and publications, and membership information.

Overview: The Center for Media and Public Affairs (CMPA) is a nonpartisan research and educational organization that conducts scientific studies of the news and entertainment industries. Since its formation in 1985, CMPA has emerged as an institution that bridges the gap between academic research and the broader domains of media and public policy. The center's goal is to provide an empirical basis for ongoing debates over media fairness and impact through well-documented, timely, and readable studies of media content.

Membership: None.

Current Concerns: Cable television programming, media coverage accuracy and bias, election coverage, violence on television, and minorities on television.

Christian Coalition of America
P.O. Box 37030
Washington, DC 20013
Telephone: (202) 479-6900
Web site: www.cc.org

Information on Web site: Biographical information, issues and legislative agenda, congressional scorecards, news, press room, merchandise, photo archives, membership information, and action alerts.

Overview: The Christian Coalition was founded in 1989 as a means to provide Christians with an avenue to be active in shaping America's government on the local, state, and federal levels. The Christian Coalition of America is the nation's largest and most active conservative grassroots political organization. The Christian Coalition's primary focus is on producing and distributing voter guides that identify pro-Christian candidates and policy positions. Before the November 2006 election the Christian Coalition of America distributed a record 70 million voter guides throughout all 50 states. The Christian Coalition also actively lobbies Congress and the White House, trains grassroots activists, and hosts pro-Christian events throughout the country.

Membership: More than 2 million members and supporters.

Current Concerns: Abortion, sanctity of life, choice in education, gambling, Israel security and defense, pornography, same-sex marriage, and religious freedom.

Common Cause
1133 19th Street NW, 9th Floor
Washington, DC 20036
Telephone: (202) 833-1200
Web site: www.commoncause.org

Information on Web site: Biographical information, state organizations, action center, blog, membership information, and issue information.

Overview: Common Cause is a nonpartisan, nonprofit advocacy organization founded in 1970 as a vehicle for citizens to make their voices heard in the political process and to hold their elected leaders accountable to the public interest. Common Cause advocates for improved quality of governance through direct lobbying, coalition forming, convening of conferences and seminars, grassroots organizing, and media outreach.

Membership: Nearly 300,000 members.

Current Concerns: Money in politics, government ethics, media and democracy, election reform, redistricting reform, and government accountability.

Consumer Federation of America (CFA)
1620 I Street NW, Suite 200
Washington, DC 20006
Telephone: (202) 387-6121
Web site: www.consumerfed.org

Information on Web site: Biographical information, press releases, publications, issue information, Food Policy Institute, state and local chapter information, and events.

Overview: Since its founding in 1968, the Consumer Federation of America (CFA) has provided consumers with information regarding the products and services that affect their daily lives. CFA gathers facts, analyzes issues, and presents information to the public and to policy makers. The CFA is an advocacy, research, and education organization. It works to advance pro-consumer policies at the state and national levels before legislatures, Congress, the courts, and regulatory agencies.

Membership: 300 allied consumer organizations.

Current Concerns: Telecommunications and media ownership, consumer rights and protection, energy policy, finance, firearms, food and agriculture, health and safety, investor protection, and housing.

Council on Foreign Relations (CFR)
58 East 68th Street
New York, NY 10065
Telephone: (212) 434-9400
Web site: www.cfr.org

Information on Web site: Biographical information, issue information, publications, research, media, and podcast.

Overview: The Council on Foreign Relations is an independent, national membership organization and a nonpartisan center for scholars dedicated to producing and disseminating ideas so that individual and corporate members, as well as policy makers, journalists, students, and interested citizens in the United States and other countries, can better understand the world and the foreign policy choices facing the United States and other governments. To accomplish this mission, the Council on Foreign Relations conducts conferences and seminars, testifies at congressional hearings, serves as an information clearinghouse, and conducts media and outreach campaigns.

Membership: More than 4,000 members.

Current Concerns: Defense and homeland security, democracy, human rights, economic development, energy, environment, international security and peace, terrorism, and nuclear proliferation.

Defenders of Wildlife
1130 17th Street NW
Washington, DC 20036
Telephone: Toll-free: (800) 385-9712. Washington, D.C.:
(202) 682-9400
Web site: www.defenders.org

Information on Web site: Biographical information, newsroom, membership information, program information, research and publications, action center, and advocacy resources.

Overview: Founded in 1947, Defenders of Wildlife is one of the nation's leading science-based, results-oriented wildlife conservation organizations. Defenders of Wildlife is dedicated to saving imperiled wildlife and championing the enforcement of the Endangered Species Act. Defenders of Wildlife is a nonprofit, membership-based organization that works across state and international borders to protect endangered and native species and educate the public about the importance of preserving and protecting native animals and plants in their natural communities.

Membership: More than 450,000 members.

Current Concerns: Arctic National Wildlife Refuge, biological diversity, Endangered Species Act, federal lands, environment, and wildlife preservation.

EMILY's List
1120 Connecticut Avenue NW, Suite 1100
Washington, DC 20036

Telephone: (202) 326-1400
Web site: www.emilyslist.org

Information on Web site: Membership information, biographical information, candidate biographies, media and news, merchandise, downloads, issue information.

Overview: EMILY's List—which refers to Early Money Is Like Yeast—a common political saying reflecting the belief that early fund-raising efforts "raise the dough" and scare off challengers and result in later fund-raising success—is the nation's largest grassroots political network dedicated to building a progressive political environment by electing pro-choice Democratic women to local, state, and federal offices. EMILY's List recruits, funds, and supports viable pro-choice women candidates by training young women and preparing them to become activists, mobilizing women voters, and training women how to run effective political and campaign organizations. The grassroots network of EMILY's List has helped elect 67 Democratic pro-choice members of Congress, 13 senators, and 8 governors. Through the Emily's List PAC, the organization spent more than $34 million on state and federal candidates during the 2006 election cycle.

Membership: 100,000 members.

Current Concerns: Reproductive rights, women's political participation, and women's rights.

Environmental Defense
257 Park Avenue South
New York, NY 10010
Telephone: Toll-free: (800) 684-3322. New York, NY:
(212) 505-2100
Web site: www.environmentaldefense.org

Information on Web site: Biographical information, membership information, programs, issues, newsroom, and research and publications.

Overview: Environmental Defense, founded in 1967, is a leading national nonprofit and nonpartisan organization representing more than 500,000 members. Environmental Defense seeks to link science, economics, and law to create innovative, equitable, and cost-effective solutions to society's environmental problems. Environmental Defense is dedicated to protecting the environmental rights of all people, including future generations. These rights include access to clean air and water, healthy and nourishing food, and a flourishing ecosystem.

Membership: More than 500,000 members.

Current Concerns: Global warming, air quality, land use, water, wildlife preservation, sustainable development, and endangered species protection.

The Federalist Society
1015 18th Street NW, Suite 425
Washington, DC 20036
Telephone: (202) 822-8138
Web site: www.fed-soc.org

Information on Web site: Biographical information, events, publications, research, membership information, and media.

Overview: The Federalist Society is a conservative organization dedicated to upholding the principles of freedom, separation of governmental powers, and judicial restraint. Founded in 1982, the society seeks to promote these ideals among law students, who they believe are heavily influenced by liberal professors and law school peers, by establishing a network of grassroots organizations that extends into all levels of academia and government. With chapters at nearly all law schools, the society funds and supports conservative legal discussions and forums with prominent academics, attorneys, judges, and elected officials.

Membership: More than 5,000 law students at approximately 180 American Bar Association–accredited law schools.

Current Concerns: Administrative law, civil rights, criminal law and procedure, federalism, separation of powers, judicial restraint, free speech, election law, intellectual property, religious liberties, and corporate responsibility.

Focus on the Family
8605 Explorer Drive
Colorado Springs, CO 80920
Telephone: Toll Free: 800-A-FAMILY (800-232-6459).
Colorado Springs, CO: (719) 531-5181
Web site: www.family.org

Information on Web site: Biographical information, merchandise, research and publications, relationship and marriage advice/ counseling, multimedia, and membership information.

Overview: Focus on the Family is a nonprofit, nonpartisan, Christian organization that produces internationally syndicated radio programs heard on more than 3,000 radio stations in North America and in 27 languages in 4,130 facilities in 160 countries. Focus on the Family broadcasts are heard by an estimated 220 million people each day. The organization also advocates for pro-family policies on the state and national levels through direct and indirect lobbying, grassroots mobilization, and media campaigns.

Membership: An estimated 220 million listeners worldwide.

Current Concerns: Marriage, promotion of evangelism, pro-life policies, sanctity of human life, and family values.

The Heritage Foundation
214 Massachusetts Avenue NE
Washington, DC 20002
Telephone: (202) 546-4400
Web site: www.heritage.org

Information on Web site: Biographical information, issue information, press and media, bookstore, and membership information.

Overview: Founded in 1973, the Heritage Foundation is a research and educational institute with the mission of formulating and promoting conservative public policies based on the principles of free enterprise, limited government, individual freedom, traditional American values, and a strong national defense.

Membership: More than 200,000 members.

Current Concerns: Tax policy, crime, free markets, education reform, environment, strengthening the family, federal spending, national security, health care, Social Security, and telecommunications.

The League of Women Voters of the United States (LWVUS)
1730 M Street NW, Suite 1000
Washington, DC 20036
Telephone: (202) 429-1965
Web site: www.lwv.org

Information on Web site: Biographical information, membership information, local league locator, issue information and alerts, research and publications, news and events, current projects/issues, and voter registration information.

Overview: The League of Women Voters of the United States is a nonpartisan political organization founded in 1920 to improve the quality of governance in the United States and affect public policies through citizen participation and advocacy. The league is largely a decentralized grassroots organization with branches in all 50 states, the District of Columbia, Puerto Rico, Hong Kong, and the U.S. Virgin Islands. The league does not make contributions to candidates for state or federal office, but it actively seeks to propose, refine, and influence legislation. Positions taken by the League of Women Voters are directed by the consensus of its members nationwide.

Membership: 130,000 members.

Current Concerns: Campaign finance reform, civil liberties, voting rights in Washington, D.C., election reform, environment, reproductive choice, ethics and lobbying reform, and health care.

Mothers Against Drunk Driving (MADD)

511 East John Carpenter Freeway, Suite 700
Irving, TX 75062
Telephone: Toll-free: 800-GET-MADD (800-438-6233). Irving, TX: (214) 714-6233
Web site: www.madd.org

Information on Web site: Biographical information, programs, take action center, news, statistics and resources, and membership information.

Overview: Mothers Against Drunk Driving (MADD) is a 501(c)(3) nonprofit grassroots organization leading the fight against drunk driving and underage alcoholism. Its mission is to end drunk driving, support the victims of drunk driving, and prevent underage drinking. It accomplishes this mission by presenting an extensive advertising and public education campaign, advocating for more strict law enforcement, and lobbying the state and federal government for strengthened punishments for drunk driving and increased use of sobriety checkpoints.

Membership: 2 million members and supporters nationwide organized into 400 chapters.

Current Concerns: Free victim services, primary seat belt laws, youth access to alcohol, enforcement of sobriety checkpoints, and reducing alcohol related fatalities and injuries.

Motion Picture Association of America (MPAA)

1600 Eye Street NW
Washington, DC 20006

Telephone: (202) 283-1966
Web site: www.mpaa.org

Information on Web site: Biographical information, press releases, issues, research and statistics, internship opportunities, and film ratings.

Overview: The Motion Picture Association of America (MPAA) represents and advocates on behalf of the American motion picture, home video, and television industries. Its members include many of the world's largest motion picture studios, including such corporations as Paramount Pictures, Buena Vista Pictures Distribution, Twentieth Century Fox Film Corporation, NBC, Universal, and Warner Bros Entertainment. Through its PAC, the MPAA donated more than $100,000 to candidates who support creative freedom and tough penalties for copyright infringement. In addition to its political involvement, the MPAA is also responsible for rating motion pictures.

Membership: All major motion picture corporations.

Current Concerns: Copyright infringement, creative freedom, digital rights management, and technology.

MoveOn.org
Web site: www.moveon.org

Information on Web site: Biographical information, membership information, issue campaign information, and media.

Overview: The MoveOn group of organizations, comprising MoveOn.org Civic Action (formerly MoveOn.org) and MoveOn.org Political Action (a federal PAC), works to promote progressive politics throughout the country. MoveOn.org seeks to bring regular Americans into the political process by providing busy but civically minded Americans a voice in a political system that is largely dominated by large money and media interests. MoveOn.org spent more than $28 million during the 2006 election cycle on state and federal elections and independent expenditures.

Membership: More than 3.3 million members.

Current Concerns: Campaign finance, civic engagement and participation, environment, energy policy, Iraq war, and media ownership.

NARAL Pro-Choice America
1156 15th Street NW, Suite 700
Washington, DC 20005

Telephone: (202) 973-3096
Web site: www.naral.org

Information on Web site: Biographical information, issues, election information, federal and state legislation information, membership information, research, and publications.

Overview: NARAL Pro-Choice America (formerly known as the National Association for the Repeal of Abortion Laws) has been the nation's leading advocate for reproductive rights for more than 30 years. NARAL Pro-Choice America works to protect pro-choice values and the freedom of privacy through advocating for pro-choice policies before state legislatures and Congress. NARAL's advocacy activities include supporting the election of pro-choice candidates, organizing grassroots support, direct and indirect lobbying of Congress, and presenting pro-choice research. Through its PAC, NARAL donated $220,000 to federal candidates during the 2006 election cycle. NARAL also operates an affiliated foundation, the NARAL Pro-Choice America Foundation.

Membership: More than 1 million members.

Current Concerns: Abortion, birth control, sex education, and civil liberties.

**National Association for the Advancement of
Colored People (NAACP)**
4805 Mt. Hope Drive
Baltimore, MD 212215
Telephone: (410) 580-5777
Web site: www.naacp.org

Information on Web site: Biographical information, issues, news and media, upcoming events, legislative action center, youth action center, legal action center, and membership information.

Overview: The National Association for the Advancement of Colored People (NAACP) is the nation's oldest civil rights organization. Its mission is to ensure the political, educational, social, and economic equality of rights to all persons and to eliminate racial hatred and racial discrimination. It fulfills this mission through advocating for achieving equality of rights, removing barriers of racial discrimination, and educating individuals regarding their constitutional rights. Although the NAACP does not operate a PAC, it seeks to influence public policy and legal rulings through litigation, grassroots organizing, media outreach, research, and voter registration and mobilization.

Membership: 300,000 members in more than 1,700 branches.

Current Concerns: Affirmative action, hate crimes, human rights, and school-choice initiatives.

National Association of Broadcasters (NAB)
1771 N Street NW
Washington, DC 20036
Telephone: (202) 429-5300
Web site: www.nab.org

Information on Web site: Biographical information, information on events, NAB merchandise, news, and research.

Overview: The National Association of Broadcasters (NAB) is a trade association that represents television stations, broadcast networks, and radio stations. With more than 8,300 member associations represented in the United States, the NAB pursues action in Congress, before the courts, and with the Federal Communications Commission. The NAB also provides its members with frequent updates on technology innovations, management trends, broadcast news, and research. Through the NAB Television and Radio Political Action Committee (TARPAC), the NAB supports candidates that are sympathetic to broadcasting.

Membership: More than 8,300 radio and television stations and broadcasting networks.

Current Concerns: Daylight savings, emergency alert systems, tax policy, media ownership, retransmission consent, and satellite radio.

National Association of Evangelicals (NAE)
P.O. Box 23269
Washington, DC 20026
Telephone: (202) 789-1011
Web site: www.nae.net

Information on Web site: Biographical information, membership information, governmental affairs, and news and events.

Overview: The mission of the National Association of Evangelicals (NAE) is to extend the kingdom of God through a fellowship of member denominations, churches, organizations, and individuals, demonstrating the unity of the body of Christ by standing for biblical truth, speaking with a representative voice, and serving the evangelical community through united action, cooperative ministry, and strategic planning. The NAE's lobby arm is a strong force in state and national politics, defeating legislation regarding religious liberties and moral issues. As a large grassroots mobilizing organization, NAE sponsors conferences, seminars, and summits.

Membership: More than 30 million members and supporters.

Current Concerns: Abortion, capital punishment, education voucher programs, environment, faith-based initiatives, global HIV/AIDS, immigration, religious freedom, poverty, human rights, same-sex marriage, stem cell research, and underage drinking.

National Association of Home Builders (NAHB)
1201 15th Street NW
Washington, DC 20005
Telephone: (202) 266-8200
Web site: www.nahb.org

Information on Web site: Biographical information, news, meeting and event information, research and position papers, publications, NAHB merchandise.

Overview: The National Association of Home Builders (NAHB) is dedicated to providing a favorable legal and regulatory environment for housing and the building industry. Founded in 1942, the NAHB is a federation of more than 800 state and local associations. It boasts a large professional staff of more than 300 full-time employees. The NAHB actively represents the building industry's interests on Capitol Hill, before regulatory agencies, and in the courts. Through its PAC, BUILD-PAC, the NAHB donated $2.9 million to building industry–friendly candidates in the 2006 election cycle. In addition to its lobbying activities, the NAHB also provides its members and the public with forecasts on economic and consumer trends.

Membership: More than 800 state and local associations with 235,000 members.

Current Concerns: Fiscal policy, immigration, affordable housing, minimum wage, and economic development.

National Association of Manufacturers (NAM)
1331 Pennsylvania Avenue NW
Washington, DC 20004
Telephone: (202) 637-3000
Web site: www.nam.org

Information on Web site: Biographical information, data and statistics, news and media, blog, member services, issue information, and membership information.

Overview: Founded in Ohio in 1895, the National Association of Manufacturers (NAM) is dedicated to advocating on behalf of manufacturers in order to promote competitiveness and economic growth and to raise the awareness of policy makers regarding the important role of manufacturing in America's national security and economic well-being. NAM hopes to encourage government to preserve American global leadership in manufacturing through investing in technology, building critical infrastructure, and providing a friendly regulatory environment for manufacturers. In addition to shaping legislative policy, NAM also serves as a primary source of information about manufacturing and its contributions to the U.S. economy, innovation, and productivity.

Membership: More than 14,000 corporations and businesses and approximately 300 affiliated associations comprise NAM.

Current Concerns: Energy security, infrastructure, global competitiveness, tax policy, health care, and human resources policy.

National Association of Realtors (NAR)
430 North Michigan Avenue
Chicago, IL 60611
Telephone: (800) 874-6500
Web site: www.realtor.org

Information on Web site: Biographical information, realtor merchandise, news and media, statistics and research, meetings and events, and membership information.

Overview: The National Association of Realtors (NAR) is dedicated to helping its members be as profitable and successful as possible. Its influence on the real estate industry is strong, as it seeks to be the leading advocate of the right to own, use, and transfer property and is a powerful supporter of free enterprise. Through its PAC, RPAC (Realtors PAC), NAR raises funds and contributes to real estate–friendly candidates and officeholders. During the 2006 election cycle, RPAC and its affiliated PACs donated more than $3.7 million in contributions, more than any other organization. In addition to campaign contributions, the NAR also seeks to influence policy through direct contact with Congress, the executive branch, and before the courts.

Membership: More than 1.3 million members.

Current Concerns: Affordable housing, consumer protection, health care, insurance policies and regulation, tax policy, and predatory lending practices.

National Cable and Telecommunications Association (NCTA)
25 Massachusetts Avenue NW, Suite 100
Washington, DC 20001
Telephone: (202) 222-2300
Web site: www.ncta.com

Information on Web site: Biographical information, media center, research and statistics, upcoming events, issues of interest, and membership information.

Overview: The National Cable and Telecommunications Association (NCTA) is the preeminent trade association representing the cable industry in the United States. It seeks to provide a unified voice to cable operators who provide 90 percent of the nation's cable television programming, equipment suppliers, and providers of services to the cable industry. The NCTA's annual trade show serves as the national showcase for innovative services such as Internet service, interactive television programming, and local telephone service. Through its PAC, the NCTA contributed more than $1.7 million to cable industry–friendly candidates during the 2006 cycle.

Membership: Not available.

Current concerns: Broadband Internet access, cable ownership regulations, copyright infringement, multicasting must carry, net neutrality, and technological innovation.

National Council of La Raza (NCLR)
1126 16th Street NW
Washington, DC 20036
Telephone: (202) 785-1670
Web site: www.nclr.org

Information on Web site: Biographical information, issues, publications, event information, and membership information.

Overview: The National Council of La Raza (NCLR) is the nation's largest national Hispanic civil rights organization and strives to improve opportunities for Hispanic Americans. Founded in 1968, NCLR is a private nonprofit and nonpartisan organization that provides policy makers and the public with a Latino perspective in five key issue areas: assets/investments, civil rights and immigration, education, employment and economic status, and health. NCLR's services include after-school programs, job training, English language courses, health centers, and homeownership counseling.

Membership: More than 300 affiliated community-based organizations.

Current Concerns: Electoral empowerment, employment and economic opportunities, civil rights and liberties, community and family wealth building, immigration, and education.

National Education Association (NEA)
1201 16th Street NW
Washington, DC 20036
Telephone: (202) 833-4000
Web site: www.nea.org

Information on Web site: Membership information, biographical information, state affiliates, current issues and events, press center, bookstore, and legislative action center.

Overview: The National Education Association (NEA) is the nation's largest professional employee organization and is dedicated to supporting public education. As a volunteer-based organization, NEA is supported by affiliates in all 50 states and the District of Columbia. The NEA lobbies Congress and federal agencies on behalf of public schools, raises funds for scholarship programs, conducts professional workshops, and collectively bargains for school employees. State affiliates are active in lobbying their respective state legislatures for continuing and increased support of public education.

Membership: 3.2 million members and more than 14,000 NEA local affiliate organizations.

Current Concerns: No Child Left Behind, achievement gaps, professional pay, special education, class-size reduction, early childhood education, school funding, school and teacher quality, and vouchers.

National Federation of Independent Business (NFIB)
53 Century Boulevard, Suite 250
Nashville, TN 37214
Telephone: (800) 634-2669
Web site: www.nfib.com

Information on Web site: Biographical information, issues of interest, news and media, membership information, and research.

Overview: Founded in 1943, the National Federation of Independent Business (NFIB) is the leading advocate representing small and independent businesses. NFIB's mission is to promote and protect the rights of business owners to operate and grow their businesses and maximize profitability. The NFIB also provides resources to its members by pooling the purchasing power of its individual members in order to provide products and services and discounted prices. Through the NFIB SAFE Trust PAC, the NFIB donated more than $3.2 million to 2,282 candidates for state and federal offices. In addition to its contributions, the NFIB also distributed voter education information supporting small business–friendly candidates.

Membership: 600,000 small business owners in all 50 states.

Current Concerns: Competition, regulatory reform, health care, immigration, labor issues, Social Security, tax policy, and technological innovation.

National Organization for Women (NOW)
1100 H Street NW, 3rd Floor
Washington, DC 20005
Telephone: (202) 628-8669
Web site: www.now.org

Information on Web site: Biographical information, action center, issues, chapter information, merchandise, research, and membership information.

Overview: The National Organization for Women (NOW) is the largest organization of feminist activists in the nation. Since its founding in 1966, NOW has led on issues of equality for women—working to eliminate discrimination and harassment in the workplace, schools, the justice system, and other sectors of society. NOW also seeks to secure and protect abortion, birth control, and reproductive rights for all women and end all forms of violence against women. Through NOW PAC, the organization donated more than $94,000 to federal candidates in the 2006 election cycle.

Membership: More than 500,000 members in 550 chapters in all 50 states.

Current Concerns: Employment discrimination, racial discrimination, same-sex marriage, domestic violence, affirmative action, and reproductive rights.

National Parent-Teacher Association (NPTA)
541 North Fairbanks Court, Suite 1300
Chicago, IL 60611
Telephone: (312) 670-6782
Web site: www.pta.org

Information on Web site: Biographical information, local PTA information, parent resources, issues and action alerts, leadership resources, and membership information.

Overview: The National Parent-Teacher Association (NPTA) is dedicated to advocating on behalf of children and youth in public schools before local, state, and federal governments. The NPTA helps develop public school policies and funding programs on the state and national levels and seeks to promote the school-home relationship to facilitate cooperation among educators and parents. Local PTAs serve as a forum where parents, teachers, administrators, and other concerned adults discuss ways to promote quality education, strive to expand the arts, encourage community involvement, and work for a healthy environment and safe neighborhoods.

Membership: 6.5 million members in 26,000 local chapters in all 50 states, the District of Columbia, the U.S. Virgin Islands, and the Department of Defense schools in the Pacific and Europe.

Current Concerns: Parental involvement in education, safe and nurturing school environments, special education, student achievement, and support for public education.

National Rifle Association of America (NRA)
11250 Waples Mill Road
Fairfax, VA 22030
Telephone: (703) 267-1000
Web site: www.nra.org

Information on Web site: Biographical information, news and media, membership, legislation alerts, merchandise, podcast, videocast, publications, programs, and membership information.

Overview: The National Rifle Association of America (NRA) is the nation's largest and foremost advocate of Second Amendment rights. The NRA also seeks to promote public safety, law and order, and the national defense and to train members of law enforcement agencies, the military, and militias and citizens in marksmanship and the safe handling of firearms. Recognizing the need to engage in direct lobbying activities, in 1975, the NRA established the Institute for Legislative Action as the lobbying arm of the NRA. In 1993, the NRA established the NRA Foundation, a 501(c)(3) tax-exempt organization that raises money to fund gun safety programs. Through its PAC, National Rifle Association of America Political Victory Fund, the NRA donated more than $947,000 to federal candidates in the 2006 election cycle.

Membership: More than 4 million members.

Current Concerns: Gun ownership rights, hunting restrictions, sportsman's issues, and wilderness and park hunting.

National Right to Life Committee (NRLC)
512 10th Street NW
Washington, DC 20004
Telephone: (202) 626-8800
Web site: www.nrlc.org

Information on Web site: Biographical information, issues, event information, legislation tracker, and membership information.

Overview: Founded in 1973 in response to the U.S. Supreme Court's decision in *Roe v. Wade*, the National Right to Life Committee (NRLC) is a nonsectarian, nonpartisan organization dedicated to restoring legal protection for unborn life. The NRLC has been successful in achieving reforms at the national level, including limiting the funding used for abortions and banning therapeutic experimentation on unborn and newborn babies. In addition to maintaining a lobbying presence at the federal level, NRLC serves as a clearinghouse of information for its state affiliates and local chapters, its individual members, the press, and the public. NRLC publishes a monthly newsletter, the *National Right to Life News,* and through the National Right to Life PAC spent more than $3 million on contributions and independent expenditures during the 2006 election cycle.

Membership: 3,000 chapters in all 50 states and the District of Columbia.

Current Concerns: Abortion, assisted suicide, euthanasia, RU-486, and Medicare.

National Taxpayers Union (NTU)
108 North Alfred Street
Alexandria, VA 22314
Telephone: (703) 683-5700
Web site: www.ntu.org

Information on Web site: Biographical information, blog, merchandise, media and news, research, issues of interest, and ratings of current elected officials.

Overview: Founded in 1969, the National Taxpayers Union (NTU) is the largest taxpayer organization, representing more than 360,000 individuals in all 50 states. The mission of the NTU is to educate taxpayers, elected officials, and the media about the importance of limited government and low taxes. To accomplish this mission the NTU uses various means, including mail, research, advertising, and lobbying. NTU is also affiliated with the National Taxpayer Union Foundation (NTUF), which produces research on economics, tax policy, and government spending. NTU does not make many donations to candidates. Through its PAC, the National Taxpayers Union Campaign Fund, NTU donated only $1,035 to candidates in the 2006 cycle.

Membership: 362,000 members in all 50 states.

Current Concerns: Alternative Minimum Tax reform, balanced budget amendment, earmarking reform, entitlement reform, Internet taxation, litigation reform, making the 2001 and 2003 federal tax relief laws permanent, congressional pay and benefits, and adoption of the consumption tax.

National Wildlife Federation (NWF)
11100 Wildlife Center Drive
Reston, VA 20190
Telephone: Toll-free: (800) 822-9919. Reston, VA: (703) 438-6000
Web site: www.nwf.org

Information on Web site: Biographical information, blogs, issue information, publications, merchandise, and membership information.

Overview: The National Wildlife Federation (NWF) serves as the champion of all varieties of wildlife and guides efforts to place wildlife refuges and endangered species. The NWF seeks to build consensus-based solutions for wildlife, going to the courts when necessary. The NWF advocates before Congress, regulatory agencies, the courts, the White House, and state and local governments throughout the nation and beyond. The organization also seeks to combat the threats posed by global warming and the environmental impact of human living and development. The NWF accomplishes its mission through advocacy, public and media education campaigns, and litigation.

Membership: More than 4 million members worldwide.

Current Concerns: Arctic National Wildlife Refuge, biodiversity, clean water, conservation, endangered species, pollution, public land policies, wetlands, and wildlife preservation.

Natural Resources Defense Council (NRDC)
40 West 20th Street
New York, NY 10011
Telephone: (212) 727-2700
Web site: www.nrdc.org

Information on Web site: Biographical information, conservation guides, issues, news, multimedia, policy proposals, and membership information.

Overview: The Natural Resources Defense Council (NRDC) is the nation's most effective environmental action organization. The mission of the NRDC is to safeguard the Earth, its people, its plants and animals, and the natural systems on which all life depends. NRDC uses the law, science, and its large grassroots membership base to advocate for the protection of wildlife and to ensure that our future generations have safe and healthy places to live. Its advertising campaigns, publications, media outreach, and Web site serve as public education tools that seek to promote conservation and wildlife protection.

Membership: More than 1.2 million members.

Current Concerns: Clean air, energy, clean water and oceans, global warming, nuclear weapons, parks, forests, wetlands, and wildlife.

People for the American Way (PFAW)
2000 M Street NW, Suite 400
Washington, DC 20036
Telephone: (202) 467-4999
Web site: www.pfaw.org

Information on Web site: Biographical information, membership information, legislative action center, news and media, publications, and reports.

Overview: People for the American Way (PFAW) serves as an advocate for the values and institutions that sustain a diverse democratic society. It seeks to counter the influence of the radical right in order to guard fundamental constitutional guarantees and freedoms. It accomplishes this mission through grassroots mobilization, education campaigns, monitoring the activities of radical right organizations, litigation, and coalition forming. Through the People for the American Way Voters Alliance PAC, PFAW donated more than $82,000 to federal candidates during the 2006 election cycle. Through the People for the American Way Foundation, a 501(c)(3) organization, PFAW provides research and publications to policy makers, scholars, the media, and the public.

Membership: More than 900,000 members.

Current Concerns: Artistic freedom, censorship, judicial nominations, civil rights, civic participation, public education, religious freedom, and voting rights.

People for the Ethical Treatment of Animals (PETA)
501 Front Street
Norfolk, VA 23510
Telephone: (757) 622-7382
Web site: www.peta.org

Information on Web site: Action alerts, biographical information, blog, lifestyle guide, media center, merchandise, and membership information.

Overview: People for the Ethical Treatment of Animals (PETA) is the largest animal rights organization in the world, and it seeks to end animal abuse of every kind. PETA focuses its attention on the four areas in which it believes the most animal abuse takes place: on factory farms, in laboratories, in the clothing trade, and in the entertainment industry. PETA works through public education, cruelty investigations, research, animal rescue, legislation, events, and protest campaigns. PETA is known for coordinating celebrity public education campaigns and high-visibility public demonstrations.

Membership: 1.6 million members.

Current Concerns: Animal testing, animal abuse, entertainment animals (rodeos and circuses), cruelty-free consumer products, hunting and fishing, trapping, ranching, leather trade, and vegetarianism.

Pharmaceutical Research and Manufacturers of America (PhRMA)
950 F Street, NW, Suite 300
Washington, DC 20004

Telephone: (202) 835-3400
Web site: www.phrma.org

Information on Web site: Biographical information, issues of interest, publications, media and news, medicines in development, and information about patient assistance programs.

Overview: The Pharmaceutical Research and Manufacturers of America (PhRMA) advocates on behalf of the nation's top pharmaceutical and biotechnology companies. In 2006, its members invested an estimated $43 billion in the research and development of new medicines. The mission of PhRMA is to advocate for policies that stimulate and encourage the discovery of new medicines and treatments by pharmaceutical and biotechnology companies. Its members include companies such as AstraZeneca, Bristol-Myers Squibb, GlaxoSmithKline, Johnson & Johnson, Eli Lilly, Merck, and Pfizer. Through its PAC, the PhRMA Better Government Committee, PhRMA contributed more than $165,000 to candidates friendly to pharmaceuticals and biotechnology in the 2006 election cycle.

Membership: More than 80 of the nation's leading pharmaceutical and biotechnology companies and research firms.

Current Concerns: Patient access to health care, price controls, intellectual property protection and incentives, medicine importation, U.S. Food and Drug Administration regulatory policies and practices, research and development, direct-to-consumer advertising, and prescription drug costs.

Planned Parenthood Federation of America (PPFA)
434 West 33rd Street
New York, NY 10001
Telephone: (212) 541-7800
Web site: www.plannedparenthood.org

Information on Web site: Birth control and pregnancy information, sexual health information, membership information, news and media, research and publications, and biographical information.

Overview: Planned Parenthood Federation of America (PPFA) was established in 1916 as the nation's first birth control clinic. PPFA believes in the fundamental right of each individual, throughout the world, to manage his or her fertility, regardless of the individual's income, marital status, race, ethnicity, sexual orientation, age, national origin, or residence. PPFA advocates for reproductive and abortion rights and provides reproductive health care and information to millions of Americans each year. PPFA believes women should have the power to control their destinies by being able to decide when to begin and terminate pregnancies. The organization also operates a PAC, Planned Parenthood Action Fund, through which it donated more than $150,000 to federal candidates during the 2006 election cycle.

Membership: An estimated 3 million supporters in more than 120 affiliates. PPFA also operated 860 clinic sites.

Current Concerns: Abortion, censorship, First Amendment rights, early pregnancy detection, family planning, patients' rights, reproductive freedom, sex education, and women's rights.

Public Citizen
1600 20th Street NW
Washington, DC 20009
Telephone: (202) 588-1000
Web site: www.citizen.org

Information on Web site: Biographical information, action alerts, press room, publications and research, and membership information.

Overview: Public Citizen is a national nonprofit consumer advocacy organization founded in 1971 by Ralph Nader. Public Citizen fights for openness and democratic accountability in government; the right of consumers to seek redress in the courts; clean, safe, and sustainable energy sources; social and economic justice in trade policies; strong health, safety, and environmental protections; and safe, effective, and affordable prescription drugs and health care. Public Citizen is operated largely through grassroots organizing, testifying before Congress, and conducting public education programs.

Membership: 100,000 members.

Current Concerns: Auto safety, congressional process, energy, global trade, health care, corporate accountability, freedom of information, consumer product safety, product liability, and occupational health.

The Rutherford Institute
P.O. Box 7482
Charlottesville, VA 22906
Telephone: (434) 978-3888
Web site: www.rutherford.org

Information on Web site: Biographical information, publications, merchandise, issue information, membership information, legal resources, news and media, and a video blog.

Overview: The Rutherford Institute is a civil liberties organization that provides free legal services to individuals whose constitutional rights have been threatened and/or violated. The Rutherford Institute also engages in public education campaigns on civil liberties and human rights, operates a toll-free hotline for those seeking legal advice or assistance, and has offices in Bolivia and Hungary. The Rutherford Institute seeks to influence state and federal policies through direct contact with Congress and state legislatures, litigation, conducting and publishing research, and mobilizing grassroots support.

Membership: Approximately 600 volunteer affiliate attorneys.

Current Concerns: Religious freedom, civil liberties, sanctity of life, free speech, parental rights, privacy rights, sexual harassment, unreasonable search and seizure, and zero tolerance policies.

Sierra Club
85 Second Street, 2nd Floor
San Francisco, CA 94105
Telephone: (415) 977-5500
Web site: www.sierraclub.org

Information on Web site: Environmental updates, membership information, press room, issue information, merchandise, research and publications, and biographical information.

Overview: The Sierra Club is dedicated to protecting America's natural beauty and wild legacy through enjoying and protecting the undisturbed places of the earth. It advocates for the responsible use of the earth's ecosystems and resources and seeks to educate the public regarding environmental protection and restoration. The Sierra Club also serves as a clearinghouse of research and information about conservation, environmentally clean living, and energy policy. The Sierra Club Foundation provides financial support to other environmental organizations and funds litigation, public education, and activist training. Through its PAC, the Sierra Club Political Committee, the Sierra Club gave more than $1 million to federal and state candidates and independent expenditures during the 2006 election cycle.

Membership: More than 1.3 million members and supporters.

Current Concerns: Global population, global warming, human rights and the environment, responsible trade, energy policy and solutions.

U.S. Chamber of Commerce
1615 H Street NW
Washington, DC 20062
Telephone: (202) 659-6000
Web site: www.uschamber.com

Information on Web site: Biographical information, media, membership information, issues of interest, publications, and event information.

Overview: The U.S. Chamber of Commerce is the world's largest association representing businesses, associations, and local chambers. The chamber is charged with advocating on behalf of business and free enterprise before government and to persuade public opinion to support free market policies. With a professional staff of more than 300 policy experts, lobbyists, lawyers, and communication strategists, the chamber is able to influence government and regulatory agency policies through direct contact with elected officials and regulatory bodies and indirect grassroots lobbying strategies. Through the U.S. Chamber of Commerce PAC (NCAP), the chamber donated $235,233 in the 2006 election cycle to federal and state candidates.

Membership: More than 3 million businesses, 800 business associations, and 100 local chambers in 91 countries.

Current Concerns: Health care, education, labor law reform, energy policy, immigration, transportation, telecommunications, infrastructure, economic development, tax policy, and biotechnology.

8

Selected Print and Nonprint Resources

This chapter provides an extensive list of books, journals, periodicals, and Web sites on interest groups, campaign finance, and lobbying. They range from the fundamental texts that established the academic field of interest group politics to Web sites that track the latest campaign finance regulations and trends to documentaries that look at current political and interest group developments. The chapter first presents the most influential books and journal articles in the field and then provides a listing of the primary academic journals, periodicals and major newspapers, Web sites, and films that cover interest group politics. The sources can be divided into several basic categories: those that examine interest group formation and membership; those that seek to quantify the power and influence interest groups wield in the lawmaking process; those that feature the lobbying profession, including how-to guides on becoming effective advocates; those that discuss the role of money in politics, including campaign finance regulations; and those that discuss the role of the media and public relations campaigns in lawmaking and elections. Each work or source that follows is accompanied by a short description of its relevance to interest group studies. Many of the sources below can be found in a well-equipped university library or are available on the Internet.

Print Resources

Books

Comprehensive Textbooks

Cigler, Allan J., and Burdett A. Loomis. 2006. *Interest Group Politics.* 7th ed. Washington, DC: Congressional Quarterly Press. 484 pages. ISBN 1933116765.

A core university textbook, *Interest Group Politics* presents a broad view of the history of interest groups as well as the effects of money, technology, and advertising on the activities interest groups engage in and the way they operate. Cigler and Loomis highlight how specific groups such as the National Rifle Association rose to power and influence in American politics and predict future trends such as the increased use of 527 and religious organizations to evade campaign contribution limits and influence election outcomes.

Gray, Virginia, and Russell L. Hanson. 2008. *Politics in the American States: A Comparative Analysis.* 9th ed. Washington, DC: CQ Press. 473 pages. ISBN 0872893421.

Politics in the American States combines excellent interest group research and a comprehensive guide to the 50 American states that touches on intergovernmental relations, elections, and the legislative process. Designed for comparative analyses between the states, the book summarizes key state issue areas such as education, law enforcement, and taxes and discusses the roles played by various interest groups in shaping these policies.

Hrebenar, Ronald J. 1997. *Interest Group Politics in America.* 3rd ed. Armonk, NY: M. E. Sharpe. 398 pages. ISBN 1563247038.

This classic university textbook presents interest group theories and data in a concise and readable manner. The book begins with a presentation of interest group formation, leadership theories, and lobbying strategies and tactics and continues on to present the interactions of interest groups with the government as well as with other interest groups. It documents the rise of the public interest groups and recent trends in lobbying before the judicial and executive branches.

Hrebenar, Ronald J., Robert C. Benedict Jr., and Matthew J. Burbank. 1999. *Political Parties, Interest Groups, and Political Campaigns.* Boulder, CO: Westview Press. 322 pages. ISBN 0813380081.

This book presents the current characteristics and the history of political parties, election campaigns, and interest groups. Rather than operating in isolated arenas, the book argues that campaigns serve as the uniting arena for political parties and interest groups, which are becoming increasingly intertwined.

Hrebenar, Ronald J., and Clive S. Thomas. 1987. *Interest Group Politics in the American West.* Salt Lake City: University of Utah Press. 157 pages. ISBN 0874802628.

Hrebenar, Ronald J., and Clive S. Thomas. 1992. *Interest Group Politics in the Southern States.* Tuscaloosa: University of Alabama Press. 432 pages. ISBN 0817305688.

Hrebenar, Ronald J., and Clive S. Thomas. 1993. *Interest Group Politics in the Midwestern States.* Ames: Iowa State University Press. 382 pages. ISBN 0813813840.

Hrebenar, Ronald J., and Clive S. Thomas. 2004. *Interest Group Politics in the Northeastern States.* University Park: Pennsylvania State University Press. 420 pages. ISBN 027102576X.

In this series, Hrebenar and Thomas present an in-depth look at regions of the United States, examining legislative and lobbying trends as well as the lobby registration and disclosure laws, campaign finance regulations, and campaign contribution trends in each state. This series is the most comprehensive attempt at presenting American states as unique arenas of interest group operations. *Interest Group Politics in the American West* covers Montana, Wyoming, Colorado, New Mexico, Arizona, Utah, Idaho, Washington, Oregon, Nevada, and California. *Interest Group Politics in the Southern States* covers Texas, Oklahoma, Arkansas, Louisiana, Mississippi, Tennessee, Kentucky, Virginia, North Carolina, South Carolina, Alabama, Georgia, and Florida. *Interest Group Politics in the Midwestern States* covers Illinois, Indiana, Iowa, Kansas, Michigan, Minnesota, Missouri, Ohio, Nebraska, North Dakota, South Dakota, and Wisconsin. *Interest Group Politics in the Northeastern*

States covers West Virginia, Washington, D.C., Maryland, Delaware, New Jersey, Pennsylvania, New York, Connecticut, Rhode Island, Massachusetts, Vermont, New Hampshire, and Maine.

Lowery, David, and Holly Brasher. 2004. *Organized Interests and American Politics.* **New York: McGraw-Hill. 320 pages. ISBN 007246786X.**

Organized Interests provides an overview of why and how interest groups form and how they influence government policy making at the local, state, and national levels. The content is presented within the context of the pluralist, transaction, and neopluralist schools of thought and is presented at an understandable college/high school level.

Nownes, Anthony J. 2000. *Pressure and Power: Organized Interests in American Politics.* **Boston: Houghton Mifflin. 288 pages. ISBN 039595150X.**

A standard entry-level interest group textbook, *Pressure and Power* offers a background of interest group theory as well as explanations of how interest groups form, recruit members, and influence legislation. Its 10 chapters touch on the evolution of interest groups in the United States, direct and indirect lobbying, how campaigns are influenced, and how interest groups form coalitions with other like-minded interests.

Thomas, Clive S. 2004. *Research Guide to U.S. and International Interest Groups.* **Westport, CT: Praeger Publishers. 544 pages. ISBN 0313295433.**

With more than 70 contributors, this work serves as a guide to studying and researching interest groups and their operations at the local, state, national, and international levels. This is a great resource for graduate and undergraduate students seeking a comprehensive guide to the field of interest group politics.

Interest Group Formation and Membership

Barone, Michael, and Richard E. Cohen. 2007. *The Almanac of American Politics, 2008.* **Washington, DC: National Journal Group. 1,850 pages. ISBN 0892341173.**

The Almanac of American Politics is published every two years and provides a brief biography of each member of Congress that includes a district profile, committee assignments, voting record, and ratings from key interest groups whose voting scorecards rate the members on their favorability to their organization's views. A popular quick reference guide to Congress, the *Almanac* allows readers to quickly gather biographical and political information.

Berry, Jeffrey M. 1997. *The Interest Group Society*. 3rd ed. New York: Longman. 267 pages. ISBN 0673525112.

A popular choice as a core text on interest groups, *The Interest Group Society* begins with a discussion of Madisonian notions of factions and pluralism and continues on to a discussion of the formation and proliferation of groups, lobbying and lobbyists, political parties, influencing public opinion, grassroots advocacy, and campaign finance laws. Berry goes into great detail in documenting the various forms of interest groups that operate in the United States—from farm and labor organizations to good government watchdog groups. Berry concludes with an examination of the corporate bias of the interest group system.

Berry, Jeffrey M., and David F. Arons. 2005. *A Voice for Non-profits*. New ed. Washington, DC: Brookings Institution Press. 210 pages. ISBN 0815708777.

A recipient of the American Political Science Association's Leon Epstein Award for its outstanding contribution to research and scholarship, *A Voice for Nonprofits* argues that nonprofits are playing an increasing role in delivering government services despite prohibitions on their participation in lobbying efforts. Berry and Arons argue that these restrictions should be eased so that the populations nonprofits serve are better represented before Congress and federal agencies.

Burns, Nancy, Kay Lehman Schlozman, and Sidney Verba. 2001. *The Private Roots of Public Action: Gender, Equality and Political Participation*. Cambridge, MA: Harvard University Press. 480 pages. ISBN 0674006607.

Several generations have passed since women gained the right to vote, yet men still dominate the world of politics and are more likely to be politically active. This book examines the gender differences in civic engagement—from the domestic demands on women's time to socioeconomic hierarchies and institutionalized barriers that complicate and deter women from entering into an active civic life. Burns, Schlozman, and Verba pull from economics and sociology to shed light on women's ability and willingness to engage in democratic politics.

CQ Press. 2006. *Public Interest Group Profiles: 2006–2007*. 12th ed. Washington, DC: CQ Press. 783 pages. ISBN 0872893448.

Public Interest Group Profiles provides a one- to four-page profile for dozens of major American public interest groups. Each profile includes biographical information as well as assessments of group effectiveness, lobbying tactics, issues of importance to the organization, leadership structure and profiles, funding sources, membership statistics, and political contribution figures. It also features information on the organization's history, publications, internship opportunities, and effectiveness. This work is an excellent reference for those seeking the ability to quickly gather core information on a variety of public interest groups.

Dahl, Robert A. 2005. *Who Governs?* 2nd ed. New Haven, CT: Yale University Press. 384 pages. ISBN 0300103921.

Originally published in 1961, *Who Governs?* countered claims by scholars that American government was dominated by elites. Rather, Dahl uses an analysis of the government of New Haven, Connecticut, to demonstrate that continuously changing and shifting groups and governmental structures aggregate, disaggregate, and reaggregate to form governing coalitions. Dahl's theory became known as "pluralism."

Garson, G. David. 1978. *Group Theories of Politics*. Beverly Hills, CA: Sage Publications. 216 pages. ISBN 080390519X.

Garson provides a historical analysis of interest group theories—categorizing the literature and determining that the existing group theory is flawed, anachronistic, and on a "process of disintegration." Garson then concludes that America is neither a participatory democracy nor a political-economic elite, but an elitist political economy.

Gray, Virginia, and David Lowery. 2000. *The Population Ecology of Interest Representation: Lobbying Communities in the American States.* **Ann Arbor: University of Michigan Press. 320 pages. ISBN 0472087185.**

Borrowing from techniques used by organizational ecologists, Gray and Lowery examine lobbying communities with the premise that environmental forces confronting these organizations directly shape group formation and activities. The book catalogues the interest group population and offers explanations for group variation and diversity, concluding that the current interest group environment is highly constraining to group formation.

Lowi, Theodore J. 1979. *The End of Liberalism: The Second Republic of the United States.* **2nd ed. New York: W. W. Norton and Company. 331 pages. ISBN 0393090000.**

Lowi offers a brief history of American public policy to argue that Congress has increasingly given the executive branch and its agencies broad yet ill-defined policy-making powers and that this threatens to undermine the separation of powers, which is fundamental to American democracy. According to Lowi, this development has resulted in increased interest group activity before the executive branch. He recommends that Congress pass narrower and more specific legislation in the future, which would leave the executive branch with little room to implement policies that are not intended by Congress.

McFarland, Andrew S. 2004. *Neopluralism: The Evolution of Political Process Theory.* **Lawrence: University Press of Kansas. 208 pages. ISBN 0700613099.**

Neopluralism is McFarland's attempt to respond to growing criticisms of pluralist theory and offer a reexamination of pluralism given recent theoretical developments. By answering the three basic questions of who holds power, how interest groups function, and how policy is made, McFarland defends pluralism's underlying assumptions and offers suggestions for refining the theory.

Olson, Mancur. 1971. *The Logic of Collective Action: Public Goods and the Theory of Groups.* **Cambridge, MA: Harvard University Press. 186 pages. ISBN 0674537513.**

Olson, a renowned American economist, was one of the first scholars to apply economic analysis to political behavior. Specifically, in his highly influential *The Logic of Collective Action*, Olson theorizes that organizations largely produce "public goods" that are beneficial to the organization's members and to nonmembers alike. Because an individual can gain the same benefits whether or not he or she chooses to participate in the collective action leads the individual to abstain, or become a "free-rider." To overcome this collective action dilemma, groups must provide "selective" incentives or "private goods" that are only available to group participants.

Petracca, Mark P. 1992. *The Politics of Interests*. Boulder, CO: Westview Press. 448 pages. ISBN 0813310016.

This book includes 16 essays from the leading interest group scholars and practitioners that document the most recent developments in interest group activities. The essays cover such topics as theories of interest group representation, American interest groups from a comparative perspective, interest group membership and organization, business interests, consumer advocacy groups, and the influence of money and technology on interest group strategies and tactics. Differing perspectives offer the reader an insider's view of the debate over interest group formation and their effectiveness in influencing the legislative process.

Putnam, Robert D. 2000. *Bowling Alone: The Collapse and Revival of American Community*. New York: Touchstone. 544 pages. ISBN 0743203046.

This highly acclaimed and widely read work argues that civil society in America is disintegrating as individuals become increasingly disconnected from the people around them and from the communities within which they live. Putnam points out that whereas in the past people formed bowling leagues, they are now more likely to bowl by themselves. Putnam argues that among the factors contributing to this breakdown in society are suburban sprawl, two-career families, technology, and changes in generational values. The book also contains a large amount of data on participation rates to back up his claims.

Rothenberg, Lawrence S. 1992. *Linking Citizens to Government Interest Group Politics at Common Cause*. New York: Cambridge University Press. 324 pages. ISBN 0521425778.

Linking Citizens provides an inside look at one of the nation's most powerful public interest groups—Common Cause. The work examines the motivations behind group members and the relationship between the membership and leadership and sheds light on the organization's lobbying agenda and role in key legislative battles.

Salisbury, Robert H. 1992. *Interests and Institutions: Substance and Structure in American Politics.* **Pittsburgh, PA: University of Pittsburgh Press. 384 pages. ISBN 0822937247.**

Salisbury presents the case for a return to examining the internal organization of institutions and how their structure affects policy decisions. *Interests and Institutions* also presents a collection of essays on the role of interest groups in American politics from leading scholars in the interest group field of study.

Schattschneider, E. E. 1960. *The Semisovereign People: A Realist's View of Democracy in America.* **New York: The Dryden Press. 160 pages. ISBN 0030106400**

The Semisovereign People describes American politics as a system dominated by powerful groups and individuals. This theory has become known as "elitism." Schattschneider presents interest groups as having undemocratic organizational structures or an "upper-class bias" and suggests that the sovereign but oppressed majority needs to balance pressure group dominance by participating in powerful political parties.

Schlozman, Kay Lehman, and John T. Tierney. 1986. *Organized Interests and American Democracy.* **Glenview, IL: HarperCollins College Division. 464 pages. ISBN 0060457929.**

Organized Interests presents the findings of 175 interviews with key members of organized interest groups, labor unions, trade associations, and corporations. The interviews reveal the makeup of the interest group universe in the United States as well as the strategies and tactics they employ. One central finding of their research is that the number of groups operating in Washington, D.C., has burgeoned, yet rather than representing new interests, these new groups are "more of the same."

Thomas, Clive S. 2001. *Political Parties and Interest Groups: Shaping Democratic Governance.* **Boulder, CO: Lynne Rienner Publishers. 353 pages. ISBN 1555879780.**

With the importance of the role interest groups play in political parties firmly established, this ambitious work examines this relationship in depth in 13 countries: Britain, France, Sweden, the United States, Germany, Italy, Israel, Japan, Spain, the Czech Republic, Poland, Argentina, and Mexico.

Tocqueville, Alexis de. *Democracy in America.* **2001. New York: Signet Classics. 320 pages. ISBN 0451528123.**

French aristocrat Alexis de Tocqueville's travels throughout the United States in the early 1830s document the remarkable ability of Americans to organize into political associations. Among other observations, de Tocqueville noted that "In the United States associations are established to promote the public safety, commerce, industry, morality, and religion. There is no end that the human will despairs of attaining through the combined power of individuals united into a society."

Truman, David B. 1951. *The Governmental Process: Political Interests and Public Opinion.* **New York: Alfred A. Knopf. 562 pages.**

The Governmental Process established the credibility of interest group theory. In it Truman offers a comprehensive definition of an interest group, describes the conditions under which groups emerge, conducts a comprehensive group-based analysis of American politics, and argues that groups should be viewed as serving an important and laudable role in American democracy.

Verba, Sidney, and Norman H. Nie. 1987. *Participation in America: Political Democracy and Social Equality.* **Chicago: University of Chicago Press. 452 pages. ISBN 0226852962.**

This presentation of a large study of citizen participation in politics seeks to answer the questions of who participates in politics, how, and with what level of success. *Participation in America* divides political participation into four categories: community activity, voting, campaigning, and direct contact with lawmakers and assesses the frequency of political participation across socioeconomic status.

Verba, Sidney, Kay Lehman Schlozman, and Henry Brady. 2006. *Voice and Equality: Civic Voluntarism and American Politics.* Cambridge, MA: Harvard University Press. 664 pages. ISBN 0674942930.

Arguing that American democracy is based on a strong ethic of civic voluntarism, this book seeks to analyze civic engagement in the United States. A survey of 15,000 individuals and 2,500 interviews reveal that civic activism moves within families from one generation to the next and varies greatly along cultural lines.

Walker, Jack L. 1991. *Mobilizing Interest Groups in America.* Ann Arbor: University of Michigan Press. 247 pages. ISBN 0472102761.

This work presents the findings of Walker's 15-year study of the organization of American interest groups and their lobbying strategies and tactics. Surveys conducted in 1980 and 1985 of more than 2,900 groups reveal that there is a surprisingly small number of groups representing the poor and weak of society. His study also reveals that some groups have reached positions of incredible power and influence in Washington, D.C., while others have not.

Wilson, James Q. 1975. *Political Organizations.* New York: Basic Books. 359 pages. ISBN 0465059368.

In this classic interest group text, Wilson argues that economic self-interest is only one of several factors leading to individual participation in interest group activities. In addition to quantifiable material benefits given to group members, Wilson adds that "purposive" and "solidary" benefits also influence individuals to join and participate in groups.

Interest Group Power and Influence

Ainsworth, Scott H. 2002. *Analyzing Interest Groups: Group Influence on People and Policies.* New York: W. W. Norton. 260 pages. ISBN 0393977080.

Analyzing Interest Groups presents interest group theories beginning with institutionalism and proceeding to pluralism and entrepreneurialism. Ainsworth also succeeds in offering a broad yet detailed look at the various venues within which interest groups operate—from the executive, legislative, and judicial branches of government to political and grassroots issue campaigns. The book provides a summary of the history of money in elections as well as a review of campaign finance laws and trends of the 2000 presidential election.

Baumgartner, Frank, and Beth L. Leech. 1998. *Basic Interests: The Importance of Groups in Politics and in Political Science.* **Princeton, NJ: Princeton University Press. 248 pages. ISBN 0691059152.**

In *Basic Interests,* Baumgartner and Leech review interest group literature from the 1940s through the late 1990s to examine the methodological problems that have hindered interest group research. They argue that during the 1970s scholars turned from analyzing the influence of groups to aspects of group activity such as membership and collective action problems. They suggest a new set of research questions—offering a path for scholarship to return to an analysis of interest group influence on governmental actions.

Bell, Lauren Cohen. 2002. *Warring Factions: Interest Groups, Money, and the New Politics of Senate Confirmation.* **Columbus: Ohio State University Press. 212 pages. ISBN 0814250882.**

Warring Factions gives an in-depth account of interest group activity in the confirmation process in the U.S. Senate. The book includes interviews with several U.S. senators, Senate staffers, and interest group leaders and argues that the confirmation process has been transformed "into a virtual circus" as interest groups battle to block or back nominees that share their organization's viewpoints.

Bentley, Arthur F. 1908. *The Process of Government: A Study of Social Pressures.* **Chicago: University of Chicago Press. 501 pages.**

The Process of Government is one of the founding works of interest group theory. In it, Bentley articulated his view—then considered novel and controversial—that understanding the composition and activities of interest groups within a society was necessary in order to have an accurate understanding of the government decision-making process and outcomes. Bentley argued that studying interest groups could not only complement traditional studies of political institutions and power structures but could also stand on its own, serving as an independent and comprehensive analytical tool.

Berry, Jeffrey M. 2000. *The New Liberalism: The Rising Power of Citizen Groups.* **Washington, DC: Brookings Institution Press. 224 pages. ISBN 0815709072.**

In this controversial book, Berry argues that liberalism is not dead, but it has transformed and is represented in the activities of citizen lobbying groups. Berry tracks the activities of these groups during the administrations of presidents Johnson, Carter, Reagan, and George H. W. Bush to argue that "postmaterial" legislative actions have increased rather than decreased. Berry also offers insights into the keys to citizen group success—attention, credibility, and organizational capacity.

Derthick, Martha A. 2004. *Up in Smoke: From Legislation to Litigation in Tobacco Politics.* **Washington, DC: CQ Press. 268 pages. ISBN 1568028954.**

Up in Smoke documents the introduction of what Derthick calls "adversarial legalism"—suits brought by state attorneys general against cigarette manufacturers for the harm done by cigarettes to the public health. The lawsuits culminated in the Master Settlement Agreement that awarded $250 billion to state governments and placed restrictions on cigarette advertising. Derthick concludes that state governments were perhaps less interested in improving public health than they were in padding state coffers.

Heinz, John P., Edward O. Laumann, Robert L. Nelson, and Robert H. Salisbury. 1997. *The Hollow Core: Private Interests in National Policy Making.* **Cambridge, MA: Harvard University Press. 448 pages. ISBN 0674405269.**

The Hollow Core is an ambitious attempt to document the influence of private interests on the policy-making process. Interviews with more than 300 interest groups, 800 lobbyists, and 300 government officials are used to assess claims that the government is controlled by private interests. The authors use a well-suited example of an oil company lobbying for a relatively insignificant revision to federal regulations to demonstrate that the effects of a lobbying campaign can be difficult to predict. In his example, the company decided to call in a big-name lobbyist to get the revision moving. However, the attention garnered by the lobbyist slowed the approval process down considerably.

Herrnson, Paul S., Ronald G. Shaiko, and Clyde Wilcox. 2004. *The Interest Group Connection: Electioneering, Lobbying, and Policymaking in Washington.* **2nd ed. Washington, DC: CQ Press. 410 pages. ISBN 1568029225.**

With 20 chapters, *The Interest Group Connection* demonstrates how organized interests gain access and influence in Congress, with executive branch agencies, and before the courts. It documents the increasingly complex lobbying tactics and recent lobbying and campaign finance developments, such as the proliferation of political action committees and 527 committees leading into the 2004 presidential election.

Jordan, Grant. 2001. *Shell, Greenpeace, and the Brent Spar.* **Houndmills, Basingstoke, UK: Palgrave Macmillan. 391 pages. ISBN 0333745469.**

This book documents the battle between Shell and Greenpeace over the disposal of the Brent Spar oil facility in the North Atlantic to demonstrate the power of a single interest group in swaying public opinion and garnering media attention. Often cited as an example of a major corporation being forced to cede to environmental concerns, Jordan reveals that Shell was more concerned about negative publicity from the controversy than about the actual environmental damage that could have been caused by the disposal of the facility.

Judis, John B. 2001. *The Paradox of American Democracy: Elites, Special Interests, and the Betrayal of Public Trust.* **London: Routledge. 320 pages. ISBN 041593026X.**

Set in the 2000 American presidential election, *The Paradox of American Democracy* documents the lackluster public participation in American politics. Judis claims that the decline in participation is tied to weakening unions and citizen organizations, which are being crowded out by conservative, elite-friendly interest groups and think tanks.

Latham, Earl. 1952. *The Group Basis of Politics*. Ithaca, NY: Cornell University Press. 244 pages.

This case study demonstrates that interest groups serve as fertile ground for analyzing governmental policy making. Latham argues that "the chief social values cherished by individuals in modern society are realized through groups" and that government serves as a referee in the battles of interest groups.

Meyer, David S. 2006. *The Politics of Protest*. Oxford, UK: Oxford University Press. 224 pages. ISBN 0195173538.

Meyer documents high-profile protests surrounding such issues as globalization, the Iraq War, and abortion. To understand these protests, Meyer argues that one must understand that protests are common to U.S. history and often represent mainstream America, not simply the fringes of society. Meyer also offers a review of protest strategies and tactics and media, public opinion, and policy responses.

Murray, Alan, and Jeffrey H. Birnbaum. 1988. *Showdown at Gucci Gulch*. New York: Vintage Books. 336 pages. ISBN 0394758110.

In *Showdown at Gucci Gulch,* Murray and Birnbaum document the passage of the 1986 Tax Reform Act. They argue that the passage of the act was a victory for Washington officials such as Bill Bradley, James Packwood, Dan Rostenkowski, and James Baker over the high-paid and lavishly dressed lobbyists of "Gucci Gulch."

Tivnan, Edward. 1988. *The Lobby: Jewish Political Power and American Foreign Policy*. New York: Touchstone Books. 304 pages. ISBN 0671668285.

This work presents an examination of the American pro-Israel lobby led by the American-Israeli Public Affairs Committee (AIPAC). Tivnan argues that AIPAC has managed to position itself as the dominant representative of American Jews on issues ranging from Israel policies toward its neighbors to relations with the Saudi government.

The Lobbying Profession

Berry, Jeffrey M. 1977. *Lobbying for the People.* **Princeton, NJ: Princeton University Press. 344 pages. ISBN 0691021783.**

In *Lobbying for the People,* Berry takes an important early step in analyzing public or citizen interest groups by gathering information on the origins, structure, and actions of these organizations. Berry also provides a definition of public interest groups, stating that they are organizations that are seeking the public good and not just benefits for its membership. The book describes 83 public interest groups, which Berry claims represent 80 percent of extant public interest organizations in 1973. It is the first comprehensive attempt to define, catalogue, and examine the public interest group movement.

Birnbaum, Jeffrey H. 1992. *The Lobbyists: How Influence Peddlers Get Their Way in Washington.* **New York: Times Books. 335 pages. ISBN 0812920864.**

In this eye-opening work, Birnbaum reveals how lawmakers work directly with former congressional or executive branch staffers turned lobbyists. Representing commercial and other special interests, these lobbyists pay for luxurious vacations and speaking fees and dish out campaign contributions in order to gain, and in some cases maintain, access to key lawmakers. Birnbaum documents these interactions to provide a realistic, albeit somewhat disturbing account of the American legislative process and the personal connections that drive the policy-making process.

deKieffer, Donald E. 1997. *The Citizen's Guide to Lobbying Congress.* **Chicago: Chicago Review Press. 304 pages. ISBN 1556521944.**

As the title suggests, *The Citizen's Guide to Lobbying Congress* is an introductory guide to petitioning government for those who are unfamiliar with lobbying and/or the legislative process. The book lays out the basic lobbying strategies and tactics such as message crafting, making contact with members of Congress and executive branch officials, and getting positive press attention. The guide also offers a description of campaign finance and lobbying laws.

Guyer, Robert L. 2003. *Guide to State Legislative Lobbying.* **Revised ed. Gainesville, FL: Engineering THE LAW. 220 pages. ISBN 096772421X.**

This step-by-step guide to state legislative lobbying helps advocates learn how to monitor and steer legislation through state legislative processes. Designed for the first-time advocate, yet insightful enough to serve the most experienced lobbyist, this guide covers such topics as assessing chances of legislative success, finding the right sponsor, hiring and working with contract lobbyists, negotiating compromises, and navigating the committee process.

Jordan, Grant, and William Maloney. 1997. *The Protest Business? Mobilizing Campaigning Groups.* **Manchester, UK: Manchester University Press. 240 pages. ISBN 0719043719.**

This book directly addresses the question of why individuals join campaigning interest groups instead of political parties. To answer this question, Jordan and Maloney use the proliferation of environmental groups in the 1980s to illustrate how a high level of membership activity can attract new members who are not attracted to political campaigns. The book offers insights into the membership energy behind campaigning groups and the impact of such groups on democracy and election campaigns.

Kollman, Ken. 1998. *Outside Lobbying: Public Opinion and Interest Group Strategies.* **Princeton, NJ: Princeton University Press. 216 pages. ISBN 0691017417.**

Outside Lobbying addresses the question of why and when interest group leaders seek to mobilize public support for their lobbying efforts. Rather than a membership recruitment mechanism, Kollman argues that this so-called "grassroots" and "astroturf" lobbying is used to take advantage of existing public opinion and to generate the appearance of public support to lawmakers.

Mack, Charles S. 1997. *Business, Politics, and the Practice of Government Relations.* **Westport, CT: Quorum Books. 288 pages. ISBN 1567200575.**

An essential for corporate government relations practitioners and aspirants, this book offers a basic guide to the legislative process from the perspective of a corporate executive. Mack urges executives to rethink their government relations strategies to implement cost-effective tactics and techniques in the areas of issue research, direct lobbying, grassroots mobilization, and interactions with trade associations.

McFarland, Andrew S. 1984. *Common Cause: Lobbying in the Public Interest.* **Chatham, NJ: Chatham House. 224 pages. ISBN 0934540284.**

McFarland documents the explosion of public interest groups in the United States and offers explanations about this phenomenon and insight into their membership, organizational structures, and impact on government policy making. A case study of Common Cause shows that public interest groups are often dominated by white, upper-class individuals even though their goals are often meant to benefit underrepresented and less powerful segments of the population.

Nownes, Anthony J. 2006. *Total Lobbying: What Lobbyists Want and How They Try to Get It.* **New York: Cambridge University Press. 278 pages. ISBN 0521547113.**

Total Lobbying provides a clear view of the lobbying profession by examining their daily actions and the results they get from all levels of government. An overview of the lobbying process is provided through case studies of lobbyists seeking policy changes, land-use rights, and procurements. The book covers the activities of lobbyists before the executive branch, the courts, and Congress and in the mobilization of grassroots public lobbying campaigns.

Richan, Willard C. 2006. *Lobbying for Social Change.* **3rd ed. New York: Haworth Press. 302 pages. ISBN 0789031663.**

Lobbying for Social Change is a guidebook to the state and federal legislative process and is geared toward social activists. Richan operates under the premise that citizens do care about government yet often lack the skills needed to track issues and become successful advocates. It provides step-by-step instructions for organizing supporters, developing a winning message, and overcoming obstacles to civic engagement and provides examples of successful campaigns.

Rosenthal, Alan. 1993. *The Third House: Lobbyists and Lobbying in the States.* 2nd ed. Washington, DC: CQ Press. 260 pages. ISBN 156802438X.

A great and understandable introduction to the lobbying profession, *The Third House* covers the strategies and tactics used by corporate, public interest, and contract lobbyists and provides a broad look at contemporary American lobbying trends. Rosenthal offers clear principles of direct lobbying and discusses the role of personal relationships in depth. Whereas most works that focus exclusively on lobbying and lobbyists usually overlook lobbying on the state level, Rosenthal devotes an entire chapter to state government relations.

Wittenberg, Ernest, and Elisabeth Wittenberg. 1994. *How to Win in Washington: Very Practical Advice about Lobbying the Grassroots and the Media.* 2nd ed. Cambridge, MA: Blackwell. 163 pages. ISBN 1557865787.

A popular how-to guide to Washington lobbying, *How to Win* offers practical advice on organizing supporters, framing the issue, attracting favorable media coverage, gaining access to lawmakers, testifying before Congress, and developing an "inside" lobbying strategy.

Wolpe, Bruce C., and Bertram J. Levine. 1996. *Lobbying Congress: How the System Works.* 2nd ed. Washington, DC: Congressional Quarterly Books. 206 pages. ISBN 1568022255.

A practical guide to lobbying on Capitol Hill, this book addresses the basics of the lobbying profession as well as more advanced techniques of writing legislation, organizing grassroots movements, framing issues, and navigating complicated parliamentary procedures and the legislative committee and floor process.

Money in Politics

Birnbaum, Jeffrey H. 2000. *The Money Men: The Real Story of Fund-raising's Influence on Political Power in America.* New York: Crown Publishers. 304 pages. ISBN 081293119X.

The Money Men documents the role of money in politics—following the individuals who give money to politicians and campaigns. Birnbaum argues that money plays an enormous role in politics and that those who dismiss money's influence have yet to hit the "moment" when they realize that moneyed interests play such a large role in American politics that understanding the flow of the money is the key to understanding the legislative process.

Drew, Elizabeth. 1999. *The Corruption of American Politics: What Went Wrong and Why.* **Secaucus, NJ: Birch Lane Press. 278 pages. ISBN 1559725206.**

Drew, a Washington correspondent for *The New Yorker* reveals and examines the corrupt roots of American politics and projects this past on the post-Watergate world of campaign financing practices. Drew characterizes the corrupt nature of American politics and argues that the public has lost confidence in its elected officials—creating an atmosphere ripe for abuses of democratic processes.

Rozell, Mark J., Clyde Wilcox, and David Madland. 2005. *Interest Groups in American Campaigns: The New Face of Electioneering.* **2nd ed. Washington, DC: CQ Press. 178 pages. ISBN 1933116242.**

The preeminent work focusing on interest group activities in electoral campaigns, this book shows that donations of money to political campaigns and mobilization and education of their membership give interest groups influence over political parties and elected officials. It also documents modern campaign finance developments, such as the rise of 527 organizations.

Sabato, Larry J. 1985. *PAC Power.* **New York: W. W. Norton and Co. 259 pages. ISBN 0393302571.**

This book by the renowned University of Virginia political scientist Larry Sabato examines the role of political action committees (PACs) in American politics. *PAC Power* documents how PACs raise funds and donate to election campaigns and describes the access and influence they receive in return.

Wright, John R., and Bruce I. Oppenheimer. 2002. *Interest Groups and Congress: Lobbying, Contributions, and Influence.* **New York: Longman. 240 pages. ISBN 0321121872.**

This work traces the evolution and organization of interest groups and provides an in-depth analysis of their contribution patterns and interactions before Congress, federal agencies, and the courts. Wright uses the case study of the Family and Medical Leave Act to demonstrate the strategies and influence of interest groups seeking to influence high-stakes political debates.

Journal Articles

Hansen, John Mark. 1985. "Political Economy of Group Membership." *American Political Science Review* **79 (1): 79–96.**

Hansen sets out to answer the enduring question of why individuals join interest groups by using empirical data rather than purely theoretical models of individual and group behavior. To do this, Hansen develops a rational model of individual group participation and then evaluates that model against aggregate changes over time in the membership of such organizations as the Farm Bureau and the League of Women Voters. Hansen concludes that subsidization is crucial to interest group mobilization.

Hershey, Marjorie Randon. 1993. "Citizens' Groups and Political Parties in the United States." *Annals of the American Academy of Political and Social Science* **528: 142–156.**

Hershey argues that a competitive relationship exists between citizen groups and political parties as they compete for loyal members and resources. This is illustrated by the decline in attachment to political parties that corresponded with the rise of citizen interest groups during the 1960s and 1970s. Hershey also presents a case study of the 1992 Republican Party platform to demonstrate these tensions within the party platform formation and presidential nomination processes.

Levi, Margaret. 2003. "Organizing Power: The Prospects for an American Labor Movement." *Perspectives on Politics* **1 (1): 45–68.**

This comparative study of labor unions demonstrates that in order to be successful, the American labor movement must reinvigorate itself as a social movement by enhancing its ground-level organizing and recruiting new members into its organizations. Levi points out that it is not sufficient for an organization to be effective in bargaining for its membership; it must also maintain an active grassroots organization.

Salisbury, Robert H. 1969. "An Exchange Theory of Interest Groups." *Midwest Journal of Political Science* **13 (1): 1–32.**

Salisbury details a model of interest group membership that is built around the idea that members receive benefits from joining an organization. These benefits may be solidary, material, or expressive and are provided by group organizers exclusively to organization members. Solidary rewards describe the social benefits individuals receive from participating in a group. Material benefits are tangible rewards, such as vacation discounts, rental car discounts, or monthly publications received in exchange for membership in the organization. Expressive benefits are the feelings of efficacy and personal expression individuals receive from joining a cause they support. Ensuring that members receive these benefits and that organizers receive continued participation, or "profit," is key to a group's success and longevity.

Salisbury, Robert H., John P. Heinz, Edward O. Laumann, and Robert L. Nelson. "Who Works with Whom? Interest Group Alliances and Opposition." *American Political Science Review* **81 (4): 1,217–1,234.**

This article presents interest group interactions in four U.S. domestic policy areas: agriculture, health, energy, and labor. The findings are based on the author's surveys with 806 representatives and 301 government officials operating in these policy areas.

Salisbury, Robert H., Paul Johnson, Edward O. Laumann, and Robert L. Nelson. 1989. "Who You Know Versus What You Know: The Uses of Government Experience for Washington Lobbyists." *American Journal of Political Science* **33 (1): 175–195.**

This article presents data on 776 interest representatives to determine how much their contacts within government from previous work experience factor into their lobbying success. Although more than half of those interviewed have such contacts, the authors conclude that policy and governmental process experience is of higher value than relationships.

Schmitter, Philippe C. 1974. "Still the Century of Corporatism." *Review of Politics* **36 (1): 85–131.**

In this article Schmitter argues that democratic and nondemocratic nations share key characteristics such as the organization of interests into a small number of elite groups for each sector of society. These peak organizations, one for business, one for labor, and so on are granted broad powers in controlling government regulation of their respective areas.

Academic Journals

American Journal of Political Science
ISSN: 00925853
Frequency: Quarterly
Web site: www.ajps.org/

Published since 1957, the *American Journal of Political Science* is the official publication of the Midwest Political Science Association and is produced by Blackwell Publishing with the support of the University of Texas at Dallas. It features articles that advance understanding in the areas of government, politics, and citizenship.

American Political Science Review
ISSN: 00030554
Frequency: Quarterly
Web site: www.apsanet.org/section_327.cfm

The American Political Science Review is the preeminent journal of political science in the United States. It is published by the American Political Science Association and features articles from leading scholars in the areas of political theory, policy, public administration, and international relations.

American Politics Quarterly
ISSN: 00447803
Frequency: Quarterly
Web site: www.uwm.edu/Org/APQ/

American Politics Quarterly is published by Sage Publications and features articles on local, state, and national politics with a focus on American political behavior, political parties, public policy, and public opinion.

The Journal of Politics
ISSN: 00223816

Frequency: Quarterly
Web site: www.vanderbilt.edu/jop/
Subscription information: www.vanderbilt.edu/jop/links

Published by Cambridge University Press on behalf of the Southern Political Science Association, *The Journal of Politics* is the oldest regional political journal in the United States. It publishes articles on American politics, political theory, and comparative politics.

Policy Review
ISSN: 01465945
Frequency: Six issues each year
Web site: www.hoover.org/publications/policyreview/

Published by the Hoover Institution at Stanford University, *Policy Review* is a leading conservative journal that addresses a wide range of theoretical and policy topics focused on American domestic and foreign policy.

Political Research Quarterly
ISSN: 10659129
Frequency: Quarterly
Web site: http://prq.sagepub.com/

Published by Sage Publications on behalf of the University of Utah, *Political Research Quarterly* is the official journal of the Western Political Science Association and publishes articles on politics, interest groups, government, and public opinion.

Political Science Quarterly
ISSN: 00323195
Frequency: Quarterly
Web site: www.psqonline.org/

Political Science Quarterly is the nation's oldest journal of political science and is published by the Academy of Political Science. Each issue features five to six articles that are edited to ensure readability across all subfields of political science and dozens of book reviews.

PS: Political Science and Politics
ISSN: 10490965
Frequency: Quarterly
Web site: www.apsanet.org/section_223.cfm

An official publication of the American Political Science Association (APSA), *PS* covers a broad range of topics within the political science field, including current political developments, the teaching profession, and news and information about the APSA.

The Review of Politics
ISSN: 00346705
Frequency: Quarterly
Web site: www.nd.edu/~rop/

The Review of Politics is published by Cambridge University Press for the University of Notre Dame. It focuses on philosophical and historical articles on political theory, literature, constitutional theory, and analysis of institutions.

Periodicals and Newspapers

Congressional Record
ISSN: 03637239
Frequency: Daily when Congress is in session
Web site: www.gpoaccess.gov/crecord/index.html

The *Congressional Record* is published daily by the U.S. Government Printing Office and contains the detailed records of congressional debates. It is relatively inexpensive compared with its rival publications, yet it does not present information in a format that is as user friendly as its more expensive alternatives.

CQ Weekly
ISSN: 00105910
Frequency: Weekly
Web site: www.cq.com

A staple of Washington insiders, *CQ Weekly* briefs subscribers on the preceding week's events in Congress and includes articles on key pieces of legislation, members of Congress, and congressional committees. It is worth the cost if you want to keep a close eye on Capitol Hill.

Governing
ISSN: 0894-3842 0894-5481
Frequency: Monthly
Web site: www.governing.com

Governing is a monthly magazine published by Congressional Quarterly, Inc. and geared toward state and local government issues and officials. It features articles on state and local government policies and administration. It boasts a readership of more than 275,000 subscribers each month and is a must read for those seeking to understand the complexity and breadth of the issues facing local governments throughout the nation.

The Hill
ISSN: 1521-1568
Frequency: Daily when Congress is in session
Web site: http://thehill.com/

The Hill is a must-read publication for Washington insiders, lawmakers, lobbyists, and observers. It delivers in-depth reporting on the legislative process, including complex parliamentary procedures and agency actions. It also informs readers on who's who in Washington, D.C., by featuring profiles on key Washington officials, staffers, lobbyists, and business leaders.

National Journal
ISSN: 0360-4217
Frequency: Weekly
Web site: http://nationaljournal.com/

The *National Journal* features in-depth stories on beltway activities ranging from legislation to committee actions and electoral politics. *National Journal* also manages several other publications tailored to specific interests. *CongressDaily* provides real-time updates on legislation, *American HealthLine* covers federal health policy, and *The Hotline* is a popular comprehensive resource on electoral politics and campaigns that features highlights of political news stories and the latest polls. *Adspotlight* gives users regular updates on the latest election commercials airing throughout the nation.

The New York Times
ISSN: 0362-4331
Frequency: Daily
Web site: www.nytimes.com

One of the nation's premier news publications, *The New York Times* features high-quality articles on current events in the areas of world politics, American politics, business, technology, sports, health, and the arts.

Roll Call
ISSN: 0035-788X
Frequency: Daily Monday through Thursday when Congress is in session
Web site: www.rollcall.com/

A leading publication of Washington news and information, *Roll Call* is published Monday through Thursday during weeks when Congress is in session. It provides real-time updates on congressional activities and procedural moves, election developments, and profiles of key lawmakers and interest group leaders.

The Wall Street Journal
ISSN: 099-9660 0043-0080
Frequency: Daily
Web site: http://online.wsj.com/public/us

Published by Dow Jones and Company, *The Wall Street Journal* primarily covers U.S. and international business and financial issues, yet it frequently has features on U.S. politics and interest groups in its Politics and Policy and Opinion sections.

Washington Monthly
ISSN: 0043-0633
Frequency: Monthly
Web site: www.washingtonmonthly.com/

Washington Monthly is a monthly magazine that features witty and engaging stories on American politics and policy by big-name writers such as Warren Buffett, Paul Krugman, Garry Trudeau, the late Molly Ivins, and Bill Clinton. It is known for its creative and artistic covers that frequently feature caricatures of leading political figures.

The Washington Post
ISSN: 0190-8286
Frequency: Daily
Web site: www.washingtonpost.com/

A leading U.S. daily newspaper and the largest newspaper in Washington, D.C., *The Washington Post* is known for its in-depth and breaking news on American politics and policy issues. The *Post* is not available for home delivery throughout the entire United States, but the online version is free and features all of the stories in the print edition.

Nonprint Resources

Internet Sites

Annenberg Public Policy Center
http://annenbergpublicpolicycenter.org

This site of the University of Pennsylvania–affiliated research center provides information on the role of advertising and the media in federal politics, including the use of issue ads in political campaigns. The site also presents the research of the Annenberg Center in the areas of political communication, information and society, media and children, health communication, and adolescent risk. This site is a great resource for those wishing to keep up to date with the latest research on the media's influence on politics and society.

Brookings Institution—Governance Studies Program
www.brookings.edu/governance.aspx

The Governance Studies Program explores the formal and informal political institutions of the United States and other democratic regimes to assess how they govern, how their practices compare, and how citizens and public servants can advance sound governance. This site provides access to information regarding Brookings Institution scholars, publications, and projects.

Campaign Finance Institute
www.cfinst.org/

The Campaign Finance Institute is a nonprofit, nonpartisan institution affiliated with George Washington University that provides research in the areas of campaign finance, interest groups and lobbying, and political parties. The Web site allows users to access figures, reports, and selected book chapters on historical and modern campaign finance trends and reform movements.

The Campaign Legal Center
www.campaignlegalcenter.org

The Campaign Legal Center (CLC) is a nonprofit, nonpartisan organization that tracks campaign finance laws, Federal Election Commission (FEC) enforcement actions, lobbying and ethics reform and enforcement, and media policy. Users can track the activities of the FEC, campaign finance litigation, and other good-governance issues such as ethics, lobbying, and redistricting reform. The CLC blog allows users to read expert commentary on developments in these issue areas.

Center for Public Integrity—LobbyWatch
www.publicintegrity.org/lobby/

The nonpartisan investigative research group's Web site provides reports on the money funding state and federal elections as well as lobbyist donations to campaigns. Its databases cover all 50 American states, dozens of foreign countries, specific issues ranging from agriculture to defense, and specific federal agencies. Users can also watch streaming video of press conferences and tutorials on the information that can be retrieved from the LobbyWatch databases.

Congressional Quarterly—MoneyLine
http://moneyline.cq.com

This Web site provides in-depth analysis and data on political action committee, candidate, and lobbyist expenditures and fundraising as well as the latest campaign finance developments. To view some articles and data a subscription is required, but crunching the numbers yourself may prove to be time consuming and difficult.

Federal Election Commission
www.fec.gov/

The Federal Election Commission Web site contains information on the members and activities of the commission and official campaign finance reports for candidates, political parties, and political action committees. One of its more user-friendly features is the interactive campaign finance maps tool that allows users to search for political contribution figures down to the zip code level.

National Institute on Money in State Politics—
Follow the Money
www.followthemoney.org/

This Web site is the only site that tracks and offers free data on political donations in all 50 states for statewide, legislative, and judicial candidates as well as for ballot measures and to political parties, political committees, and labor unions.

Opensecrets.org
www.opensecrets.org/

This Web site is an excellent and free source of data on the role of money in American politics. One can research broad election financing and lobbying trends, such as the total amount of interest group spending in the 2008 or 2006 election cycles or the nation's leading lobbying firms, as well as look up figures on specific donors, election cycles, candidates, lobbyists, industries, political action committees, 527s, and more. One can even look up all of the federal campaign donations made by residents of a particular postal code. The site also provides a general overview of current campaign finance laws.

Policy Agendas Project
www.policyagendas.org

The recipient of the American Political Science Association's 2007 Best Instructional Web site Award, the Policy Agendas Project collects and presents data on public policy outcomes in the United States since 1947. The site was created with the support of the National Science Foundation and under the direction of Drs. Frank Baumgartner, Bryan D. Jones, and John Wilkerson. Users can access an extensive database of policy outcomes and analyze them to determine government policy-making trends.

Project Vote Smart
www.votesmart.org/

This site juxtaposes campaign contributions for more than 13,000 candidates and elected officials nationwide with voting records and evaluations by special interest groups. Users can easily read about their state and federal elected officials' voting records, interest group ratings, public statements, and campaign finance information. The site also contains extensive voter information on ballot measures and legislation in each of the 50 states.

SourceWatch
www.sourcewatch.org

SourceWatch is a project of the Center for Media and Democracy that is intended to reveal the individuals and organizations influencing public policies behind the scenes and in the media. It features leading national news stories and the reality behind them. It allows users to cut through interest group and elected officials' attempts to frame issues in a favorable and misleading manner.

U.S. House of Representatives Office of the Clerk—
Lobbying Disclosure
http://lobbyingdisclosure.house.gov/

This is the official Web site of the clerk of the U.S. House of Representatives. It contains a guide to the Honest Leadership and Open Government Act of 2007 as well as a searchable database of quarterly lobbying disclosure forms.

U.S. Senate Office of Public Records—Lobbying
www.senate.gov/reference/reference_index_subjects/Lobbying_vrd.htm

This is the official Web site of the U.S. Senate Office of Public Records. It provides information on current lobbying laws, the history of lobbying and lobbyists, information on interest groups, lobbyist registration forms, and a database of lobbyist disclosure forms.

Wisconsin Advertising Project
http://wiscadproject.wisc.edu/

Affiliated with the University of Wisconsin at Madison, the WiscAds site contains studies of and coded data for campaign ads in the country's largest media markets. The site offers analysis of advertising in the 2000 and 2004 election cycles and a glimpse of the project's historic ads archive.

Films

The Big Buy: Tom DeLay's Stolen Congress
2006, Brave New Films
Format: DVD
Length: 60 minutes
Cost: $19.95

This revealing documentary, directed by Jim Schermbeck and Mark Birnbaum and featuring Tom DeLay, Jack Abramoff, Molly Ivins, Bill Ratliff, and Bill White, traces the career of Rep. Tom DeLay of Sugar Land, Texas. DeLay was known as "the hammer" for his assertive style of locking up Republican votes and seeking revenge against his fellow GOP lawmakers who failed to vote according to the dictates of the Republican Party leadership in the U.S. House of Representatives. In 2005, DeLay was indicted for conspiracy to violate election laws for diverting funds to his political action committees. This film tracks his rise to power, ties to and favors for corporate interests and conservative lobbyists and interest groups, and eventual downfall.

Dangerous Prescription
2003, PBS Frontline
Format: DVD
Length: 60 minutes
Cost: $29.98

This documentary presents an investigation into the U.S. Food and Drug Administration drug approval process and the role pharmaceutical companies play in approving and monitoring drugs. This is a great documentary to use in illustrating the activities of power interest groups before a regulatory agency.

Faith and Politics: The Christian Right
1995, Films for the Humanities and Sciences
Format: DVD
Length: 49 minutes
Cost: $89.95

This documentary focuses on the evangelical movement in the United States, which is led by figures such as Ralph Reed of the Christian Coalition, Gary Bauer of the Family Research Council, and the Rev. Lou Sheldon, who founded the Traditional Values Coalition. The film also features prominent opponents of the

Christian right and offers a debate on various social issues ranging from abortion to same-sex marriage and evolution.

The Gun Fight: The Power and Politics of the NRA
2000, Films for the Humanities and Sciences
Format: DVD
Length: 43 minutes
Cost: $89.95

This documentary traces the founding and growth of the National Rifle Association (NRA)—one of the most powerful interest groups in the United States. The late ABC News anchor Peter Jennings interviews NRA founder and executive vice president Wayne LaPierre, members of the association, gun manufacturers, and elected officials sympathetic to the NRA's cause. The NRA being a grassroots organization, this documentary asks why its membership and influence are at an all-time high despite high-profile school shootings and protests against unrestricted gun ownership. Where does the NRA derive its power from, and how does it interact with our nation's leaders in Washington, D.C.?

The Jesus Factor
2004, PBS Frontline
Format: DVD
Length: 60 minutes
Cost: $29.98

This documentary investigates the rise of the evangelical Christian movement in the United States and its strong link to conservative interest groups and politicians. The strength of the evangelical Christian movement was on spectacular public display during the 2000 presidential election, leading many to question the group's close ties to elected officials and partisan politics. This film asks the question, "How closely do Bush's religious views mirror those of the country's burgeoning—and politically influential—evangelical movement?"

K Street
2003, HBO
Format: DVD
Length: 300 minutes
Cost: $19.99

Directed by Steven Soderbergh, this weekly series, which focuses on the beltway world of powerful interest group leaders, lobbyists, and elected officials presents a fictional behind-the-scenes look at actual current political events. Filmed and produced in Washington, D.C., the series comprises 10 episodes. It ran for one season and was then discontinued.

Moyers on America: Capitol Crimes
2006, PBS
Format: DVD
Length: 120 minutes
Cost: $29.95

This film investigates the Jack Abramoff scandal—one of the biggest political scandals in American history. The Abramoff scandal is unraveled in an easy-to-follow manner as Moyers connects the lawmakers, lobbyists, consultants, political action committees, and charities used to manipulate the lawmaking process into a source of enormous individual wealth. From lucrative deals with American Indian tribes to build and/or shut down casinos to luxurious golf vacations, this film paints a bleak but accurate picture of the way power and influence hold sway on Capitol Hill.

NOW (08/25/06): Lawmakers or Lawbreakers?
2006, PBS
Format: DVD
Length: 30 minutes
Cost: $19.99

With the Jack Abramoff scandal unfolding, this film asks whether voters see their elected officials as lawmakers or lawbreakers and whether the government is accurately representing the country's fiscal situation. It looks at the issue of ethics as America entered the 2006 midterm elections and presents interviews with members of Congress regarding such issues as the federal deficit.

NOW with Bill Moyers: Kathleen Hall Jamieson on Political Advertising
2003, Films for the Humanities and Sciences
Format: DVD
Length: 36 minutes
Cost: $89.95

This documentary features an in-depth interview with Kathleen Hall Jamieson of the Annenberg School of Communication and discusses political advertising used by politicians and interest groups. The film also discusses the campaign finance regulations behind these ads and their ability to serve as unregulated forms of election campaigning in future elections.

The Other Drug War
2003, PBS Frontline
Format: DVD
Length: 60 minutes
Cost: $24.99

This documentary investigates the passage of the Medicare Prescription Drug Improvement and Modernization Act of 2003. It looks at the battle between pharmaceutical companies and an American public outraged over skyrocketing prescription drug costs. The film includes interviews with consumer advocates, lawmakers, scientists, interest group and industry leaders, and analysts. It also covers how individual states, such as Maine and Oregon, battled pharmaceutical companies to help their residents gain access to affordable prescription drugs.

The People and the Power Game
1996, Films for the Humanities and Sciences
Format: DVD
Length: 160 minutes
Cost: $269.95

This three-part series with Pulitzer Prize–winning journalist Hedrick Smith, based on his book *The Power Game: How Washington Works*, asks whether the legislative process has been "hijacked" by the media, pundits, interest groups, lobbyists, and ideological extremists. It includes interviews with elected officials, interest groups leaders, consultants, and media figures.

The Politics of Gay Marriage and Abortion Rights
2004, Films for the Humanities and Sciences
Format: DVD
Length: 22 minutes
Cost: $89.95

This short documentary that features an ABC News program discusses the legal and political ramifications of the same-sex marriage movement and opposition in the United States. On the issue of abortion rights, it focuses on the controversial stance of a Catholic bishop who declared that anyone who supports abortion rights should not be allowed to take communion.

The State Legislature: Lawmaking
1995, Films for the Humanities and Sciences
Format: DVD
Length: 30 minutes
Cost: $89.95

This program of the three-part series *The State Legislature* focuses on the state lawmaking process. It features coverage of state legislative committee and caucus meetings and dozens of interviews with state lawmakers, lobbyists, and industry leaders.

"Under the Influence" (*60 Minutes*)
2007, CBS News
Format: DVD
Length: 14 minutes
Cost: $17.95

This short piece on the politics behind the cost of prescription drugs in America features Steve Kroft and looks at the power and influence of the pharmaceutical lobby in Washington, D.C. As the piece notes, "congressmen are outnumbered two to one by lobbyists for an industry that spends roughly $100 million a year in campaign contributions and lobbying expenses to protect its profits." The piece also looks at the role of the pharmaceutical industry in the passage of the Medicare prescription drug bill and its effects on industry profits.

The Unelected: The Lobbies
1996, Films for the Humanities and Sciences
Format: DVD
Length: 42 minutes
Cost: $89.95

This film explores the behind-the-scenes world of Washington politics during the Clinton administration. The film focuses on Majority Whip Tom DeLay, lobbyists, and interest group leaders during the unsuccessful efforts of Congress to improve worker safety, which were opposed by the lobbying efforts of UPS. It also highlights the famous "Harry and Louise" ads that opposed the Clinton health care reform bill and the strategies implemented by the tobacco industry to stop unfavorable federal legislation.

Glossary

access creating tactics   Various tactics lobbyists use to create an environment that is conducive to future lobbying with a governmental official. These may include making financial contributions to a political campaign, inviting the official to social events, or providing various favors that may be of some value to the public official. The publicly stated goal is to create access or an opportunity to discuss the interest's policy objectives.

amicus curiae   A judicial brief ("friend of the court") submitted by an interest group to provide additional information or an opinion to try to influence the decision of the court.

astroturf lobbying   Contrived campaigns by interest groups and corporations to create the appearance of public support for or public outrage against an issue by spending large amounts of money to recruit citizens to contact their elected officials and the media.

bundling   The solicitation and collection of political contributions from individual donors that are then delivered collectively to elected officials, political committees, and political action committees.

candidate committee   The official political committees of federal candidates, which serve as the depositories for campaign funds.

collective action   The pursuit of a goal by more than one person. It creates a situation in which individuals have the choice of deciding whether or not to participate in the group effort.

collective action dilemma   A situation in which the benefits sought by a group are available to both members and nonmembers of the group. Because individuals can receive the benefits provided by the group's efforts without joining the group, they have little or no incentive to do so. Such individuals are commonly referred to as "free-riders."

collective benefit   A reward that is available to all members of a society regardless of their participation in collective efforts.

corporatism   A political system in which power is given by the government to certain "peak" organizations that represent professional groups in exchange for cooperation in forming policies and institutional processes.

direct lobbying   Attempts to influence legislation or regulation by directly communicating with a member of a legislative body or a governmental official who participates in formulating government policies.

disturbance theory   The theory that interest groups arise as a result of the increasing complexity of society and the tendency of society to seek a state of equilibrium. As government regulation enters new areas or as new economic sectors are created, interest groups will arise to represent the newly regulated or formed sectors.

earmark   A legislative provision that directs public funds to a specific project or organization. Earmarks can be inserted into legislation or committee reports. Earmarks are the most common legislative appropriations to be referred to as *pork*—a term that evolved out of the idea that legislators were able to "bring home the bacon" by targeting funding to their home districts and/or states.

elitism   A political system in which a small group of the economically wealthy and politically powerful hold a large share of the power over government policies regardless of the outcome of elections.

entrepreneurialism   A theory that holds that interest groups, and particularly public interest groups, form because of the aggressive actions and strong desire of individuals to form viable organizations.

exchange theory   A theory that holds that the relationship between group leaders and members is similar to the relationship between a business and its customers. The group must provide certain benefits to its members in exchange for their participation.

faction   An early American term meaning interest or interest group. Used by James Madison in Federalist No. 10.

Federal Election Commission (FEC)   The federal agency responsible for administering and enforcing federal campaign finance laws. The FEC was created by the 1974 Federal Election Campaign Act Amendments.

527   A tax-exempt organization created to influence the nomination, election, appointment, or defeat of a candidate for public office. They are formed under section 527 of the United States tax code (26 U.S.C. § 527). Although all candidate and political action committees are also created under section 527, the term *527* is usually used to refer to those committees that register under section 527 but fail to register with and be regulated by the Federal Election Commission or state election commissions.

free-rider   An individual who chooses to abstain from collective action yet still enjoys the benefits produced by that action.

grassroots lobbying   An attempt to influence legislation or regulations by organizing and mobilizing the public to contact their elected officials regarding the policy.

hard money   Money, or anything of value, that is raised by candidates, political committees, and political action committees in accordance with campaign finance laws.

indirect lobbying   Actions designed to influence government policies that do not involve directly communicating with lawmakers or government officials. It usually involves shaping public opinion through the news and organizing citizens to contact their elected officials.

interest group   A group that shares particular opinions, interests, or behaviors that make claims on other groups within society and/or on the government.

iron law of oligarchy   A term used by Robert Michel early in the 20th century to describe the tendency of organizations to create an elite hierarchy within the organization that tends to become differentiated from the mass membership and thus causes possible problems in terms of association goals and objectives.

issue advocacy   A communication that does not expressly advocate for the election or defeat of a clearly identified federal candidate. Issue advocacy ads are often used to influence federal elections but are not subject to campaign finance laws.

K Street   A major street in Washington, D.C.; it is the home of many of the most influential public relations firms, lobbying firms, think tanks, and advocacy groups.

lobbying   An attempt to influence government policies that involves communicating with lawmakers and/or public officials on behalf of an organization.

lobbyist   An individual who attempts to influence government policies by communicating with elected officials and/or public officials on behalf of an organization.

material benefits   Items or services received in exchange for group membership that can be quantified in monetary terms.

neocorporatism   A political system characterized by a high level of cooperation between government and certain interests that ensures policy and institutional process stability.

nonprofit organization   Organizations that are typically tax-exempt and formed under section 501(c) of the Internal Revenue Code. They may not use general treasury funds for contributions, expenditures, or electioneering communications, but they may establish a connected political action committee to influence elections.

pluralism   A political system in which interests and individuals have an opportunity to compete for political influence. Pluralism is characterized by access to government, fragmentation, and a competitive policy-making process. The assumption is that all interests have the ability to organize and participate in the lobbying game, even if the lobbying resources are distributed unevenly. It also assumes that almost every interest has some resources to enable them to participate.

political action committee (PAC)   Organizations independent of party and candidate committees that register under section 527 of the Internal Revenue Code and register with the Federal Election Commission and are thus subject to campaign finance laws. PACs receive donations from individuals and other PACs and then donate this money to other PACs, candidates, and political parties.

political committee   There are four general types of political committees: corporate and union separate segregated funds; national, state, and local party committees that raise and spend funds on federal elections; federal candidate committees; and organizations whose major purpose is engaging in political activities and who receive more than $1,000 in contributions and / or make more than $1,000 in expenditures.

potential groups   Interests that have not yet effectively organized to represent the interests in the political arena.

public interest group   An organization whose purpose is to represent the public will rather than a specific industry, trade, or political ideology. Oftentimes, these organizations emphasize giving the average citizen a voice in government.

purposive benefits   The rewards one receives from associating with and contributing to an organization or cause one believes in.

revolving door   This term refers to the practice of congressional members and staffers leaving elected office or employment in government to serve as lobbyists and consultants for firms, interest groups, and corporations and vice versa.

selective benefits   Benefits available only to group members. Membership is a necessary prerequisite of receipt of the benefit.

social movements   Largely unstructured groups of people seeking to challenge the existing political system. Because of a lack of conventional lobbying resources, mass movements tend to use unconventional lobbying strategies and tactics to influence public opinion to put pressure on the political officials to change public policy.

soft money   Money or anything of value that is given to or spent for federal election purposes that is not regulated by campaign finance laws.

solidary benefits   Intangible rewards one receives from the act of associating with other group members.

special interest groups   Groups that are organized to protect or represent their own private interests rather than those of the broader society.

upper-class bias   The observation that many public interest groups, while representing individuals of lower socioeconomic status, are predominantly led and made up of individuals of higher socioeconomic status.

wave pattern of interest group formation   Interest groups seem to have their dates of establishment clustered in certain decades. Explanations for this point to revolutions in communications that allow groups to be more easily formed; significant changes in society that provide advantages to some interests and disadvantages to others; the increasing complexity of society, which demands that new interests be organized to participate politically; increased governmental involvement in the economy and society; and the rise of entrepreneurs who seek to create new organizations.

Index

Note: t. indicates table.

About the Authors

Ronald J. Hrebenar is a professor of political science, the former chair of the department, and the former director of the Hinckley Institute of Politics at the University of Utah. He is the author and editor of 15 books and more than 50 academic articles and book chapters, including *Interest Group Politics in America* and *Political Parties and Interest Groups and Political Campaigns.*

Bryson B. Morgan is a law student at Harvard University and a former staff member of the Hinckley Institute of Politics at the University of Utah. He received his bachelor's degree from the University of Utah and was appointed a Harry S. Truman Scholar in 2007. He is the coauthor of several articles on the development of interest group politics in Lithuania.